COLUMBIA UNIVERSITY STUDIES IN ENGLISH
AND COMPARATIVE LITERATURE

THE EARLY LIFE OF ROBERT SOUTHEY
1774–1803

THE EARLY LIFE OF ROBERT SOUTHEY

1774 -1803

BY

WILLIAM HALLER

1966

OCTAGON BOOKS, INC.

New York

Reprinted 1966
by special arrangement with William Haller

OCTAGON BOOKS, INC.

175 FIFTH AVENUE
NEW YORK, N.Y. 10010

Ann

LIBRARY OF CONGRESS CATALOG CARD NUMBER: 66-28369

Printed in U.S.A. by
NOBLE OFFSET PRINTERS, INC.
NEW YORK 3, N. Y.

PREFACE

THERE has been no adequate detailed biography of Southey. Charles Cuthbert Southey, who compiled a *Life and Correspondence* of his father, was not qualified for his difficult task. Selections from the poet's published letters have given the leading circumstances especially of the later life, but the only approximation to a sympathetic and intelligent biography has been the characteristic sketch by the late Edward Dowden in the "English Men of Letters Series." At the same time, although it is long since many persons have read any of Southey's writings except *The Three Bears, The Life of Nelson, The Battle of Blenheim, My Days Among the Dead are Past,* and perhaps one or two other short pieces, a curiously positive, largely disagreeable and distorted impression of the man has persisted in the popular imagination. That impression I have small hope at this late day to correct, and no desire completely to reverse. My purpose is merely to supply students with a faithful account of the most interesting and least known period in the life and work of an important English writer of a momentous time in history. This book covers, therefore, only the first twenty-nine years of Southey's career — his boyhood at school and university; his reactions to literary and political movements in his youth; his early associations with Coleridge, Lamb, Wordsworth, Humphry Davy, John Rickman, William Taylor of Norwich, and others; his share in a scheme of emigration to America for the purpose of establishing there a communistic society or "pantisocracy"; his characteristics as a young man, poet, and man of letters, together with the rise of his peculiar literary and personal reputation in association with the group of men who came to be known as the "lake school";

vii

and in conclusion his settling down in what was to be his final home at Keswick.

The materials for such a study have been ample. Southey's voluminousness, indeed, has been one of the chief reasons why the public has neglected without forgetting him. The basis and most of the details for the narrative of his life are to be found in the six volumes of letters published by Cuthbert Southey, the four volumes of letters published by Warter, the *Reminiscences* of the unreliable but indispensable Cottle, the letters of Coleridge, and the correspondence between Southey and William Taylor of Norwich published by the latter's biographer. These sources have been supplemented by information drawn from the works of Southey himself, from those of his contemporaries, from the numerous books which have appeared dealing with his friends and associates, from private persons, and from unpublished letters. The mass of Southey papers left by John Wood Warter is now in the possession of Miss Warter, the poet's grand-daughter. They are not at present accessible or available for publication. They have, however, been examined in a scholarly way by the Rev. Maurice H. FitzGerald, who has kindly supplied me with what he believes to be the only important information that they contain bearing upon Southey's early life. For additional facts I am indebted to Mr. Ernest Hartley Coleridge, and to unpublished letters of Southey and Coleridge in the British and the Victoria and Albert Museums. It should be added that little information concerning the period of Southey's life covered in the present work has been derived from sources not long accessible to the public, and it does not appear likely that much more waits to be unearthed. I have had access to some unpublished letters of Southey's to which I am unable specifically to refer, and many more no doubt remain undiscovered in private hands, but judging from what I have so far found, it is probable that these date from the poet's later years and that they make few references to those exciting indiscretions of his earlier life which he never came to be ashamed of but which it pained him to recall. It is my intention, however, to continue the study here begun, and I shall be grateful to any person who will in any way supplement the information I possess concerning any period of Southey's life.

To the freemasonry of scholars I already owe several pleasurable debts. Mr. George B. Parks, Kellogg Fellow of Amherst College, ably assisted by Mr. Emery E. Neff, Cutting Fellow of Columbia University, has been skilful and indefatigable in examining manuscripts, writing letters, and interviewing persons for me in England. The Rev. Maurice H. FitzGerald and Mr. Ernest Hartley Coleridge have given me most kind assistance out of their knowledge of the subjects with which I have been dealing. Professors Ashley H. Thorndike and Ernest H. Wright have read and criticized this work while it was still in manuscript. For various courtesies I am indebted to Mr. E. V. Lucas, Captain Orlo Williams, the Rev. Canon H. D. Rawnsley, Mrs. Elizabeth D. Dowden, Professor James McLean Harper, the Rev. Walter W. Graham, the Director of the Victoria and Albert Museum at South Kensington, and above all to Mr. Frederic W. Erb and his assistants on the staff of the Library of Columbia University.

Two persons have assisted me to whom I can make no adequate acknowledgment. My wife is almost solely responsible for the compilation of Appendices B and C, and has given me other valuable help besides. Professor William P. Trent first suggested to me that such a book should be written, and in my writing of it he has given abundant aid out of his mastery of biographical research.

W. H.

COLUMBIA UNIVERSITY

CONTENTS

THE EARLY LIFE
OF ROBERT SOUTHEY

INTRODUCTION

"I have this conviction," wrote Southey, "that, die when I may, my memory is one of those which will smell sweet, and blossom in the dust." That the memory of Southey's poetry, a century after it was written, continues rather in the dust than in the bloom, — nothing in literary history is more sure. The reason is not hard to find. He did not lack the poetic impulse nor the vision of his poetic opportunity. The religion of nature, the faith in which kings were overthrown and peoples conceived in Europe and America, although it provided the most vital occasion for a great poem of idealism since Milton, had been as yet inadequately expressed in English poetry. This expression was to be achieved lyrically by Wordsworth, but Southey, a peculiarly sensitive and intense mind, also attempting it in all the new forms of poetry with which the rising generation, Wordsworth included, was experimenting, finally settled down to the more ambitious purpose of embodying his faith in epic. He failed in this where no one else succeeded, and his failure the world has found it hard to forgive. An indubitable cause for this ill-success is to be found in his inability to achieve great style. Facility, eloquence, rhetorical skill of many sorts, and noble self-devotion to his task. — these he possessed, but not the power of harmony, the crash and splendor essential for great epic verse. At his best, it must be admitted, he does not fall far short of the mark, but in such a case the proverbial miss is indeed as bad as a mile.

Yet there was another cause for failure which might have been sufficient in itself to frustrate any epic that attempted to voice the creed of the deists.   To begin with, the return-to-nature movement had no traditions, no roots in the realized past, no legends proper to itself.   The revolution in America and more vividly the revolution in France vitalized the creed into a faith, but Napoleon and disillusionment followed so hard upon hope that the idealists were unable for long to find even in the present any series of momentous events to sanction their ideals.   The effect upon Words-worth was to drive him out of the current of life into eddying mysticism, and to confine his strictly intellectual activity chiefly to a struggle for reform in the style and subjects of poetry.   The effect upon Southey was not so simple, nor his effort so limited.   Engaging in similar but even wider experimentation in poetry, he attempted to find a great story in which to embody his ideals, but sought for it, not in the life of the disappointing present, nor of the conventionally familiar past, but in the new world which travel and inquiry were opening up to the imagination.   The error was fatal for the epic poet, because this new world was too little known to be believed in as a sanction for faith, and was too soon found to be a far different world from the one he represented.   Here the fundamental weakness of the religion of nature betrayed its own apostles; they fortified their ideals by facts which they pretended to observe, but blinked.   We have forgiven Wordsworth's bad science; we have had no reason to forgive Southey's bad history.

Such is the underlying reason for the oblivion that has fallen upon the work of a man who was one of the most considerable figures of the day in which he lived.   Other causes have contributed to the gloom. The ideals of Southey's faith were being defeated in his own day upon every hand. It seemed to him that nature was being thwarted, men were therefore being corrupted, and corruption was doing and would do deadly work. First had come unnatural tyranny in France, followed by equally monstrous mob-rule and doubly monstrous usurpation. As for England, the time was not a happy one for those who believed that the industrial revolution was but increasing the corruption of an already corrupted populace to which parliamentary reform, catholic emancipation, and freedom of the press were offering increased power. "It cannot and it will not come to good," Southey cried to Carlyle at the end of life, with a passionate intensity of fear that amazed even that not uncongenial soul. Yet he did not flinch in his devotion to those ideals which were his only hope and upon which society seemed more and more to set its back. Neither did he shrink from the contemplation of danger. On the contrary, in epic and in review article, he broke lance after lance in defense of his faith against old and new evils, and even against old friends. Unlike Wordsworth, who dreamed and prosed and was afraid, Southey fought. Unfortunately for his fame, it was a losing fight, and his less simple-minded opponents misunderstood him as he misunderstood them, so that he, whose noble unworldliness kept him poor on the side of the party in power in a day of political sine-cures, saw his name become the by-word for a turncoat and a truckler for pay. This might not have been sufficient in itself to have affected his reputation down to the present had it not been that his own pugnacious Quixotism drove him into exquisitely ridiculous, not to say asinine, postures which quite fairly rendered him the butt of Byron's titanic sneer. We do not altogether trust Byron, to be sure, but Southey's poems are many and long, and the Byron that lurks in each one of us has perpetuated the sneer.

For those who have felt the injustice of this attitude, it has been difficult to find adequate argument for change. To overstate the merits of Southey's prose has not been the right way of making the truth about him known. To insist upon his virtues as a friend and the head of a household has not lessened his sins as a poet. There has remained but to examine thoroughly his life and work, and to state truthfully what is there to be found. This is a task hitherto unattempted, first because the legendary Southey has seemed so definite a figure that such a study has appeared forbidding and unnecessary, and then because the sheer labor of traversing the ramifications of the man's career and of reading his voluminous writings has deterred any who might not already have been intimidated by the tradition that he was dull. The present work attempts a beginning at the critical study of Southey, a study which, to many besides the present writer, it has seemed strange that no one has previously made. Yet the purpose of this book is not the rehabilitation of Southey's poetry, although if anything here said helps to discourage future condemnation of an author unread, so much the better. In a form of poetry in which, to succeed greatly, he had to undergo comparison with Spenser and Milton, Southey came, perhaps, nearer to success than any other Englishman up to his time, and failed. As it is, the mass of his forgotten verse contains beauties sufficient to have made the immortality of half a dozen second-rate poets who may have tempted Providence less boldly. This would have been reason enough in most cases for writing a man's biography, but Southey has more claims upon our interest. He was one of the most active spirits in a period of English history the influence of which is still alive among us. He expressed its ideals in close association with Wordsworth, and a study of his work throws some additional light upon that of the greater poet. Of even more importance, perhaps, is the fact that he entered eagerly, though half-blindly, into the great new enterprise of historical and scientific study. History in many phases was his chosen field, but his avid learning touched most of the spheres of knowledge then attainable with something of a renaissance fervor and scope. Furthermore, though he shut himself in his library in an out-of-the-way corner of England, he played a vigorous part in the discussion of important questions of his time, made himself hated as the formidable foe of some of his most famous contemporaries, and respected or loved as the friend of many others. Finally, there remains as a reason for this book the common humanity in the man himself. A high-souled youth, passing through the yeasty yearnings and awkward starts of boyhood into a manhood of self-devotion to labor and to ideals that brought him poverty, disappointment, and unfulfilled renown, but not defeat,— the story of Southey's life has among men of letters seldom been surpassed in its genuine human interest and prolonged tragic intensity.

CHAPTER I
1774–1792

BOYHOOD

I

In 1820 Southey began an autobiography[1] in which he proposed, as Coleridge did in a similar abortive attempt[2] and as Wordsworth did in *The Prelude*, to unfold "the history of his own mind," but with characteristic sensitiveness he found himself unable to continue the narrative beyond the point at which the most troubled period of his life began. In the fragment that remains, however, he tells us many illuminating things about his kindred and early boyhood.

Throughout his life, one of Southey's constant aspirations was to establish himself and his family on a firm footing

[1] *Recollections of the Early Life of Robert Southey, written by himself in a series of Letters to his Friend Mr. John May.* These constitute the first 157 pages of Volume I of *The Life and Correspondence of Robert Southey edited by his son, the Rev. Charles Cuthbert Southey, 1849* (referred to hereafter as *Life*), and are the chief authority for sections I and II of the present chapter. Where no other reference is given, they may be taken as the source of all statements of fact.

[2] *Biographia Epistolaris being the Biographical Supplement of Coleridge's Biographia Literaria with additional letters, etc., edited by A. Turnbull. London, 1911*, I, 5–22. (The editor has here republished the *Supplement* of Henry Nelson and Sara Coleridge, together with such letters of Coleridge as have from time to time been published in various other places and are no longer under copyright. Referred to as *Biog. Epis.*)

of gentility. Fruits of this aspiration we shall see both in his early revolutionary activities and in his later devotion to the established order. It is therefore interesting to note that to establish themselves had been the often baffled aim of Southey's ancestors for several generations. On the father's side they had hovered over the borders of gentility for a long time without achieving any particular distinction. Old aunts and uncles brought down traditions of a famous soldier who fought for the parliament in the rebellion, and of another who was out with Monmouth, but all else concerning both was forgotten. Indeed, so obscure was the name Southey, that the poet, who looked upon many printed pages in his day, never beheld it upon any of them except when applied to himself or his brothers. He did, nevertheless, accept his family's claim to a coat-of-arms, upon the strength of which he conjured up visions of a crusading Southey; antiquarian research[1] has shrewdly surmised that these trappings had been acquired rather by an ancestor of later date in the law who found it convenient to borrow them from another family of similar name. Old wills at the cathedral town of Wells, as far back as 1533, and according to the poet, the parish register at Wellington as early as 1696, show that the Southeys were a race of yeomen, except for an occasional weaver, clothier, lawyer, gentleman, and in one branch a few generations of noblemen with the title Lord Somerville acquired through marriage. Obscure though they were, however, the Southeys were abundant in Somersetshire for over two centuries, and many during that time were the Roberts, Johns, and Thomases that bore the name.

Robert Southey was the name of the poet's father. He had an elder brother, John, who was a surly bachelor, became a rich lawyer in Taunton, and left his fortune to

[1] Arthur J. Jewers, *Notes and Queries*, Series 8, Vol. V, 141, 202, 241.

his youngest brother, Thomas, who remained merely a surly bachelor, and took pains not to leave the fortune to his poet-nephew. Robert Southey senior, on the other hand, was apparently an amiable youth of no very forceful character, who had been taught to cipher and then apprenticed to a kinsman, a grocer in London. Standing in the shop door one day, he saw a porter carrying a hare through the street, and tears came to his eyes for love of the country sports of boyhood he had left behind. The kinsman died, and his apprentice entered the shop of William Britton, linen-draper in Wine Street, Bristol, where he stayed for twelve or fourteen years. Eventually he opened a shop of his own in the same street. There he prospered for a time, but by and by his health failed, custom left him, and he seems not to have had the ability to push his fortune. His business collapsed in 1792, and shortly afterwards he died. He was evidently a rather dull person of little importance to his brilliant son.

The poet's maternal connections are of greater interest, since they concerned themselves more actively in the affairs of their kinsfolk. They were on the whole of somewhat higher social rank, being the daughters and younger sons of small gentry of the region. Southey's grandmother came from a line of Bradfords and Crofts of Herefordshire, through whom it amused[1] him to reckon his descent from Owen Glendower, Llewellyn, and Jorwerth, and so to claim 999th cousinship with his friend Wynn. This grandmother, Margaret Bradford, was twice married, first to a gentleman named John Tyler, by whom she had three children, the most notable of whom was Elizabeth Tyler, Southey's redoubtable aunt, and then to the poet's grandfather, Edward Hill, the seventh of the name in a long line of gentlemen who lived upon their own lands in the vale of Ashton. He

---

[1] *Selections from the Letters of Robert Southey, edited by his son-in-law John Wood Warter 1856* (referred to as *Warter*), III, 516; IV, 408.

was a lawyer and a widower with two grown children at the time of this marriage, but he was also handsome, talented, convivial, and while courting the widow he made verses to express his jealousy of a certain young justice poetically denominated Strephon.

This almost middle-aged couple settled at Bedminster near Bristol in a comfortable farmhouse with a large garden where the Southey children were to spend much of their childhood. The Hills were by no means wealthy, but their son, Herbert, was sent to Christ Church, Oxford, took orders, and when about 1774 his half-sister Miss Tyler, in the course of her fashionable wanderings, went to Lisbon, he followed and eventually became chaplain to the British factory at that place after a term of service at Oporto.[1] His own sister was Margaret, the poet's mother. She was born in 1752. Her son says of her, "Never was any human being blest with a sweeter temper or a happier disposition. She had an excellent understanding, and a readiness of apprehension which I have rarely known surpassed. In quickness of capacity, in the kindness of her nature, and in that kind of moral magnetism which wins the affections of all within its sphere, I never knew her equal." In looks she was said much to resemble the beautiful Miss Tyler, but her appearance was blighted in childhood by the small-pox. She was educated by her father to dance and whistle. Her half-brother, Edward Tyler, employed in some warehouse in Bristol, brought to Bedminster a friend named Robert Southey, to whom, although we may suspect that Miss Tyler could scarcely have approved the match, Margaret Hill was married in 1772 at the age of twenty.

Robert Southey, linen-draper, had a short time previously opened a shop for himself three doors above that of his old master in Wine Street in the crowded center of the town.

---

[1] *Vindiciae Ecclesiae Anglicanae*, 4.

A legacy of £100 from a kinsman, Cannon Southey, a similar sum of his younger brother Thomas's, who seems to have engaged in partnership with him for a time, a smaller sum of his wife's, perhaps some savings of his own,— these formed the capital of the new shop, and all began hopefully. In token of his boyish love of field-sports, the linendraper took a hare as his device. Children, nine in all, came in quick succession to the Southeys. The first was a son in 1773, John Cannon, who died in infancy. The second, born August 12, 1774, was Robert Southey. Three more boys survived childhood: Thomas, who became a captain in the navy; Henry Herbert, who became a highly respected physician in London; and Edward, black sheep and rolling stone, first in the army, then in the navy, and then as an actor in provincial theaters.

It will thus be seen that Southey's kin were not in any sense distinguished people. As gentry, they were very small gentry indeed, rapidly diminishing in importance to the station of farmers and tradespeople. But they were eminently respectable and of the sort who loved respectability. Most important of all, there was on the mother's side a touch of innate ability, to which the poet thought himself indebted for his own powers, and a strong family feeling, which caused his aunt and uncle to provide for the education of the linen-draper's children.

II

Miss Tyler was in Portugal at the time of Southey's birth in 1774, but she returned soon afterwards, rented a house in Bath, and decided to take charge of her nephew's bringing up. She was now thirty-five years old, proud, domineering, eccentric, with a temper rendered more detestable by a consciousness of her own striking beauty. Her youth had been chiefly spent with her uncle, the Rev. Herbert Brad-

ford, a curate in Shobden, Herefordshire. He was a man of
wealth and intimate with a Lord Bateman of the neighborhood, with whose wife Miss Tyler became a great favorite.
Here she acquired those tastes and manners which became
her chief pride and comfort. After the death of her uncle's
wife she managed his house for him, and upon his death
she inherited a large part of his fortune, much of which, by
the time of Southey's birth, had been spent by her in fashionable vanities at watering-places. Consequently she was
henceforth compelled more and more closely to retrench her
expenditures. Her position and character, not to say her
tongue and temper, gave her an easy ascendancy, not only
over the linen-draper's young wife, who was thirteen years
her junior, but also over other relatives, friends, and servants. The picture of her suggested by Southey's autobiography and by the character of Miss Trewbody in *The
Doctor* [1] is by no means an affectionate one.

Among her other acquirements, Miss Tyler included
certain "blue-stocking" tastes and aspirations. She had
known not a few small literary men of the day, she had had
her portrait painted by Gainsborough, and through a friend
at Bath, a Miss Palmer, daughter of the owner of the
theatres at Bath and Bristol, she was enabled to pose as
patroness of the drama, to dine the players, to cultivate an
acquaintance with such people as Colman, Sheridan, Cumberland, Holcroft, and Miss Palmer's particular friend,
Sophia Lee. Possibly, one suspects, Miss Tyler hoped to
establish a little salon in the house which she now took
in Bath in 1774. It stood in the center of a walled garden,
looking out upon other gardens, the river, and Claverton
Hill. The parlor door, upon whose stone steps her small
nephew often sat, was bowered with jessamine. The interior, especially the parlor, was fitted up by Miss Tyler
at a greater expense than she could afford, and Southey

[1] *Doctor*, 157–160.

gives a curious catalogue of her treasures: a Turkey carpet; a cabinet of ivory, ebony, and tortoise shell that had come down from the great Duke of Marlborough; the portrait of Miss Tyler by Gainsborough with a curtain to preserve it from flies and the sun; a mezzotint of Pope's Eloisa supposed to resemble Miss Tyler, as well as two similar prints from Angelica Kauffman; and finally a great picture of Pombal, the first portrait of an illustrious man with which Southey became familiar.

By the time that her nephew was old enough to observe his elders, Miss Tyler's ruling passion appears to have become hatred of dirt. She commonly wore a ragged bed-gown in order to keep her better clothes clean. Her splendid parlor was never opened except for company and dusting; she lived in a kitchen with rough stone floors and a skylight, and she put her servants into a dark basement. If anyone crossed the hearth while her breakfast was preparing, the tea-kettle had to be re-filled. One whom she disliked was *ipso facto* unclean, and a cup out of which such a person had drunk had to be buried in the garden for six weeks before it could be used again. All this was, of course, vexatious to her servants, whom she intrusted with her confidences and treated now with overindulgence, now with paroxysms of rage. She would send them constantly to the playhouse, but she never forgave them if they married. Somewhat similar were her relations with her friend, Miss Palmer, and with Southey's mother.

"The authority which Miss Tyler had first exerted as an elder sister she never relaxed. My mother was one of the few persons (for a few such there are) who think too humbly of themselves. Her only fault (I verily believe she had no other), was that of yielding submissively to this imperious sister, to the sacrifice of her own inclination and judgment and sense of what was right. She had grown up in awe and admiration of her, as one who moved in a superior rank, and who, with the advantage of a fine form and beautiful person, possessed that also of a superior and cultivated understanding: withal, she loved her with a true sisterly affection which nothing could diminish, clearly as she saw her faults, and severely as at last she suffered by them. But never did I know one person so entirely subjected by another, and never have I regretted anything more deeply than that subjection, which most certainly in its consequences shortened her life."

Under such a person's care most of Southey's childhood between the years of two and six were passed, except for occasional visits to his home or to his grandmother's house at Bedminster. Miss Tyler had bought a copy of *Emile* to guide her in the education of the boy, but although in some respects she allowed him great freedom, it cannot be said that she followed Rousseau very closely.

"I had many indulgences, but more privations;" he writes, "and those of an injurious kind; want of playmates, want of exercise, never being allowed to do anything in which by possibility I might dirt myself; late hours in company . . .; late hours of rising, which were less painful perhaps, but in other respects worse. My aunt chose that I should sleep with her, and this subjected me to a double evil. She used to have her bed warmed, and during the months that this practice was in season I was always put into Molly's bed first, for fear of an accident from the warming pan, and removed when my aunt went to bed, so that I was regularly wakened out of a sound sleep. This, however, was not half so bad as being obliged to lie till nine, and not unfrequently until ten in the morning, and not daring to make the slightest movement which could disturb her during the hours that I lay awake, and longing to be set free. These were, indeed, early and severe lessons of patience. My poor little wits were upon the alert at those tedious hours of compulsory idleness, fancying figures and combinations of form in the curtains, wondering at the motes in the slant sunbeam, and watching the light from the crevices of the window-shutters, till it served me at last by its progressive motion to measure the lapse of time. Thoroughly injudicious as my education under Miss Tyler was, no part of it was so irksome as this."

Such a training would have been bad for any boy, but there were two reasons why its effects in Southey's case were not as injurious as they might have been. The first was his own innate sweetness and sanity, which are shown by the fact that neither the child nor the man writing in later years betrayed any bitterness toward Miss Tyler in spite of unmitigated disapproval of her. The other thing that made Southey's childhood not unhappy was his own resourceful imagination. At the dame's school to which he was sent to learn his letters and to be out of the way, he found playmates with whom he could concoct such grand schemes as running away to an island where there should be mountains of gingerbread and candy. Then there was a sham castle in a grove of firs on the crest of Claverton Hill within view of his aunt's garden, and a summer-house at Beechen Cliffs, and the grave of a man who had been killed in a duel, — these were goals of childish adventure. A friend of Miss Tyler had married the son of Francis Newberry, the publisher of the delectable *Goody Twoshoes* series, and for his first reading she presented the boy with twenty volumes of these books as soon as he could tell his letters. From them, Southey gravely surmises, he received the bent toward literature which determined his course in life. The most important influence of all, however, was the theater, to which the child was nightly carried by Miss Tyler and her friend, Miss Palmer, even before he could read or know what it was all about, and for occupation that should keep him out of the dirt his aunt would give him old play-bills upon which to prick letters with a pin-point. Naturally the theater came to be the most exciting joy of his childhood, though he felt at a later time that the walk home in the moonlight along the terrace of the South Parade did him more good.[1] He saw Mrs. Siddons in all her rôles.

[1] Unpublished manuscript letter of Oct. 26, 1812, to Walter Savage Landor in the Forster Library, South Kensington Museum.

He saw Shakespeare acted before he could read, and he had been through Beaumont and Fletcher by the time he had reached the age of eight. His future love of romance was shown in the fact that his early favorites were *As You Like It* and *Cymbeline*.

When he came to be six years old and tall for his age, Miss Tyler was compelled to submit to the substitution of coat, waist-coat, and trousers for the fantastic nankeen tunic with green fringe in which she had attired him, and he was sent to Mr. Foot's school, the best in Bristol, where he continued for a year. The boys seem to have been handled with great severity at this place, and young Robert was frightened out of learning the grammar they attempted to teach him. When the old man who kept the school died, Southey senior, for some reason unknown but possibly not unconnected with the fact that Miss Tyler's temper had finally led her into a feud with the linen-draper's surly brother Thomas, suddenly assumed direction of his son's education, and sent him to a school at Corston nine miles from Bristol. Upon his departure the boy found his mother weeping in her chamber, and this first sight of grief impressed him so deeply that it is recorded in his *Hymn to the Penates*, written in 1796.

The school at Corston, bad though it was, had a vivid effect upon Southey's imagination. In 1795, it would seem, he returned to look over the place again in a romantic fit of abstraction, and he composed at about the same time at least two poems inspired by his experiences there. *The Retrospect*, which gives its name to the title-page of his first volume of poems, is a description of his life at Corston, and the sonnet, *To a Brook near the Village of Corston*, is a plaintive reminiscence in the manner of Bowles; both were probably written at the same time in 1795. He returned yet again to show the place to his son in 1836,[1] and de-

[1] *Life*, VI, 311–313.

scribed it in the preface to *The Retrospect* in the second
volume of his collected poetical works. It was a little village south of the Avon and four or five miles from Bath.
Southey's father rode out with the stage-coach that carried
the boy, and left him with the master and mistress of the
school, who gave him a smiling welcome with talk of tender
care and happy sports, but after his father's form had disappeared, "never spake so civilly again."

Thomas Flower, the master of the school, was interested
mainly in mathematics and astronomy, for the sake of
which he neglected his pupils, and left them largely to the
instruction of his son, whom the boys called Charley and
whose consequence may be judged therefrom. Writing,—
the flourishing ornamental penmanship of an older day,—
arithmetic, and spelling were the subjects taught. Southey,
with a few of the other scholars, was also taught Latin by a
Frenchman who came twice a week from Bristol, and the
youngster was required, either by his mates or his master,
to help some of the older boys at their tasks. The discipline of the school was not severe; the boys were neglected
rather than abused, and although they were compelled to
sit sleepy and cold in a dark room on wintry Sunday evenings, there to listen to the droning of dull sermons, they
were given on the whole plenty of outdoor freedom for
play and getting dirty such as Miss Tyler's nephew had
never enjoyed before.

The house in which the school was kept had been the
mansion of some departed family.

"There were vestiges of former respectability and comfort . . .
walled gardens, summer-houses, gate-pillars surmounted with huge
stone balls, a paddock, a large orchard, walnut trees, yards, outhouses upon an opulent scale. I felt how mournful all this was in
its fallen state, when the great walled garden was converted into
a playground for the boys, the gateways broken, the summer-houses
falling into ruin, and grass growing in the interstices of the lozenged

pavement of the fore-court. The features within I do not so distinctly remember, not being so well able to understand their symbols of better days; only I recollect a black oaken staircase from the hall, and that the school-room was hung with faded tapestry, behind which we used to have our hoards of crabs."

This ruined magnificence made a capital playground. The boys gathered apples in the orchard; they "squailed at the bannets"— that is, threw sticks for walnuts; they flew kites and played at bow and arrow; they dammed the brook that flowed across the barton and through the orchard; and they were not much disturbed by the demands of study. At the end of a twelvemonth, however, the school came to an unlucky end, for the ablutions of the boys were conducted under no direction except their own in the ankle-deep brook in the barton. The consequences of such a system were such as to arouse the just indignation of the mothers of the boys in Bristol, and so many of the pupils were withdrawn that the school was ruined. Southey was one of those who were summoned home. He had thick, curly hair, and he was at once put through "a three-day's purgatory in brimstone."

The year of his absence had been a sad one for his mother. Another child had died during the time, and while she was away with Miss Tyler, seeking distraction in London, the death of their mother, Mrs. Hill, recalled them to Bedminster. Miss Tyler, having broken up her establishment at Bath the year before, took up her residence in 1782 in her mother's house until it should be sold, and to Bedminster also Southey was sent to be with his aunt. His grandmother's house had already been a place of many delights to the little boy, and now he was to enjoy them for the last time.

One of the ever-recurring themes in Southey's poetry, from the rhetorical *Hymn to the Penates* to some of the less pretentious, but charming minor pieces, is the love of home.

Much of the romantic yearning for escape from the world
of men simmered down in him to the plain love of a country
house where one could settle with one's books, one's wife,
one's children, and the cats. This was the impulse which
was to give us in Southey's letters that vivid picture of
Greta Hall which has made it one of the classic households
of the world, and this impulse was fostered in the boy and
the man by the memory of his grandmother's house at
Bedminster. It was a commodious, unpretentious place in
a lane two or three hundred yards off the road running
west from Bristol across the Avon and over Redcliffe Hill.
It had been built about 1740 by Southey's grandfather,
Edward Hill. The distance from the shop in Wine Street,
by a path through the fields and across a drawbridge over
a ditch at the foot of the orchard, was just two miles. The
village of Bedminster was unfortunately growing poor and
populous owing to the near neighborhood of the coal mines;
otherwise Southey would certainly have bought the house
in later years when he was looking for an establishment of
his own. As it was, after it was sold, he never saw it again,
except for one or two fleeting glimpses and for a visit with
his son in 1837.

"One ascended to the front door by several semicircular steps
into what was called the fore court, but was in fact a flower-garden,
with a broad pavement from the gate to the porch. The porch
was in great part lined, as well as covered, with white jessamine;
and many a time have I sat there with my poor sisters, threading
the fallen blossoms upon grass stalks. It opened into a little hall,
paved with diamond-shaped flags. On the right hand was the parlour, which had a brown or black boarded floor, covered with a
Lisbon mat, and a handsome timepiece over the fireplace; on the
left was the best kitchen, where the family lived. . . . [It] was a
cheerful room, with an air of such country comfort about it, that
my little heart was always gladdened when I entered it during my
grandmother's life. It had a stone floor, which I believe was the
chief distinction between a best kitchen and a parlour. The furni-

ture consisted of a clock, a large oval oak table with two flaps (over which two or three fowling-pieces had their place), a round tea-table of cherry wood, Windsor chairs of the same, and two large armed ones . . . in one of which my grandmother always sat. On one side of the fireplace the china was displayed in a buffet — that is, a cupboard with glass doors; on the other were closets for articles less ornamental, but more in use. The room was wainscotted and ornamented with some old maps, and with a long looking glass over the chimney-piece, and a tall one between the windows, both in white frames. The windows opened into the fore-court, and were as cheerful and fragrant in the season of flowers as roses and jessamine, which grew luxuriantly without, could make them. There was a passage between this apartment and the kitchen, long enough to admit of a large airy pantry, and a larder on the left hand, the windows of both opening into the barton, as did those of the kitchen; on the right was a door into the back court. There was a rack in the kitchen well furnished with bacon, and a mistle-toe bush always suspended from the middle of the ceiling."

The outer arrangements of the place were no less comfortable, and the memory of the middle-aged Southey dwelt in fond detail upon things so dear to a boy's heart as grape-vines, pigeon-houses, a pump, a barn-yard with great folding gates flanked by horse-chestnut trees, outhouses for dairy and laundry, seed-rooms, a stable, hay-lofts, coal and stick houses, sheds for carts and a carriage, clipt yews and a mounting-block overgrown with ivy. This was not all. There was also a large kitchen-garden, kept in admirable order with grass walks, espaliers and flower beds. There was wall fruit in abundance — green gages, cherries, peaches, nectarines, apricots — then an orchard beyond the garden, and a potato patch, with the crowning touch, for childhood's delectation, of the drawbridge over the broad ditch at the far end. But the flowers were the most abiding charm of the place; the syringa, the everlasting pea, and the evening primrose never ceased to remind Southey of his grandmother and Bedminster.

The plants and insects also seem to have attracted the boy, and he loved and long remembered the pictures and "fine lies" in an "old bird and beast book."[1] The grown man even speculates gravely on his narrow escape from becoming the historian of snails and cockchafers. Such amusements as these things afforded were varied by the none too successful efforts of his two odd uncles, Edward and William Tyler, to interest him in the usual boyish pursuits. These men were brothers of Miss Tyler's, younger than she and of far less importance in the family. Edward, never educated for any particular purpose, had lived aimlessly about his mother's house for a time, had then entered some trade in Bristol, and died a little later than this period, a comparatively young man. William had greater claims to interest. He was very fond of his nephew, to whom he was an unfailing source of entertainment, and who has given a delightful description of him in the character of William Dove in *The Doctor*.[2] "He was born with one of those heads in which the thin partition that divides great wits from folly is wanting." But his "was not a case of fatuity. Though all was not there, there was a great deal. He was what is called *half-saved*. Some of his faculties were more than ordinarily acute, but the power of self-conduct was entirely wanting in him." . . . "Had he come into the world a century sooner, he would have been taken *nolens volens* into some Baron's household, to wear motley, make sport for the guests and domestics, and live in fear of the rod." As it was, Uncle William spent his days in easy dependence, first on his mother and then on Miss Tyler, consorting with the servants and other humble folk, among whom he gathered an inexhaustible store of anecdotes, gossip, shrewd apothegms, folk and animal lore such as would delight the heart of a boy. One of his accom-

---

[1] *Commonplace Book*, Series IV, 193.   [2] *Doctor*, 27–29.

plishments was the power of mimicking to perfection the voices of animals.

"A London manager would have paid him well for performing the cock in Hamlet. He could bray in octaves to a nicety, set the geese gabbling by addressing them in their own tongue, and make the turkey-cock spread his fan, brush his wing against the ground, and angrily gob-gobble in answer to a gobble of defiance. But he prided himself more upon his success with the owls, as an accomplishment of more difficult attainment. In this Mr. Wordsworth's boy of Winander was not more perfect. Both hands were used as an instrument in producing the notes; and if Pope could have heard the responses which came from barn and doddered oak and ivied crag, he would rather (satirist as he was) have left Ralph unsatirised, than have vilified one of the wildest and sweetest of nocturnal sounds."

Even more fascinating to the imaginative child with his awakening appetite for romance must have been "the squire's" old saws and stories. It was from him that the saying came which, translated into Greek by Coleridge, stands at the head of *The Curse of Kehama*.[1]

"Whatever event occurred, whatever tale was current, whatever traditions were preserved, whatever superstitions were believed, William knew them all; and all that his insatiable ear took in, his memory hoarded. Half the proverbial sayings in Ray's volume were in his head, and as many more with which Ray was unacquainted. He knew many of the stories which our children are now receiving as novelties in the selections from Grimm's *Kinder und Haus-Märchen*, and as many of those which are collected in the Danish Folk-Sagn [sic]. And if some zealous lover of legendary lore (like poor John Leyden, or like Sir Walter Scott), had fallen in with him, the Shakesperian commentators might perhaps have had the whole story of St. Withold; the Wolf of the World's End might have been identified with Fenris and found to be a relic of the Scalds: and Rauf Collyer and John the Reeve might still have been as well known as Adam Bell, and Clym of the Clough, and William of Cloudslie."

[1] "Curses are like young chicken; they always come home to roost."

The delights of Bedminster came to an end in 1782 with the death of Mrs. Hill, for the place was immediately sold. At the same time Southey returned to live at his father's house in Wine Street. Miss Tyler was living with her friends or in lodgings at Bath, and the boy was with her only for his holidays. For he was now put to school in Bristol under an old Welshman named William Williams. Most of the instruction under this person, as was suitable for the sons of Bristol tradesmen, consisted in ciphering, penmanship, and catechism. For Southey there was also some meager Latin, but when he had read the *Metamorphoses* and Virgil's *Eclogues*, neither master nor usher dared trust his own Latinity to carry the boy further. For the same reason, probably, the lad was never taught to write Latin verse, and continued through life, he says, "as liable to make a false quantity as any Scotchman." Occasional English themes made up the only training in composition which he received. Of more interest, it would seem, than anything else in the school were the characters of the boys — many of them sons of West India planters — and the oddities of humanity which gathered about old Williams, an oddity himself in a dirty wig which served the boys as weather-vane for telling his temper. Yet on the whole Southey felt in later life that the four or five years spent at this school, while not unhappy, were not very profitable.

Fortunately he found plenty of intellectual food without a teacher, for his life-long passion for books had already appeared. Books were not plentiful, to be sure, during the two years that he lived in his father's house, but such as they were, he made it his business to read them. Southey senior satisfied himself with *Felix Farley's Bristol Journal*, but in a cupboard over the desk in the back-parlor there was, along with the wine-glasses, a small library. "It consisted of *The Spectator*, three or four volumes of *The Oxford Magazine*, one of *The Freeholder's*, and one of *The Town and*

Country. . . . The other books were Pomfret's *Poems, The Death of Abel,* Aaron Hill's translation of *Merope,* with *The Jealous Wife,* and *Edgar and Emmeline,* in one volume; *Julius Cæsar, The Toy Shop, All for Love,* and a Pamphlet upon Quack Doctors of George II's days, in another; *The Vestal Virgins, The Duke of Lerma,* and *The Indian Queen,* in a third. To these my mother added *The Guardian,* and the happy copy of Mrs. Rowe's *Letters* which introduced me to Torquato Tasso."

Holidays afforded the boy richer fare. They were spent with his aunt in Bath, except for a short summer visit to Weymouth when Southey had his first thrilling sight of the sea. Finally, some time about the beginning of 1785, Miss Tyler, having "lived about among her friends as long as it was convenient for them to entertain her, and longer in lodgings than was convenient for herself," took a pleasant house with a garden in the outskirts of Bristol. Thither her nephew and her brother, William, were summoned, and she resumed her usual mode of life. This was the household where Southey remembers her most distinctly, shutting up the rooms to keep them clean, living in rags in the kitchen, scolding her friends and servants, interfering with her relatives, nursing a profound contempt for Bristol society, and showing hospitality only to a stray actor or other friend from Bath. Residence with her, however, was now welcome to her nephew for sake of the additional freedom which it gave as contrasted with the cramped quarters at Wine Street. More books also fell in his way. He had long since graduated from *Goody Twoshoes;* play-going, which was resumed with joy upon his return from Corston and whenever he was with his aunt, had introduced him, as we have seen, to Shakespeare and to Beaumont and Fletcher. From these he had already learned something more than a boy's love for romance, and in Mrs. Rowe's *Letters* he had found the stories of Olendo and Sophronio and of the Enchanted Forest from Tasso. In a circulating library he soon after saw Hoole's translation of the *Gerusalemme Liberata* (1763), and a friend of his aunt's, hearing him speak of the book with delight and interest above his years, in the summer of 1783 gave him a copy of it. Bull's circulating library in Bath at once became his Bodleian. Referred by Hoole to Ariosto, he borrowed the same translator's version of *Orlando Furioso* (1783). "I do not think," he says, "any accession of fortune could now give me so much delight as I then derived from that vile version of Hoole's." Again he found an alluring reference in the notes, this time to Spenser; again he resorted to the circulating library, and asked for *The Faerie Queene.*

"My friend Cruett replied that they had it, but it was written in old English, and I should not be able to understand it. ·This did not appear to me so much a necessary consequence as he supposed, and I therefore requested that he would let me look at it. It was the quarto edition of '17,[1] in three volumes, with large prints folded in the middle, equally worthless like all the prints of that age, in design and execution. There was nothing in the language to impede, for the ear set me right where the uncouth spelling . . . might have puzzled the eye; and the few words which are really obsolete, were sufficiently explained by the context. No young lady of the present generation falls to a new novel of Sir Walter Scott's with a keener relish than I did that morning to *The Faery Queen.*" [2]

Milton came into his hands about this time also. An old widow, "mad as a March hare after a religious fashion," hearing that Southey was a promising boy, asked his mother that he might be sent to drink tea with her some evening. "Her behaviour to me was very kind; but as soon as tea was over, she bade me kneel down, and down she knelt her-

---

[1] Probably the edition of 1715, edited by John Hughes.

[2] *The Complete Poetical Works of Robert Southey, collected by himself,* *New York, 1848* 7–8 (referred to as *Works*).

self, and prayed for me by the hour to my awful astonish-
ment.   When this was done she gave me a little book called
Early Piety, and a coarse edition of *Paradise Lost*."

Such a beginning in books was now rapidly supplemented,
especially by more romances, epics, and histories.   To the
schoolboy reading of Virgil, Horace, and Ovid, were added
Mickle's *Lusiad*, Pope's *Homer*, "Arabian and mock-Arabian
Tales," Sidney's *Arcadia*, Chatterton, Gay's *Pastorals*,—
which he took seriously, — Percy's *Reliques*, Warton's *History of English Poetry*, Chaucer, the Bible,[1] and such curious
things as William Chamberlayne's *Pharonnida* (1659), of
which Southey wrote an account for *The Athenæum Magazine* in after years, as "one of the worst specimens of
versification in the English language."[2]

Here was the scholar in the making, but even before this
the poet had been putting his dreams to paper.   While still
unbreeched the boy had informed Miss Tyler's friend, Miss
Palmer, that it was the easiest thing in the world to write
a play, "for you know you have only to think what you
would say if you were in the place of the characters, and
to make them say it."   And very soon, as was natural, he
began himself the attempt to compose a drama.   "The first
subject which I tried was the continence of Scipio, suggested
by a print in a pocket-book.   Battles were introduced in
abundance because the battle in Cymbeline was one of my
favorite scenes; and because Congreve's hero in *The Mourning Bride* finds the writing of his father in prison, I made
my prince of Numantia find pen, ink, and paper, that he
might write to his mistress.   An act and a half of this nonsense exhausted my perseverance."   But the attempt did
not stop there altogether.   He even persuaded one of his
schoolmates to write a tragedy, but finding it necessary to
supply this boy first with a story, then with characters,
names, and finally with dialogue itself, he gave up in des-

[1] *Works*, 8.   [2] *Athenæum Monthly Magazine* 1807, I, 594.

pair, not, however, without attempting another tragedy for himself on the subject of the Trojan War.

Far more congenial forms soon attracted his attention, and he turned to the composition of epic and romance. Many were the heroic flights which he planned. In the covers of his *Phœdrus* at the age of nine or ten he wrote, in couplets imitating Hoole, some part of a story to be engrafted upon Ariosto, in which the Moors were to be again overthrown in Arcadia by a hero of the young author's own invention. Then at Miss Tyler's house he found the first volume of Bysshe's *Art of Poetry*, and learned the rules for making blank verse, which forthwith became his chosen medium. The Trojan Brutus, the death of Richard III and the union of the roses, the story of King Egbert, Cassibelan, a continuation of *The Faerie Queene* and another of the *Metamorphoses* of Ovid on the suggestion of Chatterton's *English Metamorphoses*, these were some of his attempted subjects. Less ambitious works were heroic epistles in rime on topics taken from classical and historical reading, translations of Ovid, Virgil, and Horace, descriptive pieces on morning in town and country in imitation of Cunningham, and a vision of Hades. In the last-named poem there was a passage perhaps ironically significant: "It described the Elysium of the Poets, and that more sacred part of it in which Homer, Virgil, Tasso, Spenser, Camoens, and Milton were assembled. While I was regarding them, Fame came hurrying by with her arm full of laurels and asking in an indignant voice if there was no poet who would deserve them? Upon which I reached my hand, snatched at them, and awoke."

Although Miss Tyler's tutelage gave the lad little chance for play, all was not bookishness in his childhood. As he grew older he found ample room for youthful exploration in the country about Bath and Bristol. The former town did not yet extend far beyond the Royal Crescent. Bathwick

Fields on the other side of the river were as yet largely open country, and from Bristol Southey was able to make expeditions to Clifton and the wilder places on the lower reaches of the Avon. Between Clifton and the sea, the river passes between precipitous and rocky banks, and there, says the poet, "I first learned to scramble among rocks, where . . . I treasured up a store of imagery and enriched my mind with sights and sounds and feelings not to be obtained anywhere but in the school of nature. These rocks and woods were my best teachers."[1] Other companions than such as these were few. Yet though there were no boys in the families of Miss Tyler's acquaintance, her housemaid had a brother, a good-natured, lively lad, named Shadrach Weeks, who proved an excellent playmate.

"At this hour, if he be living, and were to meet me, I am sure he would greet me by a hearty shake of the hand; and, be it where it might, I should return the salutation. We used to work together in the garden, play trap in the fields, make kites and fly them, try our hands at carpentry, and, which was the greatest of all indulgences, go into the country to bring home primrose, violet, and cowslip roots; and sometimes to St. Vincent's Rocks, or rather the heights about a mile and a half farther down the river, to search for the bee and fly orchis. Some book had taught me that these rare flowers were to be found there; and I sought for them year after year with . . . persevering industry, for the unworthy purpose of keeping them in pots at home, . . . Perhaps I have never had a keener enjoyment of natural scenery than when roaming about the rocks and woods on the side of the Avon with Shad and our poor spaniel Phillis. Indeed, there are few scenes in the island finer of their kind; and no other where merchant vessels of the largest size may be seen sailing between such rocks and woods."

Shad acquired considerable skill in carpentry, and this accomplishment the future author put to good use in fur-

[1] From an unpublished letter by Southey (May 27, 1819) in the British Museum.

thering his own literary interests. Before Southey left for
Westminster School, they set about making a puppet-
theatre,[1] a design that grew so elaborate as to provide for
pit, boxes, gallery, ornamental ceiling, as well as a full com-
plement of actors. Southey was to write plays for it, and
the spectator was to look through a magnifying glass behind
the gallery, but the optician told them that it was impossible to construct a single magnifier that would serve their
purpose. In spite of this disappointment, they persisted,
and even after Southey was launched at school, the theatre
still provided amusement for holiday time.

In such occupations the boy approached the age of fourteen, and the features of the mature man were becoming
distinguishable. From his father, he seems to have inherited none of that dull incompetence which was sapping
the fortunes of the linen-draper's shop, but the high spirit
of his mother's family was his to the full, that spirit that
ran to pride and ill temper in his aunt, but which led his
mother bravely through affliction. The loss of five children, the gradual disintegration of her husband's health and
little business, poverty and care for remaining children, her
own ill-health and a domineering sister who wasted on vanities what might really have helped those she sought to
govern, — the poet's mother bore her lot patiently as a
woman can. The spirit of her son, however, had as yet
undergone no trial; it was still engrossed in bookish pursuits, undisturbed by any problems of his own or others.
He was merely the romancer and the student, not yet the
moralist or the reformer. But in another year the Bastille
would fall and the spirit of this boy, like that of so many
others, would take fire. Then would appear that passionate, outspoken hate of what he thought was evil which was
to be both the strength and the weakness of the grown man.
As yet, we know merely that his mother's eye had noticed

[1] *Life*, I, 308.

that Robert as a child might always be expected to show anger at wrongdoing by the other children.

Meanwhile some provision had to be found for the youngster's future, especially as it must have long since become evident that his father was not going to be able to assist his son materially. Consequently Robert's uncle, the Reverend Herbert Hill, Chaplain to the British factory at Lisbon and unmarried, now came forward to take a more active interest in his nephew. The plan that was naturally suggested by the boy's bright promise and by the habits and connections of the Hill family was that he should go to Westminster School at his uncle's expense, thence to Christ Church, Oxford. After that clerical friends were to see that he obtained a fellowship which would lead in the usual course of events to a college living, and thus he would be settled respectably for life. Before going up to Westminster, however, it was thought well to place him with a handful of other boys under a clergyman named Lewis to be more thoroughly prepared. In this way the year 1787 was spent. The tutor's influence was small, if we may believe Southey's own statement, but greater freedom gave greater time for writing poetry. "I do not remember in any part of my life to have been so conscious of intellectual improvement as I was during the year and a half before I was placed at Westminster." This improvement came from "constantly exercising myself in English verse."

In this, however, lay ill omen for Mr. Hill's prudent and generous plan. The boy's kindred concluded from his love of books that he would take kindly to the career outlined for him. They could as yet see nothing in his reading that would lead him elsewhere, and above all they had as yet no opportunity to observe that stiff independence of character which would make it at all times difficult for others to plan for him.

"There were
Who form'd high hopes and flattering ones of thee,
Young Robert! for thine eye was quick to speak
Each opening feeling; should they not have known,
When the rich rainbow on the morning cloud
Reflects its radiant dyes, the husbandman
Beholds the ominous glory sad and fears
Impending storms! — They augur'd happily,
That thou didst love each wild and wondrous tale
Of faery fiction, and thine infant tongue
Lisp'd with delight the godlike deeds of Greece
And rising Rome; therefore they deem'd, forsooth,
That thou should'st tread preferment's pleasant path.
Ill-judging ones! they let thy little feet
Stray in the pleasant paths of Poesy,
And when thou should'st have prest amid the crowd,
There didst thou love to linger out the day,
Loitering beneath the laurel's barren shade.
Spirit of Spenser! was the wanderer wrong?" [1]

III

Our knowledge[2] of the experiences of Southey's early life
is based almost entirely upon the fragment of an autobiography written between 1820 and 1825. This narrative continues only through the early part of his residence at
Westminster, and gives practically no account of the most
interesting occurrences of those years. The bookish, high-

[1] *On my own Miniature Picture, taken at two years of age, Poems,* 1797.

[2] The main source for facts concerning the first part of Southey's
stay at Westminster is still the autobiographical fragment printed in
Life. This contains nothing, however, about *The Flagellant,* the information concerning which is drawn chiefly from the statements of
Cuthbert Southey in *Life,* I, 158–170, from Southey's letters of the
period as published in *Life* and in *Warter,* I, 1–20, and from allusions in
later letters. The records of admissions to Westminster School from
1788 through 1806 have disappeared. G. F. R. Barker and A. H.
Stenning, *Westminster School Register from 1764 to 1883.*

spirited boy was now to encounter a new kind of reading,—those books which had prepared the way for revolution,—and the revolution itself was to set this ferment working in his mind. Unfortunately his thoughts and feelings of this time, while never looked upon by himself with shame or regret, are preserved in few letters and were never thought in later life worthy of that detailed presentation which Wordsworth gave to his similar experience. Southey's autobiography was, indeed, undertaken with some such aim, but when a real beginning upon the story of these troubled, yeasty times was to be made, he shrank from the task. From the records that do remain, however, we can easily piece together a clear story of his life at Westminster which will partly account for the kind of young man who left the place and entered Oxford in the particular manner that Southey did.

In February, 1788, Miss Tyler, with thirty pounds which Southey's father had given her, glad of the excuse for a visit to London, set out on the journey to place her nephew at school. Miss Palmer was persuaded to hire a carriage and convey them with her to town. In four days they were settled in lodgings in Pall Mall which were too expensive for Miss Tyler's purse, however pleasing to her pride and taste. For about six weeks the party went to the theatres, visited friends, and had a gay time. The boy of fourteen was bored and homesick until, on the first of April, he was carried to Westminster, and entered at the school. Miss Tyler, having spent all her own money and more besides, was forced to return to Bristol before Whitsuntide.

At Westminster Southey remained for four active years, and although later he often spoke disparagingly of the system there in vogue, his schooldays were, on the whole, happy ones. Of his actual studies he tells us little, but we may assume that he progressed prosperously through the

usual course of classical reading without, however, learning
to write Latin verses. The life of the boys left a far more
vivid impression upon his mind, so vivid that in after years
he was constantly alluding to it and dreaming about it in
his sleep. The master, when he entered, was Dr. Smith,
shortly afterwards succeeded by Dr. Vincent. The school
was largely preparatory for Christ Church, and numbered
about three hundred boys, "very few upon whose countenance Nature had set her best testimonials." Most of them
were clay to the potter's hand, and the strongest hand
among them was, as usual in the public school of the day,
that of the bully and the brute. Southey, however, upon
admittance to the fourth form, was fortunately assigned to
a diligent and gentlemanly boy, named George Strachey, to
be introduced by him to the work of the form. Unluckily
Strachey lived at home, and Southey was quartered at a
boarding house kept by one "Botch" Hayes, usher of the
fifth form, who was also to be his tutor. Hayes was not
a pleasant creature, nor very efficient, and the boy was, for
a time, solitary indeed. He was placed in the same room
with a handsome young brute of an ungovernable temper
and the imagination of a fiend, who attempted to hold him
by one leg out of the window; there was a full story to
fall and stone flags underneath, but the victim struggled
manfully enough to be rescued. The room-mate then took
to pouring water into his ear as he lay asleep and to flinging
the poker and the porter-pot at him. The youngster, no
weakling in spirit, demanded to be removed from his fiend.
This was done, but peace was not yet. The tormentor,
dressed up in a sheet as a ghost, one night entered the room
to which Southey had been transferred, and attempted to ter-
rify the younger boy by rolling upon him. Nothing daunted
by the ghostly disguise, Southey seized the bully by the
throat, and clung there until the resulting uproar brought
the usher to the scene. After that he was molested no longer.

Later he engaged in pranks himself, but of somewhat different nature. A curly-headed boy was reported to have beat upon the door of a neighboring small school-master. Luckily Southey was not the only curly head in the school, and consequently escaped the reproof that he had earned. When he had become laureate,[1] writing official odes to order reminded him of the verses which at school he had regularly placed upon the tutor's table when required, and as regularly abstracted for presentation again when the next requirement should fall due. Then upon one occasion,[2] when his room-mate, Wynn, had written a theme beginning, "Pride is an insurmountable obstacle," Southey may have been the wag who secretly altered the words to "I ride an insurmountable obstacle." These Wynn read out before Dr. Vincent, much to the amusement of the boys, and if Southey was not responsible for the incident, certainly he remembered it with sufficient satisfaction to refer to it in a letter to Wynn over twenty years later.

The most precious fruits for Southey of Westminster School were the friends that he there made. Charles Watkins Williams Wynn and Grosvenor Charles Bedford were the most important of these, two men with whom he continued upon terms of unbroken intimacy throughout the rest of his life. Near the end of his days he wrote to the then Dean of Westminster, "If I were beholden to the old school for nothing more than their friendship, I should have reason enough to bless the day on which I entered it."[3] Wynn, a serious and steady youth, was the second son of a Welsh baronet of some wealth, and destined to a distinguished career in Parliament. Just when, in their course at school, the two boys met, does not appear, but they were quartered in the same boarding-house, and towards the end of the time at least shared the same room. When Wynn

[1] *Warter*, III, 249.   [3] *Life*, VI, 279.
[2] *Warter*, II, 322 and note.

left in 1791, a few months before Southey, to enter Christ Church, the latter became the head boy of the house.[1] With Bedford Southey's friendship partook less of the feeling of deep admiration and respect, more of good comradeship. He was a person of far different type,— a fellow to go on a lark with, humorous, whimsical, companionable, but distinctly beneath Wynn and Southey in natural parts. It is significant that with Wynn Bedford never appears to have maintained more than an old school-fellow good feeling. Southey met him early at Westminster, and by 1791 they had become intimate friends. Besides these, there were other congenial companions. There was a certain Combe, whom they called ἄναξ ἀνδρων, and who shared in the process of abstracting the verses from the tutor's desk. There was James Boswell, son of the immortal, whom Southey chose to be his room-mate when Wynn departed. Boswell, as one would expect, was a good-natured fellow, and when Bedford's brother, already the godson and namesake of Horace Walpole, was dubbed by the boys Dr. Johnson, Southey compelled young Boswell to write after his dictation some memoirs of this mock Johnson in mock Boswell style, and circulated them in the school. Another friend was Peter Elmsley, the classical scholar, who in later years[2] took the trip through Wales with Southey and Wynn which was to furnish the knowledge of scenery needed for *Madoc*. One of the most congenial of all these boys, probably, was Thomas Philip Lamb, son of a gentleman who lived at Mountsfield near Rye in Sussex. Immediately after his departure from Westminster, Southey wrote some of his most fulminating letters to Lamb, and spent the Whitsun holidays of 1791 and 1792[3] at Lamb's home, where he became a great favorite. There were two younger brothers and a sister of twelve. In 1838 Southey wrote

[1] *Warter*, III, 303.   [3] *Warter*, IV, 543.
[2] Preface to *Madoc*, *Works*, 325.

that he would go a long way to see Bessy Lamb. He had learned to ride upon her white pony, he had played pranks with her brother, and he had written many bad verses there, which, he says, taught him to write better, or were turned to account in *Joan of Arc*.

It would appear from all this that the reserve and withdrawal from social intercourse, which were noted traits of Southey's manhood, were chiefly acquired later. This again comes out most amusingly in the account[1] of his schoolboy delight in the stagecoach journeys that were no small part of the joys of holidays. At such times he was much interested in the human oddities to be met on the road. He traveled by day for the greater enjoyment of the adventure. A crimping-house keeper who, within earshot, recounted his profession to a companion, a deaf-mute who taught the lad the sign-manual, a village mathematician who tried to teach him how to take the altitude of a church tower by the aid of a cocked hat,— these were some of the queer fish that came to his boyish lure.

Holidays themselves were spent in various places. His visits to his friend, Lamb, at Mountsfield have already been referred to. It was doubtless upon one of these occasions that he embarked twice from Rye,[2] bent upon a week's amusement in France, but was each time prevented by the wind, a circumstance which he always regretted. Some holidays probably were spent with other school friends, and some at home where he could range along the cliffs above the Avon[3] or walk on the rocks by the sea with Wynn watching the ships go out,[4] or where he could write verses

[1] *Life*, IV, 330–331.

[2] *A Memoir of the Life and Writings of the late William Taylor of Norwich — compiled and edited by J. W. Robberds* — 1843, I, 399 (Referred to as *Taylor*).

[3] *On the Death of a Favorite Old Spaniel, Poems* 1797, 148. See also an unpublished letter of Southey's (May 27, 1819) in the British Museum.

[4] *Warter*, I, 30.

with a poetical comrade in a cave overlooking the river.
Then visits were paid to friends of his aunt,[1] the Misses
Delamare, at Cheshunt, "excellent old ladies whom it will
be a joy for me to meet in another world." They read the
poet Watts with great devotion, and looked with worshiping eyes at a summer-house in a neighboring garden where
Watts was said to have composed most of his works. The
schoolboy visitor, meanwhile, preferred to read Sidney's
Arcadia, which was also among their books.

Two of the determining traits of Southey's character have
now plainly appeared. The most conspicuous, of course, is
that passion for reading and that taste in books which led
him to pore over the *Arcadia* in holiday time. What fascinated him, that is, was not the conventional reading in
the classics, but history, romance, and narrative poetry.
One of his schoolmates, apparently George Strachey, lived
in a house so near Dean's Yard that it was hardly considered out of bounds, and Southey spent many truant
hours reading in its pleasant, well-stocked library overlooking the Thames. One of the books that he found there was
to supply him with an aspiration of no small importance.
This was Picard's *Religious Ceremonies;*[2] "The book impressed my imagination strongly; and before I left school, I
had formed the intention of exhibiting all the more prominent
and poetical forms of mythology which have at any time
obtained among mankind, by making each the groundwork
of an heroic poem."[3] Such bookishness was part of a men-
tality conspicuously alert, active, diligent, quick to feel
influences and impressions from without, but not so much
profound as venturesome and sensitive. The boyhood

[1] *Warter*, IV, 380.

[2] Bernard Picard: *Cérémonies et Coutumes Religeuses de Tous les
Peuples du Monde Représentées par des Figures . . . avec une Explanation Historique, et quelques Dissertations curieuses. Amsterdam, 1723.*

[3] *Vindiciae Ecclesiae Anglicanae*, 6-7.

writings of which he has told us are striking evidence of his impulse, stronger even than in most scribbling lads, to draw upon reading both for the substance and the form of his own composition. Few have been quicker to attempt the imitation of so many different authors; did he read Ariosto, Spenser, Ovid, he would write new *Orlandos*, new *Faerie Queenes*, new *Metamorphoses*. This courage in experimenting with literary forms was later to be of help when he would have to turn verses into guineas, but the very facility betrayed thereby was to be of doubtful value to Southey's permanent reputation.

The other trait now to be noted in the youth's character, though as yet less conspicuous, must have been already just as definite, and when not taken too seriously, strikingly attractive. It was the fearless, outspoken devotion to what he took to be his principles, and his equally outspoken hatred of their opposites. He had fastened himself terrier-like upon the throat of the bully, and had clung there regardless of consequences. This was an episode most characteristic of the future man. For it would not be far from the truth to say that Southey went on clinging to the throat of villainy all the rest of his life; he may often have been mistaken about the villainy, but there can be no doubt about the courage and the devotion with which he assailed it.

Both bookishness and the frequently Quixotic idealism now received new fuel. The young student of history and lover of Spenser found new reading, new enthusiasms, seconded by new events in the world, which were to bring ideals within his scope of action that could be fought for, and he did not shrink from fighting. The story is sufficiently told in the words that he wrote in 1816.[1] He says that he left Westminster "in a perilous state,— a heart full of feeling and poetry, a head full of Rousseau and Werter [sic], and . . . religious principles shaken by Gibbon."

1 *Life*, IV, 186, 320.

When we add that Voltaire was among the authors whose manner he was imitating at this time, and then recall that his schooldays fell within the years 1788 to 1792, we shall see that, given his temper, trouble of some sort was bound to result. The sympathy with revolutionary ideas did not in his case, as with Wordsworth, creep unawares upon a meditative spirit only slowly awakening out of boyish indifference, but came as a gusty blast to sweep a youngster off his unsteady feet. Southey was not slow to form convictions, nor having formed them, content to remain long inactive with regard to them. He was always for committing himself at once so that the world should know how Robert Southey stood, and then he was for defiantly standing by his guns. We shall see, moreover, that he rather fell in love with a vision of liberty than was convinced of a doctrine. This vision he never would surrender, and therefore he could maintain that he was conscious of no reversal in having shifted from Jacobinism to Toryism.

Rousseau, *Werther*, Gibbon, Voltaire, acting upon such a Westminster boy, led him into scrapes, for although Southey notes that among the boys there was much free and easy democracy, Westminster School at this time might have been called both negligent and tyrannical in its discipline, but scarcely liberal. We may regret that no detailed account of Southey's schoolboy exploits is available when we remember the joke on young Boswell and the prank on Wynn. The whole history might have made an amusing story. As it is, one or two vague rumors and allusions are all that we have to indicate that the final scrape which earned his expulsion was probably but the last of a series. The fact that Southey's political notions were not shared by such friends as Wynn, Bedford, and Lamb doubtless led to voluble arguments, with the result that the young radical's opinions were no secret in the school when the climax of his career there arrived.

This event was the outcome of the future laureate's first appearance in print. Some Etonians, led by Canning, had published a periodical called *The Microcosm* shortly before Southey's entrance at Westminster, and some of the boys of the latter school, during his first year, attempted to rival the Etonians in a publication called *The Trifler*. To this Southey sent anonymously by penny post an elegy on his little sister, who had just died, signing it B. In the next number he saw this notice, "B's Elegy must undergo some alterations, a liberty all our correspondents must allow us to take," but this was the last ever seen of the elegy. *The Trifler* died after forty numbers, but in his last year in the school, Southey, with Wynn, Strachey, and Bedford, planned another such paper to be called *The Flagellant*.[1] Wynn and Strachey departed before publication began, but on March 1, 1792, the first number, written entirely by Bedford, appeared. Southey never forgot that occasion. "It was Bedford's writing, but that circumstance did not prevent me from feeling that I was that day borne into the world as an author; and if ever my head touched the stars while I walked upon earth it was then. It seemed as if I had overleapt a barrier, which till then had kept me from the fields of immortality, wherein my career was to be run. In all London there was not so vain, so happy, so elated a creature as I was that day; and, in truth, it was an important day in my life. . . . "

The Flagellant purported to be the organ of four Westminster scholars who had retired to a ruined monastery in order to lash the vices of society. Bedford, under the name of Peter the Hermit, was apparently responsible for most of the first four numbers, the satire of which was mild enough and conventional enough to escape censure. But the fifth number, written by Southey under the pseudonym Gualbertus, a name ominous of Wat Tyler, was more out-

[1] *Life*, IV, 318–320. *Warter*, III, 233.

spoken and brought on grave consequences. The point of
the essay was that flogging was an invention of the devil.
Though the author wrote with little respect for dignitaries,
yet he little expected that he would give offense to anybody.
Nevertheless he confesses, "I was full of Gibbon at the
time, and had caught something of Voltaire's manner."
Cuthbert Southey could see in what his father wrote nothing but "a schoolboy's imitation of a paper in the *Spectator*
or *Rambler*." Dr. Vincent, on the other hand, saw the
traces of Gibbon and Voltaire, and it is not surprising that
his anger should have been roused. Gaulbertus began with
a supposed letter from a victim of the rod arguing for the
right of boys to think for themselves and against the assumption by schoolmasters of the divine right to flog.
There followed a brief essay which purported to be a reply
to this complaint, and upon the authority of Seneca, the
fathers of the Church, and the Bible, traced the invention
of flogging to the heathen gods and thence to the devil.
In good round terms Southey then went on to condemn the
custom as being "equally unprofitable and impious . . .
unfit to be practiced in a Christian country." As for those
disciplinarians who practiced flogging, they had merely
given their breasts as shelter for Satan.

"In this public manner, therefore, do I, Gualbertus, — issue
my sacred bull, hereby commanding all doctors, reverends, and
plain masters, to cease, without delay or repining, from the beastly
and idolatrous custom of flogging. 'Whoever shall be saved, above
all things, it is necessary that he should hold the Catholic faith.
Now, the Catholic is this, there be three gods, and yet but one God.'
Whoever denies this, cannot be orthodox, consequently cannot
be fit to instruct youth. Now, since there is but one God, whoso-
ever floggeth, that is, performeth the will of Satan, committeth an
abomination: to him, therefore, to all the consumers of birch, as to
the priests of Lucifer, ANATHEMA. ANATHEMA. *GUAL–
BERTUS.*"[1]

[1] *The Flagellant*, No. V, 88–89.

Dr. Vincent, naturally enough, resented being called a priest of the devil, and he took immediate steps to discipline his accuser by methods even more severe than flogging. It is probable, moreover, that he had previously been troubled by other evidences of Southey's uncomfortable temper and opinions. There had been a theme which he had seen fit to return to the boy "with a long row about abusing Burke in it." There had also probably been reports carried up to the doctor of a far more serious incident which, though it may unjustly have been attributed to Southey, was certainly known by so good a hand at gossip as Charles Lamb to have been connected with his name. The statue erected to Major André in Westminster Abbey had about this time been mutilated, and when Lamb lost his temper with Southey in 1823, he reminded the latter that rumor had attributed the act to some Westminster boy, "fired perhaps with raw notions of Transatlantic Freedom," and queried whether he could not himself tell something concerning the fate of André's nose.[1] Whether Lamb's intimation that Southey had been concerned in this affair be true or not, the act had apparently been charged to one of the scholars, and that Southey had been engaged in some such outbreak against authority previous to *The Flagellant* is more than glanced at in a letter written in 1818 to the same friend to whom the autobiography was later addressed. The letter,[2] which is generously cut by the editor, seems to refer to the case of some youngster recently expelled from Eton. Southey writes:

"I know something of rebellions, and generally suspect that there has been some fault in the master as well as in the boys, just as a mutiny in a man of war affords a strong presumption of tyranny

[1] *Letter of Elia to Robert Southey, London Magazine*, October, 1823; *The Works of Charles and Mary Lamb*, edited by E. V. Lucas . . . 1903 (referred to as Lamb, *Works*), I, 226.

[2] *Life*, IV, 318–320.

against the captain. Without understanding the merits of the case, it is easy to perceive that the boys believed their privileges were invaded, and fancied that the Magna Charta of Eton was in danger (the Habeas Corpus in schools is in favour of the governors — a writ issued against the subject, and affecting him *in tail*), — took the patriotic side, acting upon Whig principles. They are very good principles in their time and place, and youth is a good time and school a good place for them. When he grows older, he will see the necessity of subordination, and learn that it is only by means of order that liberty can be secured."

At this point the editorial shears have invaded the letter, but it is resumed in words that seem to indicate quite clearly that Dr. Vincent may have had something besides the paper on flogging in mind when Southey was expelled. "I have a fellow-feeling for ——, because I was myself expelled from Westminster, not for a rebellion (though in that too I had my share), but for an act of authorship."

If Southey had had his share in a rebellion, Dr. Vincent may have decided to make use of this opportunity, when the author of *The Flagellant* was to be punished, to clear off old scores with him and with insubordination in general by visiting his wrath upon the culprit caught red-handed. It was not the last time that the young man was to discover what rancors may be distilled from printer's ink. Upon this occasion Dr. Vincent immediately sued the publisher of *The Flagellant* for libel; Southey was forced to acknowledge himself the author of the obnoxious number, and reluctantly to pen a letter of apology. The matter did not rest there, but he was expelled from the school, and some time in April or early May of 1792 returned to his aunt's house in the College Green in Bristol.

This escapade had to be reported to his uncle, of course, and then there ensued six months of waiting for the word to come from Lisbon which should decide the young man's future course. It had been intended that he should enter

Christ Church,[1] where a friend of his uncle's was expected to help him to obtain a studentship, but Cyril Jackson, the dean, had heard of *The Flagellant*, and refused to admit him. This was an added indignity, for Southey had been under the impression, when he had apologized to Dr. Vincent, that the head master engaged never again to mention the affair. Consequently this treacherous tyranny made him bitter against his oppressors. It does seem, indeed, as he wrote later, that "there were more wigs than brains laid together about that poor number of *The Flagellant!*"[2]

The months of waiting from April to November, trying as they were, had no unimportant effect on the youth's development. Smarting under the sense of injury, bitter against tyranny, disappointed in his hopes for liberty in France, overtaken by family affliction and the humiliation of poverty, uncertain as to his own future, possibly already in love or soon to be, and above all with a heart full of poetry and feeling, a head full of Rousseau, *Werther*, and Gibbon, he was truly in a perilous state.

The affairs of Southey senior now arrived at bankruptcy, and the older man's health was so rapidly breaking that he died early in the following year of 1793. In this distress the son was now sent to Taunton to request financial aid from his uncle, John Southey, but the humiliating errand failed; possibly his aunt's long feud with Thomas Southey, — who would appear to have been upon good terms with his brother John, and no longer connected with the linendraper's shop,— may have had something to do with the errand's failure. At any rate, it must be said to Miss Tyler's credit that, as a result, she herself came to the rescue at this crisis.

Another circumstance that should be mentioned at this point is that, among his childhood playmates, although un-

[1] *Life*, IV, 320.   [2] *Warter*, III, 21.

mentioned in Southey's autobiographical fragment, had been the little girls of a family named Fricker, friends of Southey's mother, living on Redcliffe Hill. More will be said of these people later, but the boy's friendship with them thus early begun had been continued, and was soon to develop into love for Edith, who was about Southey's own age. In 1792, meanwhile, the troubled lad of eighteen probably went often to seek consolation under the Fricker roof, and not without success.

Dr. Vincent had failed, however, to quench the rising *furor scribendi* within him. Shortly after his departure from Westminster, Southey was writing to Bedford that the sooner they published a volume the better; "The Medley," "The Hodge Podge," "The What-do-you-call-it," or "Monastic Lucubrations" were some of their proposed titles. They would dedicate perhaps to "Envy, Hatred, and Malice," under whose sting Southey already felt himself to be smarting, or to the doctor, the devil, the king, or themselves. Such planning, of course, came to nought; still the youngster, cooling his heels if not his head in Bristol, had somehow to fill up the time. He turned to Euclid, but in spite of his good intentions, he was unable to progress without a master, and was wearied, not to say disgusted, by the confusion of triangles and parallelograms. He laid Euclid on the shelf, therefore, in order to resume "his constant study, Spenser."

Poetry and what he called philosophy, indeed, demanded most of Southey's attention. Now it was, probably, that he read the sonnets of Bowles, which had been published three years before by a Bath bookseller. The plaintive poet gave him welcome satisfaction in his own troubled mood. Now it was also that he bought Dr. Sayers's *Dramatic Sketches of Northern Mythology* (1790, 1792), the first book he had ever had money enough to order from a country bookseller. He had himself already planned poems

on similar themes while he was still at Westminster; he
had, that is, his grand scheme of writing a series of epics
illustrating the mythologies of the world, and a discussion
with Wynn[1] had suggested the composition of still another
poem on the story of the Welsh hero, Madoc. Sayers's
feeble attempts to put Percy's translation of Mallet's *Introduction à l'Histoire de Dannemarc* to poetic use, as well as
his novel verse-form, fired Southey's interest. Personal
problems pressed too closely, however, for him to attempt
any of his epic schemes at this time. Rather would he go
out to walk in the fields, alone save for his aunt's old
spaniel,[2] there to meditate and muse sadly upon the ills of
life and society in the fashion of Rousseau or *Werther* or
Bowles, and the verses that he wrote are expressive of the
feelings thus cultivated. Among his acknowledged poems
we have already an ode *To Horror*[3] dated 1791, which serves
to show the kind of thing he was learning to do in imitation of Collins, possibly even of Anna Matilda, who wrote on
the same theme. This schoolboy performance was a poem
of the sort in which, it has been said, the muse goes on the
grand tour; she here surveys the scenes of horror which are
to be found upon moss-cankered seats in old sepulchres,
beneath the abbey's ivied wall, in Greenland, on the field of
battle, or on Afric's shore where the impaled negro writhes
round the stake. In similar fashion he now sings also in
praise of *Contemplation*[4] at twilight when the shrill bat flits
by and the slow vapor curls along the ground, and the
long-shadowing smoke rises from the lone cottage. Then
is the tranquilizing Power of Contemplation to be met

[1] Preface to *Thalaba*, *Works*, 224.

[2] *On the Death of a Favorite Old Spaniel*, *Poems*, 1797.

[3] *Poems*, 1797; *Works*, 27. In the collected edition of his poetical
works (1837) Southey himself affixed the dates of composition to most
of his poems. There is every reason to suppose that these dates are
correct.

[4] *Poems*, 1797; *Works*, 127, Bristol 1792.

where the moon gleams with softer radiance over the "calmy" Ocean, or among the "pathless forest wilds" or in "the scatter'd Abbey's hallowed rounds," or in "the lone romantic glen." Nursing thus the sacred woe of reflection, the expelled Westminster boy muses upon the day now perished when hope still wove her visions, only to depart and leave him with sad REALITY [sic] to be his mate.

The scenery of the Avon supplied, of course, ample opportunity for such poetizing. High up on the face of the rocks above the river below Clifton the youth had had the joy of discovering a cave, shaded by ivy and frequented by wild bees. There, with a companion whose identity is not recorded, he would now sit for hours writing verses. The two lads called themselves Nisus and Euryalus, and the former name Southey carved upon the rock which he chose for his own particular seat.[1] A few years later he made this place the subject of one of his inscriptions.[2]

Longer tramps carried him out to the home of his forefathers the Hills at Ashton or possibly to his old school at Corston. All these occasions could serve, not merely for verse-writing, but for long, soul-outpouring letters to Bedford, and already Southey's letters are far more expressive of himself than are any of his poems. They show most clearly how all the sensitive emotionalism that went with his highly-strung nature had been set a-quiver by his romantic reading in Rousseau, *Werther*, Bowles, and their kind, but especially by Rousseau. Nothing shows this "mimosa sensibility," as William Taylor called it,[3] better than his protesting to Bedford that he had nothing of the kind. "I have undergone enough to break a dozen hearts;

---

[1] *The Correspondence of Robert Southey with Caroline Bowles to which are added: Correspondence with Shelley, and Southey's Dreams. Edited, with an Introduction, by Edward Dowden — 1881*, 15–16. (Referred to as *Correspondence with Caroline Bowles.*)

[2] *Poems*, 1797; *Works*, 180.   [3] *Taylor*, I, 256.

but mine is made of tough stuff, and the last misfortune serves to blunt the edge of the next. One day it will, I hope, be impenetrable." Of course toughness was precisely not the quality of Southey's heart, and if he ever learned to defeat pain, it was not by impenetrability but by fortitude. This innate sanity in his character was even now in evidence, for he immediately began making the effort, by means of what he called "philosophy," to check the abandonment to emotion. Upon his return from the visit to Ashton mentioned above, he sent a sketch of the church at that place to Bedford with a long letter which displays both the "sensibility" at its height and the opening wedge of that "philosophy" which was to control it.

"If you are disposed at some future time to visit the 'Verdant House' of your friend when he shall be at supper, — 'not when he eats, but when he is eaten,' — you will find it on the other side of this identical church. The very covering of the vault affords as striking an emblem of mortality as would even the mouldering tenant of the tomb. . . . My pilgrimage yesterday was merely the result of a meditating moment when philosophy had flattered itself into apathy. I am really astonished when I reflect upon the indifference with which I so minutely surveyed the heaving turf, which inclosed within its cold bosom ancestors upon whom fortune bestowed rather more of her smiles than she has done upon their descendants, — men who, content with an independent patrimony, lay hid from the world too obscure to be noticed by it, too elevated to fear its insult. Those days are passed. . . . Were you to walk over the village (Ashton) with me, you would, like me, be tempted to repine that I have no earthly mansion here, — it is the most enchanting spot that nature can produce. My rambles would be much more frequent, were it not for certain reflections, not altogether of a pleasant nature, which always recur. I cannot wander like a stranger over lands which were once my forefathers', nor pass those doors which are now no more open, without feeling emotions altogether inconsistent with pleasure and irreconcileable with the indifference of philosophy."

Here is the welter of sentimentality, but here also is the suggestion that Southey does not wish to go on fondling his emotions indefinitely. The rest of the same letter gives us still more of the healthy reaction toward self-control.

"What is there, Bedford, contained in that word [philosophy] of such mighty virtue? It has been sounded in the ear of common sense till it is deafened and overpowered with clamour. Artifice and vanity have reared up the pageant, science has adorned it, and the multitude have beheld at a distance and adored; it is applied indiscriminately to vice and to virtue, to the exalted ideas of Socrates, the metaphysical charms of Plato, the frigid maxims of Aristotle, the unfeeling dictates of the Stoics, and the disciples of the defamed Epicurus. Rousseau was called a philosopher whilst he possessed sensibility the most poignant. Voltaire was dignified with the name when he deserved the blackest stigma from every man of principle. Whence all this seeming absurdity? or why should reason be dazzled by the name when she cannot but perceive its imbecility?"

The answer to such questions was at least partly conveyed in a letter which the writer of them received at the very moment that he was asking them. The long-awaited word had at last arrived from Lisbon; "It is such as I expected from one who has been to me more than a parent; without asperity, without reproaches." Southey, consequently, is immediately more cheerful, and continues the discussion of philosophy in hopefuller vein; "I can now tell you one of the uses of philosophy; it teaches us to search for applause from within, and to despise the flattery and the abuse of the world alike; to attend only to an inward monitor; to be superior to fortune. . . . Do give me a lecture upon philosophy, and teach me how to become a philosopher. The title is pretty, and surely the philosopher S. would sound as well as the philosophic Hume or the philosopher of Ferney."

A book which the young man was reading about this

time shows its influence plainly in these passages. This was Elizabeth Carter's translation of Epictetus. To go about as he had done with his heart upon his sleeve was patently uncomfortable, and like a sensible man, Southey proposed to minimize discomfort. Epictetus especially appealed to him, and although it was not for some time to come that he was completely emancipated from Rousseau, if indeed he ever became so, yet the leaven of stoicism was at work; he says that in the next few years he literally wore out a copy of Mrs. Carter's book with carrying it to and fro. By 1799 he could write, "I counteracted Rousseau by dieting upon Godwin and Epictetus; they did me some good, but time has done me more. I have a dislike to all strong emotion, and avoid whatever could excite it."[1]

Southey's political feelings were merely a phase of the view of life so far revealed. Nations he thought of as being like individuals; both might be tyrannized over, their feelings pained and thwarted of expression, by the rule of schoolmasters, kings, and aristocrats. Political freedom meant a republicanism derived from reading of ancient history in the pages of Gibbon, Lucan, and Rousseau, as well as in the classical texts, and vivified by the example of America; it meant a people free from its tyrants, happy as a schoolboy free from his Dr. Vincent. Southey's hopes are for a state in France like that across the Atlantic or like that in ancient Rome before the rise of a Cæsar. His heroes, therefore, are men like La Fayette and the milder constitutionalists such as the Girondins. His real ignorance of the history and causes of contemporary conditions in France is only a little greater, at first, than his ignorance concerning England. Even at this time, however, he was aware of certain differences between the two countries, and as time went on he was to feel these to the point of obsession. Hence would arise the charge of turncoating. Now

[1] *Taylor*, I, 261; *Life*, IV, 186.

that the Jacobins were clinching their hold upon the country's throat, he was already growing disgusted with the French people. Having obtained freedom, they must be corrupt indeed if freedom failed to bring the happiness expected. Thus he writes to his friend Philip Lamb: "Time has justified all your prophecies with regard to my French friends. The Jacobins, the Sans Culottes, and the fishwomen carry everything before them. Everything that is respectable, every barrier that is sacred, is swept away by the ungovernable torrent. The people have changed tyrants, and, for the mild irresolute Louis, bow to the savage, the unrelenting Pétion." He recognizes, of course, that such statements may make it appear that he has lost faith in the cause of freedom. "After so open a declaration of abhorrence, you may perhaps expect that all sanguine dreams of romantic liberty are gone forever. It is true, I have seen the difficulty of saying to the mob, 'thus far and no farther.' I have seen a structure raised by the hand of wisdom, and defended by the sword of liberty, undermined by innovation, hurled from its basis by faction, and insulted by the proud abuse of despotism." In spite of all this, however, he asks: "Is it less respectable for its misfortunes?" Moreover, as proof of his faith in liberty, he writes, upon inviting Bedford to witness the installation of a chancellor at Oxford, "The spectacle is only inferior to a coronation. . . . It will be worth seeing, as perhaps coronations, like the secular games, will soon be a tale that is told."

Nevertheless, he does not lack hope for England; she is better, for all her sins, than France, where the people are tigers and apes, and than Prussia, where they are slaves. In England, at any rate, "Peg Nicholson is only in Bedlam; Tom Paine is treated with lenity," although "woe be to him who dares to attack the divine will of schoolmasters to flog, or who presumes to think that boys should neither be treated absurdly nor indecently."

In the midst of such fulminations the letter arrived from
Lisbon, and the handful of *Flagellants* was dispatched by
request to Mr. Hill. The young man was now ready to
begin his residence at Oxford, but not all his perplexities
had been settled by his uncle's kindness. The latter's expectation that Southey would take orders upon graduation
was not express in its terms, but was none the less understood by his nephew, who, although he knew of no alternative, was not inclined to reconcile himself gracefully to the
prospect. He looked upon his brother Tom as more fortunate because Tom had given up any idea of the university
in order to become a midshipman in the navy, "a method
of education in my opinion far better." The problem of
finding some congenial career for himself was to grow momentous before long, but for the present he had to content
himself with protesting to his friends. "Is it not rather
disgraceful, at the moment when Europe is on fire with
freedom — when man and monarch are contending — to sit
and study Euclid or Hugo Grotius? As Pindar says, a
good button-maker is spoilt in making a king; what will
be spoilt when I am made a fellow of Balliol?" . . . "Four
years hence I am to be called into orders, and during that
time . . . how much have I to learn! I must learn to
break a rebellious spirit, which neither authority nor oppression could ever bow; it would be easier to break my
neck. I must learn to work a problem instead of writing
an ode. I must learn to pay respect to men remarkable
only for great wigs and little wisdom."

CHAPTER II

1793-1794

I

SOUTHEY'S career at Oxford[1] was not to be such as he would recollect with pleasure, but the influences then working upon him and the steps to which he then committed himself determined his whole future. He entered Balliol the boy who had been reading Rousseau and had been expelled from Westminster; he departed the pantisocrat and a poet of the new era. Now was to develop in him a mind which would display the aspirations of Englishmen of his generation more profusely than the mind of any contemporary except Coleridge, though generally without understanding and almost never in enduring form. Southey lacked profundity and penetration; but he had a sensitiveness which rendered him singularly quick to feel new impulses. With this quickness he united a vehement facility of expression and a diligence of application which enabled him to accomplish more in mere bulk of composition than all but a very few authors in any age. These traits made him an unusually copious channel of expression for the mental life of his time, and these are the traits which, by 1795, were fixed upon him.

It was but natural, therefore, that Southey should have absorbed with avidity the books which had shown the way

---

[1] The main facts of this period of Southey's life are to be found in *Life*, I, 162–209.

to '93. Political conditions and the methods of Locke had led in England to the disintegration of the old religion of Protestantism. In its place had come a bloodless attempt on the part of the Deists to construct by argument a new religion of nature, an equally bloodless attempt of the orthodox by the same means to reconstruct conventional theology, and in the Wesleyan movement a genuine resurrection of faith. In England conservatism scored a Pyrrhic victory over Deism, but in France the belief in a just and benevolent god of nature was informed with life as an expression of the revolutionary opposition to that established order which sanctioned itself by insistence upon a god above and contrary to nature. To many English youths the revolution in France made this new religion the great reality of life even after they had ceased to believe in France as its embodiment. It is important to think of all this in terms of religious experience, for it was a religious mood in which Southey spent his life, and which he sought in all his writings to express. That romantic emotionalism, that "mimosa sensibility," so characteristic of the time was not merely a disturbance in the spirit, superficial or profound as the case may have been, induced by Rousseau, *Werther* and other fashionable books as we makers and readers of books are prone mistakenly to think. In passionate natures it was rather symptomatic of genuine needs in the human soul and of the failure of English Deism and common sense theology to meet these needs by their specious efforts to explain away the mysteries of life by dehumanizing the imagination, or, as they said, making religion reasonable.

In order, therefore, to understand the youth who went up to Balliol in 1793 it is necessary to refer to the more intangible but none the less human origins of the sensibilities and ideals which he shared with all the more active spirits of his generation. In the first place we must bear in mind the

intensity of his emotions.   For all his stoicism he never
achieved steady self-control, as Carlyle, who saw him still
quivering and flushing under gray hairs, vividly testifies.
His feelings were always on the raw long after he had forsworn Rousseau, and would have been so had he never
read Rousseau.   There were many influences at work
in England to intensify this sensitiveness.   Rationalism,
although certain souls managed to live by it, had not stilled
the obstinate questionings of deep natures.   On the contrary, without settling the old, it had raised new questions
bound to augment an already latent excitement.   When
romanticism, therefore, challenged common sense, it was
not a movement of mere reaction, not merely a recrudes-
cence of "enthusiasm" and "superstition," but a consistent
fulfilment of rationalism itself.   The age of common sense
grew curious about matters upon which common sense had
delivered a fiat of condemnation.   Dr. Johnson did not
believe in ghosts, and he disapproved of the Scotch, but he
went to Cock Lane and to Scotland nevertheless.   The
eighteenth century might sneer at "Gothic" things, but it
began the study of them; it prated about this best of all
possible worlds, but studied to improve its imperfections.
Thus men rediscovered two potent sources of excitement;
they found the joy, rendered permissible by the decay of
old authority, of indulging freely the impulse to theorize
and to dogmatize with or without knowledge, and fortunately they found also the joy of seeking knowledge with
or without reference to theory and dogma.   Now although
the man of common sense wished above all things not to
be disturbed, these new pursuits could not but offer disturbing questions, prospects of dazzling hope and abundant
opportunities for "enthusiasm."   That this should have
been partly the effect of irrational dreamers like Rousseau
has, of course, been obvious; we must not forget, however,
that the mind has its adventures no less thrilling than those

of irresponsible reverie, and Gibbon also had a share in putting schoolboys into a perilous state.

Of the complex inconsistencies which resulted in individuals from such a blending of opposing influences, Southey was an excellent example. Fear of the unknown, which skepticism and theology had vainly tried to argue away, hunger for the knowable upon which reason feeds, both feelings, so characteristic of his generation, were present in him with unusual intensity. Yet he was more deeply moved by religious passion for certain ideals, a passion which served in the end to negative all his endeavors after knowledge. Like other believers in the religion of nature, he did not perceive that nature, never wholly known and remaining forever to be investigated, may be affected by man's ideals but has no care concerning them, that none of the facts and forces of existence is either good or bad save as man's thinking makes it so. Consequently Southey insisted upon an *a priori* division of nature into the natural or the good, so called because it appeared intentionally to agree with his ideals, and the unnatural or the bad, so called because it appeared intentionally to oppose them. He failed, that is, to know nature at all, and in the scientific sense of the word never grew free to investigate anything. He was, to be sure, passionately afraid of the unknown, but this he identified with the unnatural and wrong, and although courageous enough to attempt inquiry, his fears were always beyond control, he lost his temper with the nature he failed to understand, believed himself righteous to the extent that it was evil and himself angry, and continued to seek only such half-knowledge as would confirm and not allay his fears. Yet so indefatigable was he in his search for this knowledge, such as it was, so wide in his scope, that only so fundamental a limitation could have prevented him from the highest scholarly achievement. In all this he was a true son of his age; times of war and revolution are those in which sound learning, especially in the fields that Southey chose, may be most ardently desired but is seldom prosperously sought.

The experiences that prompted Southey's cravings for an explanation of life to which he could give religious and poetic faith were in essence those that all humanity shares. There was first the phenomenon of death, and there was also the phenomenon of evil, which could not, now that nature was believed good, be assumed as the primal justification of death, but had to be conceived as both a corruption in man's nature and as the results of that corruption embodied as society; evil, that is, became "man's inhumanity to man." It was envisaged, not so much in personal as in political and social wrong-doing on the part of the corrupt, of kings and mobs acting by tyranny or by some vague cataclysm of terror. These things overspread Southey's life with fear and hate, but it must be added to his credit that he also possessed an unfailing curiosity concerning mere disconnected facts of experience in all times and places, even when they betrayed for him no moral import whatever. It was only when he sought to explain the facts he had collected that his perturbation of soul became evident.

Such were Southey's dominating emotions. They were expressed in the terms of his own day, but what the terms were it is not difficult to discern. In the first place the pain and mystery of death was a far more frequent experience to the men of the eighteenth century than we are prone to realize in this more advanced day of medical science. Southey's acquaintance, before as well as after 1793, with death in his own family, — and his experience may be paralleled by many other cases — was such as would appall any person of similar extraction and temperament to-day. He was one of nine children; five died in infancy, and of these, four were a poignant part of his own boyhood memories. The schoolboy elegy which has been mentioned was an expression of personal grief, and he always remembered the long dead sisters with whom in childhood he had strung jessamine flowers in his grandmother's garden. In his schooldays, his grandmother and, at the beginning of his Oxford career, his father died, the latter under circumstances peculiarly distressing and in the prime of life. At the height of the pantisocracy excitement suddenly died Southey's most admired college friend, Edmund Seward. The last person to bid him farewell upon his departure to Portugal in 1795 was his friend and brother-in-law, Robert Lovell; the first news to greet him when he returned, eager to join his bride, was of Lovell's death from "fever." The widow and child, as inmates of his household for many years, kept this loss alive for him. A dearly loved cousin, with whom he had lived as with a sister in his mother's house, was to languish and die of consumption under his own roof in 1801. There too and possibly of the same cause his mother was shortly after to die before her time. His own first child, named Margaret like his mother and cousin, died in 1803, just when the fascinations of a year-old baby were beginning to unfold. All these deaths were to occur before Southey was thirty, and others in circles only a little less remote might be added to the list. Later he was to lose three more children, — the baby Emma; Isabel, the beauty of the family; and Herbert, a son of brilliant promise. Of course less sensitive natures toughened under such trials; Southey endured but never ceased to wince. It was with less joy than sorrow that, on the threshold of his old age, he informed his friends of the approaching birth of another, and, as it turned out, his last child and only surviving son. "Death," he wrote, "has so often entered my doors, that he and I have long been familiar."

The passing away of nearly all these friends and kindred was sudden and unaccountable. A child might be apparently strong and well; then would come some unusual brightness, tantalizing the hopes of its parents, some preternatural activity of eyes or limbs, and in a few hours death amid the utter helplessness of all. Beyond some vague notions about drugs and climate, knowledge often worse than none, their ignorance was complete. How many men of twenty-nine to-day with. Southey's intelligence and capacity for feeling have known the deaths of twelve near friends and relatives, nearly all of them in youth, only one in old age, and all but this one from some vague disease? The fact that our little rush-light of science has left us still with many dark questions to face should not keep us from realizing that it has also dispelled for us death-fears without number; otherwise many of us might well have paralleled the experience of Southey. Finally, we should remember in all charity that it was the struggle to find escape from such and so frequent trials that was the source of many of the extravagances as well as of many of the accomplishments of that romantic temperament of which he possessed so large a share.

Religion, except in the classes appealed to by Wesley, was inadequate to satisfy the emotions of this struggle. Death itself, as it appeared more and more frequently the physical result of unknown, unseen forces which were vaguely named disease, and less and less the result of dramatic violence, no longer suggested even a show of its own cause. The fading of the Protestant religion from the imagination deprived men of the comforting thought that there was an angry God whose vengeance for sin was death. Deism, on the other hand, even when made concrete by revolution, offered nothing as tangible in its place, and when a man like Southey ran upon the dubious regions of his faith, he had to live in his helplessness by a stoic steeling of his nerves and by promising himself a hereafter where the pains and losses of this life were not understood but canceled.

Similar reasons account for Southey's fear of evil, which, true to his time, he always thought of as being personified in a monster of despotism, mob-violence, or conscious deviltry. We must remember that besides Gibbon no man in England, not even Hume or Burke, had so far attained the historical point of view. Unless men could live mystically, therefore, like Wordsworth in his happy moments, by dodging the logic of facts, they were compelled to abide, in spite of their faith in the benevolence of nature, in constant terror of some disruption of nature by evil which was none the less terrible for being unnatural. Consequently Southey, a far more courageous soul than Wordsworth, facing facts was forever fighting monsters, — afreets, and teraphim; kings sitting upon thrones of blood-cemented skulls, peoples turned tiger like the French, men turned Satan like Byron. Bugaboos haunted him all the days of his life, but he fought them with Quixotic devotion. In his youth they were the kings and aristocrats, but quite naturally they became a Jacquerie, a Napoleon, an Irish jesuitism, freedom of the press, parliamentary reform, and modern industrialism. Such was the effect of the religion of nature in Southey. Had his scientific understanding kept pace with his thirst for information, he might have realized his expectation of surpassing Gibbon even without the advantage of Gibbon's leisure, and he would have been a happier man. As it was, he studied, as I have said, only to confirm his fears.

Such an impression is strikingly reënforced by the description of the man that grew out of such a youth. It is written by one whose own dour spirit possessed many of the same characteristics. "Southey was a man towards well up in the fifties;" says Carlyle, "hair gray, not yet hoary, well setting off his fine clear brown complexion; head and face both smallish, as indeed the figure was while seated; features finely cut; eyes, brow, mouth, good in their kind — expressive all, and even vehemently so, but betokening rather keenness than depth either of intellect or character; a serious, human, honest, but sharp, almost fierce-looking, thin man, with very much the militant in his aspect — in the eyes especially was visible a mixture of sorrow and anger, or of angry contempt, as if his indignant fight with the world had not yet ended in victory, but also never should in defeat." [1]

If the little understood phenomena of disease and social maladjustment engendered emotions which no faith or science was able to still, so also did the new intellectual freedom of the eighteenth century. Even to young men who forswore its authority, rationalism had opened new vistas for exploration by the intelligence, and these new vistas thrilled their souls with longing for those new voyages into the unknown which were to be pushed forward by the nineteenth century, and which form not the least romantic chapter in the history of mankind. The whole field of historical, scientific, literary, social, and political research, invention, and discovery, save for a pioneer here and there, lay before the young student who went up to Oxford in 1793, like a virgin continent in which only trails had been blazed. Though he knew that death and the passions of men were things to be feared, he knew also that there were other things to be known without fear, and this knowledge was a thing to stir passions as genuine if not as compelling as those that ignorance roused. The expansive plans of a Coleridge, the scope of a Goethe, even a Southey's tireless activity, are proof that not since the Renaissance had such a prospect and passion for learning come to man.

Southey was thoroughly awake to the existence of this world that lay before him. Certain of his interests in it that took permanent hold upon him will have to be discussed in detail elsewhere; at this point it is necessary to under-

[1] Carlyle, *Reminiscences*, New York, 1881, 516.

stand how the opportunities for intellectual adventure at this time added greatly to the emotional excitement and intensity of a young man who was alert to them. We must not forget that any youth who stood at the threshold of nineteenth-century research, realizing, even though vaguely, what lay in the immediate future, could not fail to be moved with a deep and compelling excitement. If he were a Coleridge, all his energies would be consumed in contemplation and expatiation on the prospect, his will overwhelmed with the wealth of opportunity displayed to his intelligence. If he were a Southey, with a passion for getting work done, he would be fired to accomplish, even though uncritically, what he saw was still undone. The failures of both men to achieve any great finished work differed but in complementary way. The excitement of the prospect palsied Coleridge; it overstimulated Southey, and eagerness to be doing rendered him too easily content with the half done. Excursions which he thought momentous explorations into new continents of knowledge turned out to have been merely landing parties guided by false reckoning. The important thing to be noted at present, however, in order to gain a notion of the state of mind of the young Oxford student, is that there was in him, even thus early, an eagerness for inquiry in a great variety of fields steadily centering upon certain chosen subjects without ever confining itself to them exclusively.

The intellectual activities which Southey undertook or thought of undertaking between the ages of nineteen and thirty comprise most of the subjects of modern research. One of the first to be noted was his interest in scientific investigation, especially in its bearing upon medical knowledge. At Oxford he was to think of entering the profession of medicine, giving up the idea, characteristically, partly because of the inability to steel himself to the sight of suffering. In 1798 he was to form a friendship with

Humphry Davy, then a young assistant to Beddoes at his "Pneumatic Institute" in Bristol, where they experimented with gases in the hope of finding a cure for consumption. In the course of this work Davy discovered nitrous oxide, the dentist's laughing gas, and Southey, dyspeptic from sedentary sins, allowed himself to be experimented upon. At a still later time he took great interest in the work of his younger brother, Henry, who became a physician, and whom he urged with delightful self-consistency to devote his professional energies to the discovery of the cause and cure of consumption while writing a history of the crusades in his leisure moments. Here was a particularly good example of the way in which Southey and others of his time perceived the fields of research without realizing the extent of the labor and the difficulties involved in reaching them.

Southey's interest in scientific matters, although more evidence could be cited to show its continuance, never developed into anything more than amateurish curiosity. The subjects that most fascinated him were the history and literature of the past. In such study, far more than in the writing of poetry, he himself came properly to feel that his true vocation lay. Here again the blending impulses of reaction and progress make their presence known. Eighteenth-century judgment had erected classical literature into a canon, and in its passion for order and modernity had thrust what was not classic according to the canon into an outer darkness as something "Gothic" or otherwise to be contemned. Yet the fine intelligence of the eighteenth century could not rest content with that, and by Southey's time the impulse to investigate the non-classical was already well developed. Already, too, there had been attempts to utilize other mythologies and other histories and literatures than those of the Greeks and Romans as material for poetry. From these came inspiration to the Westminster schoolboy to plan epics for all the gods not of Olympus. The older literature of England and the Germanic peoples attracted him, but he also planned and in some part accomplished something in Arabian, Hindu, Persian, Welsh, American, and Spanish learning. Finding such study to be his chosen field, he settled down to the study of Spain and Portugal, and planned to write an account of the latter country, a history of its explorations and colonies, as well as of Portuguese and Spanish literature, and of monasticism. These works were never accomplished, but the indefatigable author did manage to achieve, out of all these labors, some notable translations, a finely conceived epic on the origin of the Spanish nation, and histories of Brazil and the Peninsular War. Southey's attitude grew to be that, since there was so much to be known about the history of the past, it was mortal sin for him not to write upon it all. To his list of subjects could be added church history, travel, the position of women, the manufacturing system, missions, religious psychology, literary history and biography, all that mass of learning represented by his *Quarterly Review* articles, *The Doctor*, and the four tomes that were printed out of his commonplace books. In our day Southey, with — it is to be hoped — certain radical changes in his point of view, might have become a research professor of high rank, for no Ph.D. ever surpassed his encyclopedic capacity for information. That he possessed a true philosophic and imaginative sympathy for the times and peoples about whom he knew so much is as little true of him as of many in our day learned after the same fashion. Yet this failure to illuminate as well as to inform was not a failure of intention, for he made a noble effort to be as true as he could within his limitations to the life and spirit as well as to the facts of other times and places. It was rather a failure in learning itself, for his attitude toward life and his duties as chief provider for the many mouths that were to be fed out of one ink-well in Greta Hall combined to prevent Southey from becoming genuinely and profoundly intelligent in any subject.

II

We must return to the youth of nineteen in whom the traits that we have been discussing were already well developed, and were soon to be fixed.   Alert, sensitive to a fault, stiffly independent, full of multifarious reading, his head whirling with the wine of new doctrines and the vision of new fields of knowledge, his temper little willing to brook the restraints of circumstance or college dignitaries, he began his residence at Balliol in January, 1793, having been registered in the preceding November.   "Behold me, my friend," he wrote at once to Bedford, "entered under the banners of science or stupidity, — which you please, — and like a recruit got sober, looking to the days that are past, and feeling something like regret."   Balliol is said to have occupied at the time an inferior reputation in the university.   Southey's rooms were reputed to have been situated in a rambling old building called, with reason, the "Rat Castle" near the head of Balliol Grove, and were pointed out as his until the building was torn down.[1]   The state of the university was, of course, little to the taste of a young stoic and democrat, although, except for a few such regulations as that students must wear shoes and not boots with the gown, he was allowed to do much as he pleased. His tutor, indeed, a certain Thomas Howe, probably aware of the young man's political notions, expressed similar ones himself and added, "Mr. Southey, you won't learn anything by my lectures, Sir; so, if you have any studies of your own, you had better pursue them."   This man was

[1] *Quar. Rev.*, v. 88, 203.

an exception, however, and for the most part, Oxford appeared to exhibit only "waste of wigs and want of wisdom."

As contrasted with Westminster, Southey found Oxford a very aristocratic place. School was truly republican, and social distinctions had been there unregarded. The most respected boy was "the best bruiser," next came the best cricketer, next the cleverest, and next the best scholar, but these ranks were attainable by all regardless of worldly position. At college, however, Southey discovered[1] that feelings of equality were to be got rid of; that old schoolfellows might pass him in the street as if they knew him not, staring him full in the face to assure him that it was not done through inadvertence; that young men with whom he had eaten at the same table, studied in the same class, perhaps slept in the same chamber might demand the ceremony of introduction before continuing his acquaintance. The pursuits of these youths were also of the usual aristocratic order. Fashions of dress and behavior were set by those of greatest wealth or rank, and the most universal interest was the sowing of wild oats. Some years later[2] (1807) Southey gave his impressions of certain of the Oxford undergraduates with great gusto. Such beings passed, he said, for human because it pleased God to set them upon two legs, to give them smooth skins and no tail, and to enable them to talk without having their tongues slit. They were sent to Oxford in order that they might proceed through their course of shooting, horse-racing, whoring, and drinking out of sight of their families and without injury to their characters. Incidentally, they would come away with the name of having been at the university and with a qualification for undertaking the cure of souls.

It may be seen that Southey's opinion of Oxford in his day was not high; swimming, according to his own asser-

---

[1] *Letters of Don Manuel Espriella, Letter XLVI.*   [2] *Ibid.*

tion, was the only useful thing he learned there. "My college years," he said, "were the least beneficial and the least happy in my life."[1]   At a later time still, the man of forty-two looked back and thought that the boy of nineteen had suffered grave danger at this time.   It seemed to him that when he left Westminster he had had nothing to discipline his character properly except adversity.   Yet his actual behavior at college was both innocent and characteristic enough.   When the college barber waited upon him in the regular course of duty to dress and powder his hair, the young republican, like Wesley in 1728,[2] sent the astonished man packing, and insisted upon wearing his long curls in their native liberty.   *The Edinburgh Review* appropriately points out that in 1793 refusal to use hair powder "was a token of disaffection to Church and State."[3]   Southey also refused to drink more wine than suited his inclinations and principles.   He condemned the excesses of the undergraduates with the stern eye of the disciple of Epictetus and Rousseau.   "As for me, I regard myself too much to run into the vices so common and so destructive.   I have not yet been drunk, nor mean to be so.   What use can be made of a collegiate life I wish to make; but in the midst of all, when I look back to Rousseau, and compare myself either with his Emilius or the real pupil of Madame Brulenck, I feel ashamed and humbled at the comparison.   Never shall child of mine enter a public school or a university.   Perhaps I may not be able so well to instruct him in logic and languages, but I can at least preserve him from vice."

Academic formalism seems to have pleased Southey as little as the behavior of undergraduates.   Upon the installation of the Duke of Portland as chancellor of the university the young man indulged in another bit of radical

[1] *Life*, IV, 194.   [3] Review of *Life*.   *Edin. Rev.*, v. 93, 376.
[2] *Life of Wesley*, I, 60.

unconventionalism. All other pens in the institution had been versifying for the occasion:

> "For three whole days I heard an old Fur-gown
>   Bepraised, that made a Duke a Chancellor;
>   Bepraised in prose it was, bepraised in verse;
>   Lauded in pious Latin to the skies;
>   Kudos'd egregiously in heathen Greek;
>   In sapphics sweetly incensed; glorified
>   In proud alcaics; in hexameters
>   Applauded to the very galleries,
>   That did applaud again, whose thunder-claps,
>   Higher and longer, with redoubled peals,
>   Rung when they heard the illustrious furbelow'd
>   Heroically in Popean rhyme
>   Tee-ti-tum'd, in Miltonic blank bemouth'd;
>   Prose, verse, Greek, Latin, English, rhyme and blank,
>   Till Eulogy, with all her wealth of words,
>   Grew bankrupt, all-too-prodigal of praise,
>   And panting Panegyric toil'd in vain,
>   O'er-tasked in keeping pace with such desert." [1]

It was Southey's boast that he was not guilty of a single line to that old fur-gown, but he did compose some verses that he might have offered upon this occasion if praise of peace and railings against war and desolation, which he alleged were brought upon peoples by the great, had been welcome in 1793 at a time when England under Pitt had gone to war with republican France. In the circumstances he could only remain in his room while the rest were installing the chancellor, and address his verses to the cat of Rat Castle, a good democratic beast with claws and an independence of character that might serve as excellent example to spaniel man.[2]

[1] *Written the Winter after the Installation at Oxford* (1793), *Annual Anthology*, 1799; *Works*, 172.

[2] *Verses, intended to have been addressed to His Grace the Duke of*

The social distinctions which Southey has described seem really to have interfered with his happiness less than he imagined. Wynn, who had preceded him at the university, was at Christ Church, and their old friendship was continued. In addition to this hardly a week had elapsed after his arrival before there had gathered about him a little party of men "glad to form a sober society." Conspicuous among them was Edmund Seward. "I used to call him *Talus* for his unbending morals and iron rectitude."[1] With this man Southey became closely intimate, and revered him all his life as one who exercised over him a decisive moral influence at this "perilous time" in the development of his character. "I loved him with my whole heart, and shall remember him with gratitude and affection as one who was my moral father, to the last moment of my life." This youth seems, indeed, a little impossibly virtuous, but to Southey he was admirable as a true philosopher, one whose example as a stoic inspired imitation. Two years before Seward had forsworn wine, butter, and sugar from a resolution to abridge the luxuries of life. Now he drank only water and breakfasted upon tea and dry bread. In spite of this and in spite of an odd and uncommon appearance, Southey felt that Seward's manners were most pleasing. His philosophy, however, was his chief claim to attraction. He had begun to study assiduously at the age of fourteen, and when Southey asked him whether his attention did not flag over Hutchinson's *Moral Philosophy* in Latin, adding the opinion that "if our tutors would but make our studies interesting, we should pursue them with pleasure," Seward replied, "Certainly we should, but I feel a pleasure in studying them because I know it to be my duty." This Southey

Portland, Chancellor of the University, etc. On his installation, 1793. Published in *Annual Anthology*, 1799, and suppressed in later editions of Southey's poems.

[1] *Life*, IV, 320.

took to be true philosophy because it tended to make man happy by first making him good.

There were several others in Southey's "sober society" with whom he was also upon excellent terms, and among whom he could spend his time "alternately studying and philosophizing, railing at collegiate folly, and enjoying rational society." Nicholas Lightfoot seems to have been his nearest neighbor in Rat Castle; with him, he says nearly thirty years later, he practically lived; they read together, breakfasted together, passed every evening together, and agreed in their views and feelings. Lightfoot became a country schoolmaster, and continued Southey's lifelong and admiring friend.[1] Another member of this group was Robert Burnett, of whom we shall hear more anon. Charles Collins would have been made by Southey the occupant of the chair of Plato in an ideal university. Robert Allen was the one with whom Coleridge was to make a notable visit a few months later. Then there was a certain Cooke Rogers,[2] who vigorously defended Southey against a man who, from not understanding a "metaphysical conversation," had accused him of blasphemy and atheism. The conversations of this group as a whole, however, need not be supposed to have been exclusively metaphysical or even rational. That lighter matters sometimes engrossed them is shown when Southey writes, "The fiddle with one string is gone, and its place is supplied with a harpsichord in Burnett's room. Lightfoot still melodizes on the flute, and, had I but a Jew's harp, the concert would be complete."

[1] *Correspondence with Caroline Bowles*, 27.   [2] *Warter*, II, 195.

III

Southey now threw himself with characteristic energy
into the business of reading and writing. History, philosophy of his own particular kind, and poetry claimed his
attention, and in long declamatory, sophomoric letters to
a former schoolmate, he poured forth descriptions of his
pursuits and impressions of what he saw and read. As
for writing, we shall see presently how his pen busied itself.
In emulation of the philosophic Seward he made the pious
resolution of rising every morning at five to study, equip-
ping himself for the purpose with an alarm clock and
tinder box. He describes the scene to the appreciative
Bedford: "This morning was the first. I rose, called up
a neighbor, and read about three hundred lines of Homer,
when I found myself hungry; the bread and cheese were
called in as auxiliaries, and I made some negus: as I spiced
it my eye glanced over the board, and the assemblage
seemed so curious that I laid aside all for your letter,— a
lexicon, Homer, ink-stand, candles, snuffers, wine, bread
and cheese, nutmeg grater, and hour-glass."

The long epistolary effusions also show that neither such
a life nor the example of Seward had as yet completely
effected Southey's conversion to stoicism. Far from adopting the tenets of any cynic or sophist, he declared that his
sentiments should be colored by fancy, nature, or Rousseau.
He would found no school of disputants or doctors; ideas
rose up with the scenes he viewed, some passing away with
the momentary glance, but some remaining engraved upon
his memory. "My heart," he adds, "is equally easy of
impression with that of Rousseau, and perhaps more tena-
cious of it," and he recommends Bedford to read *The Man
of Feeling:* "Few works have ever pleased me so painfully
or so much." But the leaven of the stoic was working, for

he immediately says, "It is very strange that man should be delighted with the highest pain that can be produced. I even begin to think that both pain and pleasure exist only in idea. But this must not be affirmed; the first twinge of the toothache, or retrospective glance, will undeceive me with a vengeance." It is evident from much of this that the young man's reading was now extending itself widely among other philosophers, and he mentions enough concerning not only Epictetus, but Plato, Aristotle, Epicurus, Seneca, Plotinus, to show that he had formed some acquaintance with them. How all this was to affect his poetry and his plans of life will appear very soon.

For poetry was by no means neglected in the midst of all this active reading. In December of 1793 the poet calculated that he had composed up to that time about 35,000 lines of verse, of which 10,000 had been burnt or lost, another 10,000 preserved, and 15,000 more kept but thought worthless; this count excluded letters of great length written in doggerel. It included notably one long narrative poem, *Joan of Arc*, and a host of minor pieces, most of them written during Southey's school and college years. This activity culminated in the publication of a volume of shorter poems with Robert Lovell at the beginning of 1795, and of *Joan of Arc* at the end of the same year. Yet it is noticeable that the facility shown in all this output was nearly equaled by its feebleness; the interest for the modern reader lies almost solely in the sensitiveness shown by the young writer to all the swarming new ideas in the life and literature of the time. Hardly a single poetic experiment was being attempted by any versifier of the day which Southey, in his exuberant youth, did not initiate, or share, or join. Hardly a new view of life or a feeling of the coming generation escaped some expression in his copious scribbling. He made use of all the notable new verse forms of the day as rapidly as they appeared; the sonnet, the various ode forms including some of his own invention, the elegiac quatrain, blank verse for the purpose of satire, reflection, drama, and narrative. He gave expression to the worship of nature, the love of retirement, the aspirations for freedom, the sympathy with the common people and the poor, the attraction toward the past and the distant, — Gothic, Oriental, American. Of the examples set by Gray, Mason, Collins, Chatterton, Thompson, Sayers, Cowper, Darwin, Akenside, Young, Glover, Crabbe, Gay's *Pastorals*, the inevitable Gessner, Thomas Warton, Bowles, — not one failed to be noted by him, and at a later time at least, probably even at this, he took cognizance of such obscurities as Hole, Polwhele, Russell, Bampfylde, Dermody, Emily, Knowles, and others of the same order of magnitude.[1]

So abundant were the poetic influences upon Southey at the very beginning of his career that it is difficult to decide how they should be distinguished or in what order presented. Modeled upon the more conventional eighteenth-century forms, undoubtedly, were many of the thousands of verses that had been destroyed as well as a few that have been preserved. *The Retrospect*, written on the occasion of a visit to his old school at Corston, is in heroic couplets and reminds one in tone and manner of Goldsmith.[2] *Rosamund to Henry*[3] plainly harks back to *Eloisa*, and *The Triumph of Woman*[4] to *Alexander's Feast*. Here too might be mentioned a feeble imitation of Gray's *Elegy* in *The Miser's Mansion*, but this form was dearer to Southey's poetical associate, Lovell. A far more striking influence, however, the importance of which he constantly

---

[1] *Life of Cowper*, Chap. XII. See also Southey's review of Dr. Sayers's *Collective Works*, Quar. Rev. Jan., 1827, v. 35.

[2] *Poems*, 1795; *Works*, 154.

[3] *Poems*, 1795; omitted from *Works*.

[4] *Poems*, 1797; *Works*, 98.

acknowledged in later life,[1] was that of William Lisle Bowles. Many, without doubt, as compared with the number of sonnets that Southey preserved in his printed poems, were those that he committed to the flames. Bowles, the indigent son of a clergyman who had left a widow and seven children, had, in 1789, knocked three times at the door of one Cruttwell, a printer in Bath, before he could gain admittance and submit for publication a sheaf of fourteen sonnets. Cruttwell at first declined to accept them, but finally consented to publish one hundred copies at a cost of about five pounds. The young man left his manuscript and went back to his unpaid bills at Oxford, little expecting to hear again from his poems. They appeared as *Fourteen Sonnets written chiefly on Picturesque Spots during a Journey,*[2] and in six months Bowles received a letter from Cruttwell saying that an edition of five hundred could be sold. This was immediately issued (1789), seven new sonnets having been added by the author, and it was followed in a few years by three more editions (1794, 1796, 1796). The wine of Bowles was thin, to be sure, but it had the true Pierian flavor to young men who longed to be stirred in such ways and by such causes as Bowles had found. Coleridge, then a youth at Cambridge, had come upon the volume (probably the second edition, 1789), had written a letter of commendation to the author, and had transcribed copies of the work to give away to his friends. Meanwhile Southey, too, although there is no evidence of the fact in his letters and although the earliest of his sonnets is dated merely 1794, had undoubtedly picked up Bowles's volume in Bath or Bristol, and had begun to try

---

[1] *Works, Preface.*

[2] *Poetical Works* of W. L. Bowles, ed. by Gilfillan, Vol. I. *Introduction* by Bowles to the edition of his poems of 1837; Vol. II, *Introduction* by the editor. Coleridge *Biographia Literaria*, ed. by J. Shawcross, Vol. I, 8, and note.

the new experiment for himself. A few years later he became entirely disgusted with the form,[1] and suppressed many of the specimens which had appeared in his early volume. In the main he followed his model quite closely. Bowles's plaintive self-pity and moralizing upon nature fitted in well with his own moods. Nothing conduces more to the composition of poetry of this kind than to be in love and have poor prospects of marriage, to be dissatisfied with the way the world is run, to be addicted to versifying, and to be twenty years old; this was Southey's state when Bowles fell in his way. Consequently there is preserved a goodly number of sonnets which were composed by him in 1794 and the years following, and published in his three early volumes (1795, 1797, 1799). They doubtless represent some earlier attempts in the same form which had been destroyed. They descant upon nature, the wickedness of society, the goodness of Edith Fricker, and the longing for domestic retirement far from the haunts of men. Southey added other characteristic themes,— ruined castles, the attractions of Chaucer, the unhappy Werther, the iniquities of the slave trade. The sincerest tribute to Bowles, however, was paid in 1795. Bowles writes[2] that Cruttwell, the printer, reported to him that he had been visited by "two young gentlemen, strangers, one a particularly handsome and pleasing youth, lately from Westminster School, and both literary and intelligent." They spoke, says Bowles, "in high commendation of my volume, and if I recollect right, expressed a desire to have some poems printed in the same type and form." The "handsome and pleasing" youth was, of course, Southey, and on the strength of such a proffer, perhaps in the hope of such another good stroke as he had achieved with Bowles, Cruttwell accepted the poems submitted by the two young men.

[1] *Poems*, 1797, *Preface*.
[2] Bowles, *Poetical Works*. Introduction to Vol. I, as above.

For another poetical experiment which Southey attempted at Oxford (1794) the model appears to have been
less direct than in the case of the sonnets. He had, as we
have seen, read Gay's *Pastorals* as a boy and taken them
seriously, and in an obscure provincial collection of poems[1]
he had seen a translation of one of Gessner's *Idylls* which
made, to be sure, but little impression upon him at the
time.[2] The effect of these slight suggestions was now to
afford an easy and rather amusing vehicle for some of his
radical vaporings in a handful of compositions called *Botany
Bay Eclogues*, written at Oxford in 1794. Four of them
were published in 1797[3] with a motto from Bowles, and
a fifth saw the light only over a pseudonym in *The
Monthly Magazine* in 1798.[4] In these efforts the young
disciple of Rousseau made use of the so-called eclogue to
describe, in easy anapests and with satirical flings at government, how the wickedness that had been bred by society
in the poor creatures transported to Australia might be
there cured by solitude and nature. Hardly more than
jeux d'esprit, these little poems, if they can be called that,
are interesting as forerunners of later, more important
attempts in the eclogue vein, and because they were not
suffered to go unremembered by the critics of the day.

We pass for the present, however, to still more important compositions which are a development of Southey's
schoolboy interest in literature, history, and mythology. I
have already described the effect upon the boy's imagination of the little volume of Sayers's which had been published in 1792. Among the influences which blended with
the appeal of this book to affect one of the most important
phases of Southey's work, none is more notable than that

---

[1] *Poems, chiefly by Gentlemen of Devonshire and Cornwall* [ed. by
R. Polwhele], 2 vols., Bath, 1792, I, 85.

[2] *Taylor*, I, 214.   [4] *Month. Mag.*, Jan., 1798, v. 5, 41.

[3] *Poems*, 1797; *Works*, 113.

of the ode as it had been written in various forms and on various themes during the preceding generation. Although he wrote in 1799, "I never attempt the ode, it is the kind of poetry I like least,— perhaps because it was the last I understood,"[1] and although he stated in the preface to his volume of poems published in 1797, "I now think the Ode the most worthless species of composition, as well as the most difficult; and [shall] never again attempt it," nevertheless he made many experiments with the form in the years 1793 and 1794, experiments which were closely connected with his interest in the work of Sayers.

In the first place, like Sayers himself, he had been impressed by the beauty of Collins's *Ode to Evening;* "Everyone who has an ear for meter and a heart for poetry, must have felt how perfectly the meter of Collins's *Ode to Evening* is in accordance with the imagery and the feeling."[2] Youthful admiration for this poem resulted, of course, in imitation. *To Hymen*[3] (composed at Oxford, 1794) is a creditable attempt at the same stanza, and in such pieces as *Written on the First of December* (1793) and *Written on the First of January* (1794),[4] as well as in many later ones, we meet experiments with variations upon Collins's model. Of more far-reaching importance for the young writer was the influence of the so-called Pindaric or Cowleyan ode in several forms and derivatives. This was in part due to the fact that Collins, Gray, Mason, and Sayers all made use of the ode more or less extensively in their attempt to employ the imagery and "machinery" of other literatures and mythologies than the classical, especially those of the northern or "Gothic" nations. Here was a twofold interest, a verse form to be tried and a favorite field of inquiry to be invaded at the same time.

Although Southey drew upon Gray and Collins for models

[1] *Taylor*, I, 265.
[2] *Works, Preface.*
[3] *Poems*, 1795; *Works*, 145.
[4] *Poems*, 1797; *Works*, 131.

in writing his odes, it was Sayers whose inspiration was more direct and impelling, and may be considered first in importance. His *Dramatic Sketches*, says Southey, was "the first book I was ever master of money enough to order at a country bookseller's."[1] Sayers[2] himself was a leisured, not to say indolent, dilettante and an intimate of William Taylor of Norwich, by whom he and his book were much overrated. In publishing *Dramatic Sketches*, Sayers's motive, so far as it went, was characteristic of the time. He regretted in his preface that English poetry was devoid of any but a few "traces of the splendid and sublime religion of our Northern Ancestors." Yet he showed little desire to do more than capitalize for purposes of poetry a new mythological "machinery" in the hope of affording the relief of variety to the old Olympian scheme. His own studies never carried him beyond what was, even in his day, a superficial knowledge of "northern antiquities," and he frittered away his time filing and polishing the few slight pieces that he had managed to compose, in the opportunist's not the scholar's fashion, out of the little that he knew. Taylor, his intimate friend from boyhood, and largely the instigator and inspirer of his literary work, had traveled in Germany and acquired the most extensive knowledge of German language and literature possessed by any Englishman up to that time. He undertook to teach German to Sayers, and they construed together Goethe's

[1] *Taylor*, I, 447, Jan. 23, 1803.

[2] *Dramatic Sketches of Northern Mythology* was published in 1790. It reappeared with some additions in 1792, and again in 1803, in 1807, and in the *Collective Works* edited with "Biographic Particulars" by William Taylor in 1823. Sayers published, besides, in 1793 *Disquisitions Metaphysical and Literary* containing an essay on English metres, and in 1805 *Miscellanies, Antiquarian and Historical* containing a not very profound article on English medieval literature. It is to be noted that Southey wrote the review of his old master's *Collective Works* for *The Quarterly Review* in 1827.

Proserpina, Voss's *Luise,* portions of the chorus dramas of Klopstock, odes and at least one ballad of Stolberg which Sayers translated under the title, *Sir Egwin.*[1] Taylor also reports that his friend had read the Greek tragedians with "agitated feeling." This reading in German, although "he did not, however, persevere in the study of the German language, . . . nor was he a warm admirer of the literature," probably suggested the notion of imitating the Greek form of the drama in English, an idea strengthened by models nearer home. "Percy's *Northern Antiquities,*"[2] says Taylor, "supplied some of the costume and colouring." Southey added[3] that Gray's versions of the Runic poems[4] aided by Percy's translations[5] "of the more celebrated remains of the Skalds" had also "strongly impressed the rising generation of poets."[6] He further added a list of others who, to his knowledge, had before or after attempted to make use of similar material in poetry; "Minor pieces, drawn from the stores of Scandinavian antiquity, had been composed by Miss Seward,[7] by Mr. Polwhele, and by others of the contributors to a collection of poems,[8] chiefly by

[1] Sayers, *Collective Works,* xxxviii-xxxix.

[2] *Ibid.* xxxix; Thomas Percy, *Northern Antiquities, — or a description of the manners, customs, religion, and laws of the ancient Danes. . . . With a translation of the Edda and other pieces from the Islandic tongue . . . Translated from Mons. Mallet's Introduction á l'Histoire de Dannemarc, etc. (1755–1756). With additional notes by the English translator and Goranson's Latin version of the Edda.* 2 vols. 1770.

[3] *Quar. Rev.* v. 35, 204–205.

[4] *The Fatal Sisters* and *The Descent of Odin,* pub. 1768.

[5] *Five Pieces of Runic Poetry translated from the Islandic Language,* 1768.

[6] For the whole subject see especially F. E. Farley, *Scandinavian Influences in the English Romantic Movement.*

[7] Anna Seward, *Llangollen Vale and other Poems,* 1796, containing *Herva at the tomb of Argantyr.*

[8] *Poems, chiefly by Gentlemen of Devonshire and Cornwall* [edited by Richard Polwhele], 1792, including *The Incantation of Herva* and other poems on Scandinavian subjects.

gentlemen of Devon and Cornwall, which appeared just at this time; and Mr. Hole, a little before, had founded,[1] upon the Runic mythology, a poem of more pretensions in its extent and structure, than anything which had appeared since the *Leonidas* and the *Epigoniad*."

In his use of the Greek dramatic form Sayers was not, as has been suggested, dependent alone upon the example of the Germans or his reading of the classics. He had also in mind the work of a "Greek school" of English poets among whom he classed himself. Gray and Collins he named as the founders of this school, apparently for no reason save that they wrote odes upon "Gothic" or allied subjects which served as models for the choruses of Mason's efforts to throw the same material into the form of the Greek drama. Southey, therefore, names Mason, rather than Collins, as Gray's associate in founding such a school and also includes[2] Gilbert West and, "with strong shades of individual difference," Akenside and Glover. The treatment of the ode form by these men is their most interesting characteristic as a "school." Sayers, in the essay on English meters in his *Disquisitions*, which is mainly a series of citations from former writers in defense of his own use of rimeless and more or less irregular verse,[3] refers to the experiments with similar forms by Peele in *The Complaint of Œnone*, by Spenser as he supposed in *The Mourning Muse of Thestylis*, and by Sidney, Milton, Watts, Collins, and by Glover in the choruses of his *Medea*, an attempt earlier than Mason's in the Greek dramatic form. The "Greek school" was supposed to continue these experiments principally in its adaptations of that type of the ode which employs some kind of long and fairly complicated,

[1] Richard Hole, *Arthur, or the Northern Enchantment. A Poetical Romance*, 1789.

[2] *Quar. Rev.*, v. 35, 205.

[3] Saintsbury, *History of English Prosody*, III, 39.

sometimes varied, stanza or irregular verse paragraph. These adaptations were several in number. There was the original "Pindarick" with its complicated, irregular, riming verse paragraphs; there was the type with varied, regular, but fairly complicated riming stanzas recurring in strophic balance; there was the type using throughout a single form of long, complicated, riming stanza; and finally there was the possibility of using any one of these forms without rime. As thus developed this verse-form was to be one of the many to attract Southey's imitative and experimental zeal and to receive further interesting development at his hands.

Mention has already been made of the impression created upon young writers by Gray's "Runic" poems. Although these pieces were simpler in form than the ones we are discussing, they were called odes by the author, and being similar in subject-matter, were associated with *The Bard* and *The Progress of Poesy*. The two latter were composed in the strophic arrangement, and the same poet's *Ode for Music* in the irregular riming stanzas, but Gray published no experiments with the rimeless forms. A uniform long stanza was used by Collins in his ode *On the Popular Superstitions of the Highlands of Scotland*, and here too were famous references to "northern antiquities." In his ode *To Liberty* the strophic arrangement appears, but that on *The Passions*, called an "ode for music," is in the irregular stanza like Gray's later *Ode for Music*. Finally, in the *Ode to Evening*, Collins achieved his great success with the rimeless stanza. Notice should here be taken also of the odes of Thomas Warton, because of the influence which Southey[1] acknowledges that Warton, along with Gray, Mason, and,— he might have added,— Collins exercised upon his own schoolboy verses. Warton's odes,[2] fourteen

[1] *Works, Preface.*

[2] A collected edition of Warton's poems appeared in 1777; there were several later editions, and in 1802 Richard Mant edited his *Poetical Works*.

in number not including his laureate productions, are smooth and simple in form. They show no great power of poetic imagination, but they refer to such matters as Arthur, Hardyknute, the *Faerie Queene,* the crusades, and ruined abbeys. It does not appear that Warton was at all associated by Sayers and Southey with their "Greek School."

The most important member of the group was really William Mason, Gray's somewhat insufferable friend and imitator. His odes, sixteen of them published between 1756 and 1788, though painfully imitative of Gray and like his using the strophic form except for two in the irregular verse paragraphs "for music," do not deal with "Gothic" subjects at all. It was his two plays *Elfrida* (1752) and *Caractacus* (1759) that ventured into this field. Both of these pieces purport to deal with ancient English or British history, but rely for their information mainly upon Tacitus, Cæsar, and other classical authorities, or possibly upon Camden's *Brittania* and Drayton's *Polyolbion.* They are frankly experimental, and betray a curious kind of inconsistency between critical conservatism and innovation. Each professes to be a "dramatic poem, written on the model of the ancient Greek tragedy," and therefore introducing a chorus and following the three unities, firmly established, according to the author, by Aristotle. Since Shakespeare had surpassed all possible competitors in native genius, Mason avowedly chose to make use of art as a means to outrival him.

By art Mason explains that he means the use of an elaborate and ornate imagery and diction. For his subject-matter he offers no apology, but he was plainly trying to lay claim to the charm of novelty in using non-classical material. The result of his endeavors is not very happy. Of the manners and customs of the ancient Saxons or Britons he was, of course, profoundly ignorant. It has been pointed out that Gray[1] was the first poet of the eighteenth century who drew, not upon Gothic architecture, but upon Gothic literature for his materials, and Gray, while he may not have produced the true ring of the Edda in English, at least achieved a note that was striking and original. Mason scarcely draws even upon Gothic architecture, and attains at best merely a pale resemblance in plot and motivation of character to Beaumont and Fletcher. His British and Saxon mythology is simply the classical system done over into terms of Druid and Odin. He had no notion of adapting the legends of the older literatures themselves as plots, but his scheme was solely to utilize, as part of that "art" by which he was to rival Shakespeare, the names of the northern gods and as much as he could learn without labor concerning the northern peoples. The impulse to find a new mythology for poetry was stirring, however, even in Mason. Yet it was long before faith would be strong enough to render any mythology the poets might use more than were "machinery." The situation was well described by Southey in his review of Dr. Sayers when he said that the gods of the Greeks and Romans had grown stale, that angels and demons had proved but a poor substitute, and that poets seemed well disposed to transfer their devotion to the gods and heroes of Valhalla.[2]

The suggestions that Mason offered to Sayers, and in a more general sense to Southey, are apparent. Here was both the idea of writing upon "Northern Mythology" and of doing so in the form of the Greek drama. For his dramatic passages Mason had used blank verse, but added the slightly novel device of using odes in the manner of Gray for the chorus of virgins in *Elfrida* and of bards and

[1] For Gray's knowledge of old Norse see *Appendix* by G. L. Kittredge to the *Introduction* to *Selections from Thomas Gray*, edited by W. L. Phelps.

[2] *Quar. Rev.*, v. 35, 204.

druids in *Caractacus*. These are mostly in the strophic balance, with one or two exceptions in favor of the irregular form "for music." Such treatment of the chorus contained the most important idea which was to be derived from Mason by Sayers and Southey.

The two plays we have been discussing were presented [1] at Covent Garden, *Elfrida* in 1772, with alterations by Colman, and *Caractacus* in 1776. Southey says that they were well received, and he remembered having as a child seen Mrs. Siddons in the rôle of Elfrida at Bath.[2] Mason's chief influence, however, was upon Sayers, whom Southey commends for taking such a model,[3] adding that, if he had been one of the mocking-birds of Parnassus, he would have followed rather the example of Cowper, Darwin, or Merry, "then each in full sail upon the stream of celebrity, which very soon floated two of them, by a short cut, into the dead sea."

The purpose of Sayers which distinguished him so strikingly from the followers of the men just named, especially in the mind of a boy with such tastes as Southey's, was frankly "mythological." The preface to his *Dramatic Sketches* opens with the statement: "Among the variety of mythological systems which have contributed at different periods to decorate the poetry of England, it is much to be lamented that we should discover only the faintest traces of the splendid and sublime religion of our Northern Ancestors." Gray he distinguishes as the only one who had "deigned to notice the sacred fables of the Goths."

"It is certain, however, that the most magnificent features of Scandinavian superstition have hitherto been chiefly concealed in the Sagas of Iceland, or have appeared only in the tragedies of Klopstock and a few other pieces, little known except among the Germans and Danes to whom they owe their existence. This being

[1] *Eng. Poets*, ed. by Alexander Chalmers, v. XVIII, 309–310.
[2] *Quar. Rev.*, v. 35, 195 and note.   [3] *Quar. Rev.*, v. 35, 197.

the case, I am tempted to publish the following Sketches, with a view of giving some slight idea of the neglected beauties of the Gothic religion, and of recommending a freer introduction of its imagery into the poetry of the English nation."

Sayers's only contribution, however, to the illustration of "northern antiquities," beyond what he had derived from Percy, was the presentation of a small part of the information to be obtained from his source. Even the form of the Greek tragedy was chosen, not because of any particular predilection for the form itself, but "as affording in its chorus the most favorable opportunity for the display of mythological imagery." [1]

In the handling of his choruses or, as he called them, odes, we find the other source of interest for Southey. These did indeed use the terms of northern mythology with some show of familiarity, which must have had the charm of novelty, but they were chiefly notable for their metrical form. Sayers used, in partial imitation of Mason, the loose ode with an effort to adapt the movement of the verse and the length and arrangement of the lines to the feelings expressed. More than this, however, acting upon the example of Klopstock and Stolberg, he abandoned the use of rime entirely, "both because," as he says, "it was less conformable to the [Greek] model imitated, and because it appeared unnecessary, if not prejudicial in this species of poetry." This departure of Sayers made an immediate and striking impression upon Southey. Always interested in versification, from his imitative youth onwards, he has himself in various places pointed out the difficulties that beset the composition of this type of meter.[2] Irregular blank verse is always liable to fall into mere prose cut up upon the page into unequal lines of print, or into regular

[1] *Dramatic Sketches, Preface.* See also *Preface* to *Moina.*
[2] *Correspondence with Caroline Bowles,* 51, 53–54, 58–59.

blank verse similarly abused, or it may give the impression that the author has simply measured off his lines according to some preconceived pattern and then forgotten to rime. Southey does not fail [1] to note that Collins had been the only one to succeed notably with a rimeless lyric measure in English poetry; he, perhaps rashly, deemed that Milton had lost his meter entirely in *Samson Agonistes*, and that Glover, in the rimeless stanzas of the choruses to his *Medea*, had counted his verses off on his fingers. Sayers, on the contrary, had avoided all pitfalls.

"[He] never employed a strongly-marked measure unless it was peculiarly appropriate, and then he constructed his verses so (having the language at his command,) that they required no humouring from an indulgent reader, but that in the easy and natural pronunciation of the words, the accent should necessarily fall where the harmony of the line required it.   Neither did he err . . . in subjecting his unrhymed lyrics to a rule of uniformity, rendering the composition more difficult, and the effect less pleasing.   He arranged them, according to his own perception of metrical harmony, in lines of such length and cadence, as, by suiting the matter and the passion, should at once satisfy the judgment and content the ear."

Later criticism [2] has truthfully pointed out that, in comparison with *Thalaba*, Sayers's success was not as great as it is here represented, but Southey was comparing the author of the *Dramatic Sketches* with other poets whom he thought to have been even less successful; therefore the impression made upon him by Sayers was much enhanced, and he was not slow in his Oxford days to attempt the imitation of these rimeless odes.

The influence of the subject matter of the *Dramatic Sketches* upon the youth who was planning mythological

[1] *Quar. Rev.*, v. 35, 211–213.
[2] Saintsbury, *History of English Prosody*, III, 39–41.

epics must not be overshadowed by that of the meter. The
paucity of real knowledge betrayed by Sayers did not, of
course, trouble Southey at the time. It was enough to be
encouraged by the example of another poet who had actually accomplished something in a small way like that which
he had himself dreamt of doing. In his first edition (1790)
Sayers had published three pieces. The first and slightest
of them was a thin adaptation of the story of Balder dead,
derived from the version of the prose *Edda* as distilled
through Mallet and Percy from Goranson's Latin translation. Sayers called this poem a masque; it had no chorus,
and is interesting only as an attempt to present this story
in English verse. *Moina* purports to be a full drama with
a chorus of bards. It is the tragedy of a Celtic woman
who has been made the Sabine wife of Harold, a Saxon
warrior, and is condemned to be buried with her husband's
body after the alleged Saxon custom, instead of being permitted to rejoin the Celtic lover from whom Harold had
taken her, and with whom she had been unable, for reasons
of propriety, to flee before her proper husband's death.
Needless to say, this plot did not come from Percy, and
neither did that of the other tragedy, *Starno*. *Moina* was
supposed to present a Saxon theme, and *Starno* attempted,
like the "admirable tragedy of Caractacus," [1] to deal with
a British one. Starno is a British chieftain who has regained his daughter from the Saxons, aided in the rescue
by the maiden's Saxon lover, who has fled with her to
British strongholds. The druids, who compose the chorus,
demand the lover for sacrifice to their gods, and although
Starno is persuaded by his daughter to deny the demand,
the Saxon youth refuses to accept safety on the intercession
of a maid, and is slain. In the second edition of his book
(1792) Sayers attempted another experiment in form in the
"monodrama", *Oswald*. This dealt with the same kind of

[1] Sayers, *Collective Works*, I, 99.

material, but can best be discussed at another point. [1] These four pieces made up the little book that fell in so pat with Southey's youthful tastes and aspirations, and to which he refers so often in later life with gratitude.

The weakness of these efforts of Sayers was not long, however, in becoming at least partially apparent to their admirer, for Southey wrote to William Taylor in 1803: [2] "Perhaps Dr. Sayers has not chosen his subjects well: the tale of Moina would have done equally well for a Hindoo or Peruvian drama." Here was exactly the trouble; Dr. Sayers's purpose was to "illustrate" Gothic religion and mythology, but his knowledge of the people and literature, not to mention the religion and mythology, was so slight that his "subjects" are inappropriate and absurd. Southey was to do better than Sayers in this respect, but not even he ever escaped from the semididactic notion that he must "illustrate" without vitalizing mythology or some other little known field of information. As for Sayers, the most that can be said for him is that his book, to such a boy as the one whose development we are tracing, was not untouched by the glamour of the past, that his wine, though thin and new like that of Bowles, nevertheless smacked of the muses' own hillside.

When we turn to the odes that Southey composed between the years 1791 and 1794, we find that the few specimens preserved traverse in imitation much of the evolution of the ode here presented. It has already been noted that he had attempted several pieces after the mode of Collins's *Ode to Evening*. Gray and Mason and Thomas Warton had used also the other types for the description of nature or the expression of their reflections upon life. Southey now in turn put his own romantic yearnings into similar form in such pieces as *To Contemplation* [3] (1792), *To a Friend* [4]

---

[1] See below.
[2] *Taylor*, I, 447, Jan. 23, 1803.
[3] *Poems*, 1797; *Works*, 127.
[4] *Poems*, 1797; *Works*, 128.

(1793), *Urban* [1] (published 1795), the two poems *To Lycon* [2] (published 1795), *Written on Sunday Morning* [3] (1795), and possibly the obscure *Mortality* published only with the signature S. in *The Monthly Magazine* of July, 1796. Over these somewhat vapid juvenilia we need linger only long enough to note that Southey used either a fairly simple stanza or, when indulging in more grandiose sentiments, the loose irregular form.

More interesting, as in the end more characteristic, are three odes in which, as in Gray's *Progress of Poesy* and Collins's *Ode to Liberty*, the muse goes on a grand tour. The first of these, *To Horror* (1791), has already been sufficiently discussed. *Romance* and *Hospitality* (both published 1795) [4] are also suggestive of *The Bard*, and are especially to be noted for the evidence they show of youthful erudition in Southey's favorite fields. "Romance" is beheld as a "wildly beauteous form," "lovely in horror," taking her stand on the "bicrowned hill" of Parnassus. From that point she speeds to the various lands in which her sway has been felt, footnotes explaining the references. These include "fictions of Romance, popular in Scandinavia at an early period"; Heliodorus, who "rather preferred to be deprived of his see than burn his Ethiopics"; Regner Lodbrog, of whom Southey had read in Percy; Arthur, Lancelot, Tristram, the paladins of France, Archbishop Turpin "instead of forging the life of a saint . . . better employed in falsifying the history of Charlemagne"; "Arabian fictions ingrafted on the Gothic romance"; Godfrey, Cœur de Lion, the Romance of the Rose, Spanish prose romances, Cervantes, Sidney, Spenser, and lastly Rousseau, to whom the grateful muse would fain "pour forth the energic thanks of gratitude." *Hospitality*, opening with even stronger echo of *The Bard*, pursues its subject in fashion similar to *Ro-*

[1] *Poems*, 1795.
[2] *Poems*, 1795.
[3] *Poems*, 1797; *Works*, 132.
[4] *Poems*, 1795.

mance. "Hospitality," as formerly seen in the monasteries destroyed by Henry VIII, in "proud Avalon," in the Arab's tent, among the savage Indians beside the Oroonoko, is contrasted with the niggardliness to be met "in fashion's circle, far from nature's laws." All three of these poems are in the loose form of the ode and show a palpable effort to accommodate the verse to the varying emotions expressed.

The idea of using the ode for narration had, of course, been represented in Dryden's *Alexander's Feast,* and is imitated with boyish facility by Southey in *The Triumph of Woman* (1793),[1] where the subject matter is drawn from the *Apocrypha,* and the sentiments accord with *Joan of Arc.* Narration is also implicit in the odes of Gray and Collins and especially in those of Sayers. Having read the *Dramatic Sketches,* Southey says that he convinced himself, "when I had acquired some skill in versification, that the kind of verse in which his choruses were composed was not less applicable to narration than to lyrical poetry." [2] Consequently we find the element of story more pronounced in the remaining odes to be discussed. The subjects are drawn either from "northern mythology" or from biblical legend, and the latter fact points to an additional source for Southey's style in this vein of writing. The swinging parallel structure of Hebrew poetry, which he had seen effectively adapted in Ossian, a book that had not failed to impress him, continued, especially in connection with the verse-form derived from Sayers, to be one of the characteristics of Southey's verse narratives.

In the two poems based upon "northern mythology," however, it is interesting to note that he had not yet taken the full step after Sayers, but was still following Gray, except that, although riming, he always used the irregular rather than the strophic form of the ode. *The Race of Odin* [3] is again a palpable imitation of *The Bard.* It recounts the

----

[1] *Poems,* 1797; *Works,* 98.   [2] *Works, Preface.*   [3] *Poems,* 1795.

fabled expulsion of Odin from the east by Pompey, and prophesies the vengeance to be taken by Odin's descendants in the overthrow of Rome when the world will again be free. In *The Death of Odin* [1] the meter is mainly the vigorous staccato movement of Gray's *Descent of Odin;* the story, like the previous one, drawn from the indispensable Percy, is of Odin choosing to die by his own hands in order to obtain the eternal reward of the warrior.

In the three odes drawn from Hebrew sources, Sayers is the model rather than Gray. *The Death of Joshua,* [2] which never attained the honor of being printed anywhere save in *The Monthly Magazine* over the signature S., is unmistakably an attempt of Southey's, though in rime, at something in the vein of Sayers. *The Death of Moses* [3] and *The Death of Matathias,* [3] however, are at last rimeless, and the tone and meter of *Thalaba* begin to be manifest. These two efforts in imitation of Sayers show a facility in the use of verse already equaling, if not surpassing, their model. They avoid the difficulties to which the form is liable, and they show greater freedom in varying the harmony to suit the changing moods of the speaker in the poem. There is also present that rhetorical skill which was to become one of Southey's most conspicuous merits both in verse and in prose.

Among the *Dramatic Sketches* was one entitled *Oswald* and called by the author "a monodrama," "a species of play, which has not yet, as far as I am able to discover, been attempted by English writers." [4] Sayers's immediate model was probably Goethe's *Proserpina,* which he had construed under Taylor's tutelage, but he also states that such poems were common "both in the closet and the

---

[1] *Poems,* 1795.
[2] *Month. Mag.,* Oct. 1796, v. 2, 730.
[3] *Poems,* 1795.
[4] *Dramatic Sketches; Preface* to *Oswald.*

theater" among the French and Italians.   Jean Baptiste
Rousseau [1] seems to have been the first to introduce the
Italian "cantata" into France in a series of poems upon
classical subjects, of which one, entitled *Circe*, became famous
and served to suggest the type.   This was a kind of lyrical
dramatic monologue written to be accompanied by music
after the fashion of the cantata   and representing Circe
declaiming to the sea-waves her desolation at the departure
of Odysseus.   *Circe* had many imitators.   Jean Jacques
Rousseau himself essayed a similar piece in *Pygmalion*,[2] for
which music was written by Horace Coignet and which was
actually presented at Lyons in 1770 and at the Comédie
Française in 1775.   With German attempts at this form,
however, we are more concerned.   Taylor says that the
first of these was H. W. von Gerstenberg's *Ariadne auf
Naxos*,[3] and translates it in his *Historic Survey of German
Poetry*.[4]   This was a close imitation of *Circe*, and according
to Taylor was declaimed in the theatre at Hamburg with
intervals of music.   Shortly afterwards K. W. Ramler composed several pieces of the same sort, notably *Ino, eine
Cantate*,[5] and Goethe, in his *Triumph der Empfindsamkeit*
(1787), introduced the cantata or, as it seems now to have
been called, the monodrama, *Proserpina*.   Both of these
poems were also translated by Taylor,[6] and it was undoubtedly he who taught both Sayers and Southey to experiment

[1] *Les Œuvres choisies du Sr. Rousseau, contenant ses Odes, Odes
Sacrées . . . et cantates.*   Rotterdam, 1719.   There were many later
editions during the eighteenth century.

[2] John Grand-Carteret, *J. J. Rousseau*, 353.

[3] *Ariadne auf Naxos, Eine Kantate* in his *Vermischte Schriften von
ihm selbst gesammelt*, 1815–1816.   The date of the poem is here given
as 1765; Taylor gives it as 1785.

[4] William Taylor of Norwich, *Historic Survey of German Poetry
Interspersed with Various Translations*, 1829–1830, III, 3.

[5] *Oden, Zweyte Auflage*, 1768.

[6] *Historic Survey*, I, 325–328; III, 312.

with the same form. The odes that have just been discussed, especially those derived from *The Bard*, have all of
them some of the characteristics of the dramatic monologue, and in the hands of Taylor's two pupils the monodrama was but a by-development of the ode. It was
always written by them in blank verse, was always concerned, like several of Southey's odes, with the suicide of
some mythological or heroic personage under stress of circumstances of great pith and moment, and consisted of his
or her parting words setting forth the occasion of the agony
and concluding with the death stroke itself. Sayers's *Oswald* dealt with the theme of Odin's death, which Southey
also treated, possibly on this suggestion, in his ode on the
same subject. In his second edition Sayers added another
monodrama called *Pandora*. Southey was quick to take
up with the new idea. His *Sappho*[1] was written in this
form in 1793, and was followed by similar pieces at various
later times: *Orthryades*[2] and *Aristodemus*, both published
only over the signature S. in *The Monthly Magazine* for
August, 1796, and April, 1797, respectively, *The Wife of
Fergus*[3] (1798), *Ximalpoca*[3] (1798), *Lucretia*[3] (1799), *Frances
De Barry*[4] (1799?), and *La Caba*[5] (1802). Interest in these
things rests solely in the additional evidence they give of
Southey's erudition, of his passion for experimenting with
new forms, and his fatal facility for touching feebly upon
themes and styles that were later to have golden development in other hands than his.

Of the rest of Southey's minor productions during his
Oxford period, we have few remains, but their general

---

[1] *Poems*, 1797; *Works*, 121.

[2] The name is also spelt *Othryades*.

[3] *Annual Anthology*, 1799–1800; *Works*, 122–123.

[4] Daniel Stuart, *Letters from the Lake Poets*, 444–447.

[5] *Works*, 123.

character may be surmised. Of such *jeux-d'esprit* as *The Chapel Bell* [1] (1793) there were probably not a few. More important to be noted is the fact that there were two other poets to whose influence upon his youthful work he makes acknowledgment. These were Akenside and Cowper. Southey wrote many inscriptions a few years later in imitation of the former's poems of the same kind, and indeed his *For a Tablet at Godstow Nunnery* [1] and his notorious *For the Apartment in Chepstow-Castle where Henry Marten the Regicide was imprisoned Thirty Years* [2] may have been composed as early as this. Akenside's influence as a whole, however, may be discussed at a later point with more appropriateness. As for Cowper, his satire of corrupt society, his love of nature and domestic life, his sympathy for the poor, his touch of political radicalism, his religious feeling if not his Calvinism, all these notes found appreciation in Southey. We therefore meet the blank verse of *The Task* in the two poems already referred to upon the installation of the Duke of Portland as Chancellor in 1793 and in not a few other pieces of later date which no doubt represent a mass of similar work which had previously been consigned to the flames.

We have seen indeed that all the poems so far discussed as the work of Southey's Oxford period were but the winnowings out of thousands. Yet when we include *Joan of Arc*, they probably show quite justly the tenor and forms of the author's poetical activity up to the age of twenty and also, in a general way, of his after life. Their worth intrinsically and as expressions of his personality is inferior to that of his letters. Their significance is in the evidence they give of his favorite pursuits and of the intimate connection between his versifying and all his other aspirations and activities.

For the first of his epic attempts to embody in poetry

---

[1] *Poems*, 1797; *Works*, 130.   [2] *Poems*, 1797.

the religion of nature and revolution Southey was now in several ways busily preparing. First of all he was continuing to read all the narrative and epic poetry he could find with special attention to certain particular works which were to provide him with models. Ossian was among his books, and when he thought (Easter Sunday, 1793) of a trip to Scotland, he wrote: "We will wander over the hills of Morven, and mark the driving blast, perchance bestrodden by the spirit of Ossian." But there were other writers than MacPherson who obtained even greater interest. The prime favorite at this time was Glover's *Leonidas,* which Southey declares (Nov. 13, 1793) that he had read perhaps more frequently than any other composition, not for sake of "thoughts that breathe and words that burn," but for sake of the subject. This seemed to him "certainly the noblest ever undertaken," and he cited Milton, Homer, Virgil, Lucan, Statius, S. Italicus, V. Flaccus, Ariosto, Tasso, Camoens, Voltaire, "and our own immortal Spenser" in comparison.

To such reading the young man now added the active study of English and French history in all the works then to be had. The result of his delving was soon to appear in the composition of *Joan of Arc.* In the meantime he was keenly alive to the historical associations of the neighborhood of Oxford and other places which he visited upon his vacation rambles. Scenes from the past came thronging about him: he thought of Alfred marking Oxford to be a seat of learning; of Latimer and Ridley[1] burnt upon the spot before his window where he now wished for a monument to religious liberty; of Godstow Nunnery,[2] which roused in him such sensations as Carthage or Troy might

[1] *For a Monument at Oxford opposite Balliol Gateway,* composed 1797, *Annual Anthology,* 1799; *Works,* 181.

[2] *Rosamund to Henry, Poems,* 1795; *For a Tablet at Godstow Nunnery, Poems,* 1797.

inspire, for was it not "memorable in the annals of legendary, yet romantic truth." Then in the Easter vacation of
1793 he walked with Seward to the latter's home in Herefordshire, and longed for the pen of Rousseau "to describe
the various scenes which have presented themselves to me,
and the various emotions occasioned by them." Wood-
stock they visited, Evesham Abbey where he thought of
Simon de Montfort and "The Blind Beggar of Bethnal
Green," Worcester, and an old mansion, ". . . mouldering
away, in so romantic a situation, that I soon lost myself
in dreams of yore, — the tapestried room — the listed fight
— the vassal-filled hall — the hospitable fire — the old
baron and his young daughter, . . . a most delightful day-
dream. How horrid it is to wake into common life from
these scenes! at a moment when you are transported to
happier times to descend to realities!"

IV

After his Easter holiday with Seward, Southey, by the
help of his busy reading, managed to pass the time of his
next term at Oxford until spring brought the long vacation
of 1793. He then paid a short visit to his home,[1] and went
again in July to visit Seward, with whom as before he spent
several weeks tramping about Herefordshire. Then in
August he went down to Surrey to visit Bedford at Brixton
Causeway, about four miles from London. This friend, it is
clear, did not share Southey's political principles, but he
was a sympathetic and appreciative companion, and the
three months which the two boys spent together were filled
with happiness, with hearty discussion, with still heartier
fun no doubt, and with poetry. For now the first draft
of *Joan of Arc* was composed.[2] The subject had been suggested by Bedford himself a short time previously, and

[1] *Works, Preface.*   [2] *Works, Preface to Joan of Arc.*

Southey, after his usual habit, had promptly sketched out a plan, and had written the first three hundred lines. With leisure and encouragement he now took up the poem again. The home of Bedford's parents was a quiet, retired tradesman's house in what were then the rural environs of London. There was a garden at the rear, and at the end of the garden stood four lofty linden trees under which was a summer-house with chairs and a desk. This place was allotted to Southey for his work, and there, interrupted occasionally by the necessity of shooting at wasps with horse-pistols loaded with sand, twelve books of *Joan of Arc* were completed in six weeks.

Joan of Arc was the fullest expression of Southey's boyhood enthusiasms. Before publication it was completely revised in consultation with Coleridge, but the latter probably did little to alter the structure of the poem, and even less to alter its ideals, though he did, doubtless, supply encouragement and metaphysical arguments in their support which the author may not have understood and did not retain. When the two men met in the spring of 1794, Southey was already making "the adamantine gate of democracy turn on its golden hinges to most sweet music," [1] and the revision of his poem in 1795 was merely for the improvement of the style and the enhancement of the decorations. The first edition, therefore, may safely be taken as an expression of the feelings that engrossed the poet in 1793 and for several years to come. It reflects with all the overemphasis of vibrant youth the author's intellectual tastes, his temper, his literary gifts, his convictions in politics and religion. He dedicated the poem to "liberty," and that word recurs constantly upon his pages. What he meant by it is not far to seek. Being young, he wanted to be freer to live as he chose, and to marry whom and when

---

[1] *Letters of Samuel Taylor Coleridge edited by Ernest Hartley Coleridge,* 1895 (referred to as Coleridge, *Letters*), I, 72.

he chose. Society, to be sure, offered him the prospect of
a fellowship and a college living, but these he did not want,
and he was made of such mettle that he would not take
them, especially since there was now a faith that sanctioned
their rejection and put the blame upon society, where it
seemed so justly to belong. Liberty, then, meant liberty
for himself, that liberty of opportunity which was ultimately made for him, after a fashion, by *Joan of Arc*. It
meant also political liberty, the liberty of a people, thought
of, not so much as being made up of separate individuals
with separate characters and wants, but as being itself an
individual with wants and a character of its own. The
romantic revolutionist, of course, had, first and last, much
to say about the final obliteration of the lines of creed and
nationality in the freedom of democracy, but the net result
of such notions was to imbue any given revolutionist with
even stronger sense for nationality than before, especially
as nationality was opposed by the individualities of governors or of other nations seeking to impose their unwelcome will upon it. Several things contributed, in the case
of Southey, to feed these notions. He was, as we have
seen, interested as a boy in history, but like Rousseau,
though not so narrowly, his studies were at first almost
solely of Greece and Rome. And here he was particularly
impressed by the story of compact, unanimous Sparta
ranged with liberty-loving Athens against the tyrannical
Persia, or of republican Rome overthrown by despots, or of
the unfortunate Jews crushed and scattered as in the
pages of Josephus. We have just seen that he thought the
subject of Glover's *Leonidas* one of the finest possible for
an epic poem, and the notes to *Joan* were to contain
references to Thomas May's translation of Lucan's *Pharsalia*. All the epics, in fact, which Southey read so widely
in his boyhood, were full of the same feeling of national
unity and national will or destiny. It was natural, there-

fore, that he should constantly have been planning poems upon such themes, and that three of his most ambitious efforts, *Joan of Arc*, *Madoc*, and *Roderick*, should all have dealt with the account of a people rising as one man to oppose or flee from some form of tyranny.

Lastly, and most important, since they gave the spark to all this tinder, were the actual political revolution then moving in the world and the opposition rising against it. In the preface to the final edition of *Joan* (1837) Southey says that the poem was written when he "was ignorant enough of history and of human nature to believe that a happier order of things had commenced with the independence of the United States, and would be accelerated by the French Revolution." In such cold accents does the old laureate set down the fiery influence which set him free to run the course that he did. Several years before (1824) he had written[1] to Miss Bowles: "Few persons but those who have lived in it can conceive or comprehend what the memory of the French Revolution was, nor what a visionary world seemed to open upon those who were just entering it. Old things seemed passing away, and nothing was dreamt of but the regeneration of the human race."

> "Bliss was it in that dawn to be alive,
> But to be young was very heaven,"

and Southey sat down on the day after his nineteenth birthday to write *Joan of Arc* in Bedford's summer-house during six weeks of the long vacation.

Joan of Arc was to give its author a reputation in England which helped him greatly in his later struggles. That it did so was due to the expression that the poem gave to this age-old passion of the young for free room in which to live, and to the passion for national liberty which had made many Englishmen sympathize with the American

---

[1] *Correspondence with Caroline Bowles*, 52.

revolution, and now with the new French republic. Here indeed was an epic subject ready to the young poet's hand far more moving than that he had praised so highly of the ancient Spartans fighting Persia. War began between France and her enemies with the foolhardy attack of Austria in April 1792, the republic was proclaimed on September 22, in January Southey had entered Balliol, and in February the English government under Pitt ranged itself among the foes of liberty. It will be remembered that the idealists of England saw nothing as yet in the horrors of 1793 to shake their faith in the revolution, and Southey's feelings would have agreed with Wordsworth's as that poet sat "with alien heart" listening to English prayers or praises for victory, and "fed on the day of vengeance yet to come." It is unfortunate that the aged Wordsworth edited *The Prelude* before its final publication; in Southey's case we have only evidence even less direct of his feelings at this time, for his copious letters, which must, after his fashion, have told passionately how he felt, have been carefully expurgated of nearly all references to passing events. The nature of his reactions, however, is abundantly evident in *Joan*.

Southey notes [1] that among the chance causes for the success of the poem with the public was the fact that it was the first work of such pretentions published since Glover's *Athenaid* in 1787, or rather, — so cold did that fall from the press,— since the same author's *Leonidas* in 1737.[2] Southey's interest in *Leonidas* has already been described. What Glover had done was to expand Herodotus's account of the defense of Thermopylae into a blank verse epic of twelve books with some sentimental additions to the plot and with emphasis upon the patriotism and unbroken freedom of the Greeks in contrast to the slavish hordes of

---

[1] *Works, Preface* to *Joan of Arc.*
[2] Southey here disregards Wilkie's *Epigoniad*, 1757.

Xerxes. The work was dedicated to Lord Cobham, praised by Lord Lyttleton, a little patronized by Frederick William, Prince of Wales, and taken up as an expression of their principles by the insurgent Whigs who opposed Walpole. This gave the poem a vogue which carried it through three editions in its first two years, not to mention a French translation in 1738, a German one in 1766, two later editions in the author's life, and three more after his death. There is no distinction whatever in Glover's work. If Southey found it interesting chiefly for its subject matter, we may truthfully say that it is interesting, if at all, only for that. The characters are wooden, and the blank verse is blanker prose save for an occasional declamatory rise in praise of virtue or freedom. Southey wrote at a later time that both Virgil and Glover were characterized by a levelness of manner, "the one never rising, and the other never dismounting from his stilts." [1] It is difficult now to see why such éclat should have attended such a poem, but be that as it may, the work took its place in the public mind as representing what a later editor called the "zeal, or rather rage, for liberty."

Southey's procedure closely followed Glover's. The latter had versified Herodotus; Southey did the same for Holinshed, Hume, Rapin-Thoyras, Monstrellet, Fuller, and similar sources. [2] Glover represented an heroic leader at the head of his people in a picturesque struggle for political liberty which was, though remotely, applicable to the struggles of the British politicians of his day. Southey saw in Joan a similar heroic person leading her people in a similar struggle but with an application to his own day even more pertinent. It was the French people that she led in the struggle for liberty against the English.

Of the real woman, Jeanne Darc, he was, of course, completely ignorant, but no less so than were his only available

[1] *Taylor*, II, 95.   [2] See Appendix B.

sources of information.[1] Caxton (1480) and the Burgundian Monstrellet (1500?), while presenting the leading facts, were noncommittal with regard to Joan's character, but Fabyan, Hall, and Holinshed developed the notion which appeared in Shakespeare that she was a witch deservedly burnt for her sins. ` Thomas Fuller (1642) was not certain that she was not a saint; Richard Baker (1643) showed her merely as a charlatan. Through the eighteenth century the usual notion, as given in Hume and Rapin-Thoyras, was that Joan was the dupe and tool of courtiers, and Voltaire's *La Pucelle* served to vulgarize her story in popular imagination. Two men, however, whose works we have no evidence that Southey knew, suggested a new note. William Guthrie, in his *General History of England* (1647–51), defended Joan as a saint and martyr, and when Wesley wrote a sketch of English history for his people, he copied Guthrie's remarks on Joan with an expression of his belief in her "enthusiasm." Southey's originality consisted in taking the legend as meagerly and on the whole meanly presented by his sources, and making, not a saint or martyr out of her, but a heroine, a kind of female Leonidas.

Southey's interest in his heroine was, of course, as a political rather than as a human figure. As De Quincey pointed out,[2] he shows her merely doing, never suffering. He invents an infancy and childhood for her, makes her share the terrible effects upon the poor country people of the English invasion, and gives her a romantic education with a hermit in the forest. Roused to action by visions, an angel, and reports of the horrors of war perpetrated by

[1] For the whole subject of the history of the Jeanne Darc legend in England see Pierre Lanery D'Arc, *Le Livre d'Or de Jeanne d'Arc Bibliographie Raisonnée et Analytique des Ouvrages Relatifs à Jeanne d'Arc* . . . 1894; James Darmesteter, *Jeanne d'Arc en Angleterre* in his *Nouvelles Etudes Anglaises* . . . 1896; and Félix Rabbe, *Jeanne d'Arc en Angleterre*, 1891.

[2] *Collected Writings*, edited by David Masson, V, 400.

her country's enemies, she resolves to save France. She meets Dunois wounded, cures him, convinces him of her mission, and is led by him to the king at Chinon. There she convinces also the court and clergy in the traditional manner, leads an army to the relief of Orleans, repulses the English, defeats them at Patay, and crowns the king in triumph at Rheims. There Southey's interest in Joan stopped, for from that point on her story is personal rather than political. The French people had conquered in the fight for liberty against the English, and that was sufficient for his purposes at the time. It is necessary to add, however, that even if he had not been so preoccupied with this aspect of the story, the other was little likely to have occurred to him or to anyone, even to Shakespeare. The reason for this was that the marvelous detailed documents relating to Joan's sufferings and displaying her most intimate nature became generally accessible only in 1790 in the work of L'Averdy,[1] who made the first scholarly effort to study the sources of Joan's history, and superseded all other works on the subject until the monumental publications of Quicherat[2] (1841–1849) made Joan a world-wide heroine. Of the existence of L'Averdy's work, Southey was informed, as he tells us in the preface to his first edition (1796), but he appears never to have seen the book itself, certainly never, in later editions, to have made use of it.

The general outline of the story, as given in the poem, was thus easily applicable to the situation obtaining in 1793. It also offered many opportunities for pertinent and, at the time, startling allusions to the ideas and affairs of

[1] See Appendix B.

[2] Jules Quicherat, *Procès de condamnation et de réhabilitation de Jeanne d'Arc dite la Pucelle d'Orléans, publiés pour la première fois d'après les manuscrits de la Bibliothèque royale, suivis de tous les documents historiques qu'on a pu réunir et accompagnés de notes et d'éclaircissements* . . . Paris, 1841–1849.

the same momentous year.   The exigencies of the narrative compelled the author to represent the triumph of a king, but the facts of history also permitted him to depict the awakening of a people to national consciousness and the resolution to throw off a tyrant Englishman; as for Charles VI, he was a fit object against whom to vent republican spleen, and he consequently makes a sorry figure in Southey's hands.   He is a king always eager to order a fast for the people and a feast for the courtiers, who are said [1] to be "insects," "summer-flies," "blood-suckers" sprung from the "court dunghill," and loath to do battle against the invaders.   Joan, on the contrary, assisted by her follower Conrade, a figure supplied by Southey, is the voice of the people urging the king to burst his fetters and lead the nation against the common foe.   Charles trembles at her words, but the implication is that he is incapable of becoming the hero she intends herself to be.   Thereupon her satellite Conrade calls down destruction upon the heads of those mighty ones, those "prime ministers of death" (no uncertain reference to the prime ministry of England at the time), who send thousands to massacre merely in order to rear pyramids of glory out of the bodies of the innocent.

> "Oh groves and woodland shades
> How blest indeed were you, if the iron rod
> Should one day from Oppression's hand be wrenched
> By everlasting Justice! come that hour
> When in the Sun the Angel of the Lord
> Shall stand and cry to all the fowls of Heaven,
> 'Gather ye to the supper of your God,
> That ye may eat the flesh of mighty men,
> Of Captains and of Kings!' Then shall be peace
> When . . . author of all ills that flesh endures,
> OPPRESSION, in the bottomless abyss
> Shall fall to rise no more!" [2]

---

[1] *Joan of Arc*, 1796, Bk. IV, 88–91.   [2] Bk. V, 470–480.

In the ninth book Southey sends Joan in a dream on a journey to a kind of purgatorial inferno, where she beholds, chief among other marvels, the monarchs of the earth, "the MURDERERS OF MANKIND," enthroned under a black dome, and "each bearing on his brow a crown of fire." In this gallery sit Nimrod, Alexander, Cæsar "accurst liberticide," Octavius, Titus "the Conqueror of the Jews," and lastly Henry V, who addresses her on the pertinent subject of invading France. He confesses that he might have reigned in happiness, peace, and prosperity if his appetite for glory had not been tempted by the spectacle of France, torn by faction and apparently an easy prey. Therefore, though himself a man of temperate life, he sent forth murder and rape to work for him, and persecuted those who taught new doctrines which, albeit true, opposed his wishes. He can now have no hope of escape from punishment until the whole human race is as happy as the French were by him rendered wretched, until it forms "one brotherhood, one universal family of love."

Such principles could not be made the sole basis of the action of the poem, but they could be enforced by many such prophetic strains looking forward to the poet's own day. Thus he refers to Brissot and Madame Roland as martyred patriots who have sowed by toil and manured by blood a mighty tree beneath which the sons of men hereafter will pitch their tents in amity.[1] Or he alludes to the Bastille as a hell-house of France before the sublime, almighty people dashed the iron rod from their tyrant's hand.[2] In the bolder tones of a funeral speech by Joan over the dead on the field of Patay, Southey brings home the application of all this to England by making his heroine pray to the God of peace and love to forgive the blood-guilty men who came to desolate France and compel its people to bow the knee before a tyrant, and by making

[1] Bk. III, 70–82.   [2] Bk. IX, 28–31.

her prophesy that England's chiefs will drain their people's
blood and wealth in vain if they attempt to force by arms
the yoke of slavery upon France, who will repel the mer-
cenary thousands sent upon her and blast the despots with
the thunderbolt of vengeance.[1] Finally, the concluding
scene of the poem consists of a warning and a prophecy
to the king of France. Let him remember to be a friend
to the weak and lowly; let him not shroud himself in his
robes of royalty when hunger is abroad in the land; let him
protect his people; he will then be heaven's true representative, and never need hireling guards fleshed in slaughter to
fight in vain defense of a tottering, blood-cemented throne.
If he should fail to follow her advice, may God be merciful
to him when the spirits of the murdered innocent cry out
for justice! The poet concludes the whole work with a last
fling at England; the maid has redeemed her country, and
the hope is uttered that the arms of "FREEDOM" may
always meet with such success.[2]

For his conception of Joan as an heroic figure in a struggle for popular liberty, Southey was not indebted to any
previous treatment of the story. Chapelain's *La Pucelle*
(1656) did, indeed, attempt to treat Joan seriously, but
could hardly be so read. Southey knew [3] of the existence
of this poem from Boileau at the time of the composition
of his own work, but was unable to obtain a copy of it
until the publication of his second edition (1798). At that
time, with his passion for giving information, he printed
an analysis of Chapelain's work which, he there says,
"comprises all the beauties, and most of the absurdities of
twelve thousand lines. I believe no person less interested
than myself in the story could persevere through it." As
for the ribald burlesque that Voltaire produced after Chapelain, Southey had now long since passed out of the mood

[1] Bk. X, 115–131.
[2] Bk. X, 728–748.
[3] *Joan of Arc*, 1796, *Preface*.

in which he could take the cynic sympathetically, and he wrote,[1] "I have never been guilty of reading the *Pucelle* of Voltaire." These words were not printed, however, until the second edition, for the benevolent Cottle could not speak harshly even of a dead Voltaire, and altered the statement in the preface of the first edition to "The *Pucelle* of Voltaire I have not read." Southey's inspiration and model were really to be found in *Leonidas,* and, we should add, Lucan's *Pharsalia,*[2] a great favorite with all the young romantic revolutionists.

To these influences and to these sentiments must be added others more far-reaching. Joan is the champion of popular liberty only because she has grown up in the freedom of nature. For this notion, of course, Southey was indebted not only to revolutionary theories sweeping in upon him from all sides, but also to that "head-full" of Rousseau which he got at school. Yet references to Rousseau in his extant letters are few and, except in one or two cases, never specific. It was rather the poet Akenside[3] to whom he acknowledged a direct obligation for the principles that had imbued his youthful mind. This almost forgotten writer bears a striking relation to all the romantic nature-poets which betrays much concerning the origin of their ideas. Akenside attempted the impossible task, in which Pope had already failed, of building poetry out of the thin notions of Deism before Deism was more than the *a priori* theology and shallow optimism of Bolingbroke and Shaftesbury. The poetic problem was to provide their doctrine of a vague, all-powerful, beneficent deity with images as concrete as the dramatic mythology of the Christian trinity, saviour, devil, and judgment day. Akenside, always theoretical and never apprehending religion by faith, flounders badly, but strikes out the main lines that later

[1] *Life,* I, 283.   [2] Bk. II, 266–272.
[3] *Works, Preface.*

poets of natural religion were to follow. Through nature the deistic god makes men good, and through nature he manifests himself. Akenside conveys all this by an adaptation to his needs of the classical mythology, as in the *Hymn to the Naiads*, or by the new mythology of personifications in *Pleasures of Imagination*. The theme of the latter poem is in crude form that theory of the poetic function later elaborated by Coleridge and Wordsworth minus the notions about using the language of the middle and lower classes of society. The imagination, according to Akenside, is the faculty by which man perceives and reveals the divine, — or the good, the true, and the beautiful, — as it exists only in nature. Consistently with his theories, he has much to say in addition about liberty and the rights of man, but his theories were never sufficiently fused within him by passion to make him a poet. Deism ran off by other channels to France, and there became the religion of popular revolution. When it returned flaming to England, ardent spirits like Southey and Coleridge, welcoming it, rejoiced to find their hopes already expressed in Akenside, to whom they frequently refer,[1] and plunged at once to the enterprise so coldly attempted by the older writer of representing the religion of nature poetically. The artistic problem was still the same, — to find an imagery that would make their religion concrete, — and the same solutions were tried. For Akenside's warmed-over classical mythology Southey merely substituted history in *Joan* and nonclassical mythology in later poems, and like Wordsworth, fused most, but, like Wordsworth again, not all of Akenside's demi-deities of personification into the grand personification of Nature. If Southey failed to become a great poet, it was in part due

---

[1] The mottoes prefixed to Southey's *Poems*, 1797, to Coleridge's *Moral and Political Lecture*, 1795, and to Coleridge's *Religious Musings*, as it appeared in the 1796, 1797, and 1803 editions of the author's poems, were all drawn from Akenside.

to the fact that revolutionary Deism lacked roots and body for great epic, and found its final expression only in the lyric of Wordsworth.

With Akenside as an authority, therefore, the poet makes Joan owe all her power to the fact that she has been educated by nature to be natural, or in other words, good, and that good is naturally omnipotent; consequently she has but to confront the wicked, unnatural English in order to drive them pell-mell into annihilation. The weakness of this faith was, of course, the weakness of the poem; there can be no struggle, because one party is invincible, the other unhuman, and neither is interesting. In describing the education of Joan, then, Southey accepts whole-heartedly the theory that in the blest era of the infant world, "ere man had learnt to bow the knee to man," love and happiness had gone hand in hand.[1] Honesty then reigned; vice had not yet appeared; gold, and hence avarice, had not yet been discovered; the worship of justice had not yet given way to the worship of wealth and power; only when that occurred did oppression and poverty, parents of misery, appear. Nevertheless this decay was ordained by the "All-Wise" for the best, for man would thereby learn to regain and keep by means of wisdom that state of bliss which he had lost through ignorance. For Joan, the lucky circumstances of her education insured this happy state so far as it could be attained in her own experience. Her parents had been driven by the English from Harfleur, her mother was dead, she was left alone as a child beside her father's body in a forest, and there a holy hermit with the educational principles of Rousseau had found her and brought her up. Her infancy was spent in the forest. The hermit taught her to pray to an all-gracious God as her creator and preserver, taught her also in seraphic rapture to behold God in the works of nature about them.

[1] Bk. II, 266–272.

The faith which Joan thus learned she also learned to preach, for when she is examined by the priests [1] endeavoring to determine her divine inspiration, and is asked whether she has duly attended divine confessional, her reply is unhesitating. To be sure she admits that she knows not the abstruse points of nice religion, the subtle and narrow bounds of orthodoxy, but condemns all forms of devotion, chaunted mass, altar and robe, wafer and cup, priest-created Gods, storied panes, trophied pillars, the imaged cross. These things have waked in her no artificial awe. But she has beheld the eternal energy pervading the boundless range of nature; morning and evening her soul has been called forth to devotion by the sun and flowers. The priests reply that nature is sinful, but she flouts the suggestion. Nature cannot teach sin; nature is all benevolence, all love, all beauty. Only if it be sin to bind the wounds of the lamb and bathe them in tears, has nature taught sin, for this is what nature has taught her to do. Suggestions to the contrary are blasphemous. There is no vice in the greenwood, no misery, no hunger, such as will one day plead with damning eloquence against the rulers of society.

In the second edition of the poem (1798) Southey made still further use of the teachings of the romantic thinkers. He there attempted to eliminate from his narrative all the miraculous elements included in the earlier form. Where an angel comes, therefore, in the first edition, to inspire Joan with her lofty mission, in the later version her inspiration more consistently rises from nature through a romantic reverie or trance. There is a lonely spring called the fountain of the fairies. It is deep in the forest, with no sound except of the passing wind or murmuring stream. Here Joan's soul may enjoy solitude, freedom, holy quiet, and escape from human kind. While sitting in this place one

[1] Bk. III, *passim.*

night she is enveloped in a storm and filled with the glory of tempest, thunder and lightning, so that all thought is annihilated in her, her powers suspended, and she herself "diffused into the scene." In this state it occurs to her to save France. Such was the romantic machinery of the natural supernatural.[1]

Before leaving the discussion of *Joan of Arc*, it must be noted that the choice of a female hero by the young poet was no accident, though of feminine characteristics she displays none. But among Southey's sympathies for the oppressed was the sympathy for the lot of woman. The *Inscription for a Tablet at Godstow Nunnery*[2] in memory of Rosamund gave some indication of this, and it is signallized still more by the composition, during this very visit at Brixton Causeway, of *The Triumph of Woman*[3] with a dedication to Mary Wollstonecraft which coupled her name with that of Joan, Madame Roland, and Charlotte Corday. The poem itself was simply a variant upon the same theme and situation as the epic just composed.

The poetical qualities of *Joan of Arc* are easy to distinguish. They are a faithful reflection of the qualities of Southey himself. The poem has vigor, but coupled with a certain stridency, an unstoical lack of restraint. At best, it has the qualities of good rhetorical declamation and clear narrative, but it is too hurried, in spite of being also too long, to achieve beauty of phrase or rhythm. The blank verse, indeed, is scarcely distinguishable as such; it never sings, yet it shows promise of developing into swift and lucid prose. Contrary to expectation, the poem as a whole is not dull so much as thin, and sharp with the sharpness of unripe fruit. All these are qualities rising naturally from the character of the young author. He was a lean, greyhound creature with hawk-like head, and the quick inten-

---

[1] *Joan of Arc*, 1798, Bk. I, 127–129.   [2] *Poems*, 1797.
[3] *Poems*, 1797; *Works*, 98. The dedication is dated 1795.

sity of an animal highly bred for speed. His passion for headlong expression and for committing himself conspicuously, his constitutional incapacity for patience, — which is a different thing from persistence or fortitude, — are all here displayed. The character of Joan herself is a projection of Southey. Her self-confidence, her self-assertiveness, her lack of humility, her vehemence, her voluble preachiness, her unrestrained impulse to be doing, — these are the traits of an eager, overstimulated, unreflecting boy, and such a boy Southey was when he wrote himself into his poem; unreflecting, for the whirl of romantic and revolutionary ideas came to him, not as things to be apprehended and weighed by the intelligence, but as impulses to be caught by the emotion. What Southey had as boy and man were not so much opinions and judgments, as sympathies and antipathies. Hence he contributed nothing to the revolutionary notions he had received except immediate, vigorous, copious expression in words and also in actions. We are interested in *Joan of Arc*, therefore, as the first full manifestation of Southey's personality, and as a sharp delineation of the rising current of the age in which he lived. The latter consideration gave the poem a contemporary reputation of an obvious nature which inevitably and rapidly faded.

V

In October the long visit with Bedford came to an end, and the author of *Joan of Arc* returned to his aunt's house in Bristol. From that place we find him writing on the 26th in great perturbation over the delay of the baggage containing his clothes and, far more momentous, his manuscript. He did not keep the following term at Oxford, but remained at home still reading and writing "till my eyes ache." For his failure to return to the university at this time his son and biographer can assign no reason, but reasons there were, weighty and not far to seek.   At least two circumstances might well give him pause before he continued in his Oxford course.   In the first place, opinions such as were expressed in *Joan of Arc* were not expected of an Oxford graduate, a fact which he well knew; "What is to become of me at ordination heaven only knows!   After keeping the straight path so long the Test Act will be a stumbling-block to honesty."   In the second place, he was now busy falling in love with Edith Fricker, an occupation highly incompatible with the prospects of a candidate for an Oxford fellowship.   It is not strange, therefore, that we find the young man remaining at Bristol during the autumn of 1793 in a great quandary concerning his own and the world's affairs.

That his engagement to Edith Fricker was not the result of worldly prudence goes without saying.   Old acquaintance, the excitement under which he was laboring, these supplied occasion for the attachment, but the ardor of Southey's personal devotion to the woman he afterwards married was much greater, and lasted longer into the settled years of wedlock, than his published letters[1] indicate. Nevertheless there is probably a reference to the young man's state of mind at this time in a letter written years afterward in 1832 touching upon Mary Colling, the maidservant, pet, and poetess of Mrs. Bray.   Southey expresses a fear lest "someone with as much romance in his heart and head as there was in mine when I began life as a poet should fall in love with that sweet countenance of hers, and this should end in a marriage."[2]

[1] I am indebted to the Rev. Maurice H. FitzGerald for the information that letters of Southey to his first wife, now in the possession of Miss Warter but not available for publication, are those of a lover, full of affectionate inquiry and regret at not hearing from her sufficiently often, and repeating what a difference marriage has made to his whole life.

[2] *Correspondence with Caroline Bowles*, 243.

End in a marriage, he was bound it should in 1793, and hence more difficulties arose. Upon entering Balliol he had said, "If I can one day have the honour of writing after my name Fellow of Balliol College, that will be the extent of my preferment." Such preferment, however, now that he wanted a wife, became insufficient to his hopes. In his *Letters of Don Manuel Alvarez Espriella* he gives an interesting summing up of the practical objections to the system of clerical promotion then in vogue at the university. By successful study a young man might expect to obtain a fellowship. After that he would become eligible in the order of seniority to one of the benefices of the college, but he must not in the meantime marry, on pain of losing his place. If his affections were already engaged, his condition seemed to Southey pitiable. He would spend his years enviously waiting for his elders to die, while the woman wore away her youth in dependent expectation; "and they meet at last, if they live to meet, not until the fall of the leaf." [1]

Southey's perplexities under the circumstances were not lessened by the worldly state of the family [2] with which he planned to ally himself. In social position the Frickers were members of the same class of yeomen, small professional and trades people to which he himself belonged and which was, if anything, superior to that of Coleridge, but they were also very poor. Stephen Fricker had begun life with some means derived from inheritance and from his wife, and was thus enabled to engage in business and to give his children advantages of comfort and education. According to Cuthbert Southey, he had at one time carried on the manufacture of sugar-pans at Westbury, but the

[1] *Espriella*, Letter XLVI.

[2] Byron, *Works, Poetry*, VI, 175 note by E. H. Coleridge; *Letters*, VI 112–113 note by R. W. Prothero: *Memoir of Sara Coleridge*, I, 9–12. For further information concerning the Frickers I am indebted to the kindness of Mr. E. H. Coleridge.

war of the American Revolution put an end to this enterprise. He became subsequently an innkeeper and a potter
in Bristol, but migrated to Bath, where, during the last
six years of his life, he owned and managed a coal-wharf.
He appears to have been a man of high character, but he
was betrayed by subordinates and died bankrupt about
1786. His widow and six ungrown children, unused to
poverty, were left penniless. What happened to them
during the next eight years is somewhat uncertain. They
returned to Bristol, and there Mrs. Fricker opened a school,
assisted in some way by her two younger daughters, Martha
and Elizabeth, then small children. Of the three older
girls, Mary became for a time an actress, and married
Robert Lovell in 1794. Edith and Sarah earned money by
work of some sort in the houses of friends; they may even
have been apprenticed to a milliner, but it would appear that
they were not, as Byron said, "milliners of Bath" at the
time of their marriage. Each of the three possessed beauty,
Edith particularly being said to have had "a fine figure and
quietly commanding air," and for women of their time and
class, sufficient education and refinement to make them
suitable wives for the men they married. When nearly
ninety Mary was still keeping up her Latin by reading
Horace and her French by reading Madame de Staël.
Sarah wrote tolerable verse, though not that published as
hers by her husband, and she taught her daughter Italian.
Edith probably received the same education as her sisters,
but her later life gives less evidence of bookish tastes; she
appears, indeed, to have taken almost no share in her
husband's intellectual activity.[1] Her character was one of
unstinting devotion to those she loved, fortitude in afflic-

---

[1] It is probably not safe to trust Coleridge's opinion upon such a
matter without reservation, but he was frequently just as well as keen
in his analysis of character. In the Forster Library in the South Kensington Museum there is preserved a fragment of a letter, unsigned and

tion, and a capacity for shrewd management in household affairs which she had but too abundant opportunity in youth to learn and as the poet's wife to practice. Unfortunately she also manifested a tendency to depression[1] of spirits which frequently saddened her life for her, and clouded her last days with melancholia.

Our impression of all the Frickers, finally, is probably to be completed by the description given by Sarah's daughter, Sara Coleridge, of her mother's younger sisters, Martha and Elizabeth.

"Without talent, except of an ordinary kind, without powerful connections, by lifelong perseverance, fortitude, and determination, by prudence, patience, and punctuality, they not only maintained themselves, but, with a little aid from kind friends, whom their merits won, they laid by a comfortable competency for their old age. They asked few favours, accepted few obligations, and were most scrupulous in returning such as they did accept, as soon as possible. They united caution and discretion with perfect honesty and truth, strict frugality and self-control, with the disposition to be kind and charitable, and even liberal, as soon as ever it was in

undated but in Coleridge's hand, dealing with marriage, "a subject so full of regretful anguish to me." "[Mrs. Southey] loves her husband almost too exclusively, and has a great constancy of affection, such as it is. But she sympathizes with nothing, she enters into none of his peculiar pursuits — she only loves *him;* she is therefore a respectable wife, but not a companion. Dreary, dreary would be the Hours passed with her. Amusement, and all the detail of whatever cheers or supports the spirits, must be sought elsewhere. Southey finds them in unceasing authorship, never interrupted from morning to night but by sleep and eating." To this may be added Shelley's statement (Jan. 2, 1812) that Mrs. Southey "is very stupid; Mrs. Coleridge worse. Mrs. Lovell, who was once an actress, is the best of them." *Letters of Percy Bysshe Shelley,* edited by R. Ingpen, I, 209.

[1] Unpublished letters of Southey's in the possession of Miss Warter, written in December 1801 and February 1802, refer to the "miserable depression," "beyond anything you can imagine bad," from which Edith had then recently been suffering.

their power. Their chief faults were pride and irritability of temper."

It is plain that Southey's early intimacy with the Fricker family now ripened into love for Edith. His sense of honor, to be sure, kept him from plighting his troth until the following summer,[1] but Cuthbert Southey states that in August, 1794, his father had been for some time engaged,[2] and certainly the two young people must have then long known how their hearts stood. Through the Frickers Southey met Robert Lovell, and as early as December, 1793, wrote a letter of introduction for him to present to Bedford in London. In this the poet says that Lovell's "intended bride I look upon almost as a sister, and one should know one's brother-in-law."

Such were the circumstances that kept Southey at Bristol and away from Oxford in the fall of 1793. He was not, he thought, ambitious; all that he asked for in the letters and in the sonnets and other verses upon love and Edith which he wrote in great numbers during these months was that he might shun the crowd and retire to the solitude of nature with his wife. Yet even retirement required funds, and he felt compelled to cast about for some honorable way of establishing himself in a gentlemanly calling other than the church. When he returned to Oxford in January, therefore, it was at first with the intention of studying medicine rather than divinity. Consequently, during the next six months he went through a course of anatomy, and read some medical books. But his heart was in literature, and his sensibilities could not endure the dissecting room; he learned enough to be able to kill men correctly in *Joan of Arc*, and to render himself miserable in after life without avail when his children fell ill.[3] Medicine abandoned, he tried to realize something upon his hopes for part of the

---

[1] *Warter*, I, 42.   [2] *Life*, I, 216.

[3] *Correspondence with Caroline Bowles*, 101.

fortune of a grand-uncle upon his father's side who had married an heiress of the Cannon family. This couple's son had left an obscure will entailing upon the Southey line a certain estate, to which the young poet expected eventually to succeed, but Lord Somerville, the incumbent at this time, so managed that his distant cousin ultimately fell heir to nothing but a chancery suit. It was the reversion to this inheritance which Southey now tried to sell. The effort was vain, and he attempted, instead, through Wynn and Bedford, to obtain some official position at London. In this he promptly desisted when reminded that his well-known political principles would not commend him to the favor of government; "My opinions are very well known. I would have them so; Nature never meant me for a negative character; I can neither be good nor bad, happy nor miserable, by halves. You know me to be neither captious nor quarrelsome, yet I doubt whether the quiet harmless situation I hoped for were proper for me: it certainly, by imposing a prudential silence, would have sullied my integrity." (June 25, 1794.) Authorship was the one sure possibility, but even for this some independent provision was needed. The natural accompaniment of such a situation for a lad of nineteen was, of course, ill humor with the world, and he railed at not having been trained up to be a carpenter instead of being devoted to pursuits useless and unimportant. "Every day do I repine at the education that taught me to handle a lexicon instead of a hammer, and destined me for one of the drones of society." Suiting practice to theory, Southey one night spent three hours with Shad, his aunt's servant, "cleaving an immense wedge of old oaken timber without axe, hatchet, or wedges; the chopper was one instrument, one piece of wood wedged another, and a third made the hammer. Shad liked it as well as myself, so we finished the job and fatigued ourselves." (Dec. 22, 1793). Nineteen years he has lived and been of no service to mankind. "Why, the clown who scares crows for twopence a day is a more useful member of society; he preserves the bread which I eat in idleness." Yet the real trouble was with the world, not with himself. "The more I see of this strange world, the more I am convinced that society requires desperate remedies. The friends I have . . . are many of them struggling with obstacles, which never could happen were man what nature intended him."

This dejection was not rendered less meanwhile by the application of remedies to society in France, remedies grown desperate indeed. Upon the execution of the French queen (Oct. 16, 1793) Bedford wrote, using this bloody deed as the occasion for a reproof to his friend's republicanism, and the latter, though not surrendering his political faith, replied warmly that to suppose that he felt otherwise than grieved and indignant at the fate of the unfortunate queen was to suppose him a brute, and to request an avowal of his feelings was to imply that he had none. "You seemed glad, when arguments against the system of republicanism had failed, to grasp at the crimes of wretches who call themselves republicans, and stir up my feelings against my judgment." At the same time (Oct. 30, 1793) he wrote to another friend that he was sick of the world and everyone in it. The execution of Brissot (October, 1793) and of the other Girondists so harrowed up his feelings that he could not sleep,[1] and he was thereby driven to believe that virtue could aspire to content, happiness being out of the question, only in obscurity. Everywhere the strong tyrannized over the weak, and depravity was to be seen upon all hands. The only difference between nations was that in Turkey the agent of tyranny and corruption was a "grand seignor," in France a revolutionary tribunal, and in England a prime minister.

[1] *Life*, VI, 356, Dec. 1837.

In a society so bad as this, what should a penniless young philosopher-republican do who was twenty years old and wanted to get married? Perhaps it was Rousseau who had suggested to him that he should repine at not having been reared a carpenter, and perhaps Rousseau also suggested a remedy for the present situation. This was, briefly, to run away from it. "O for emancipation," Southey writes (May 11, 1794) when he should have been composing a college declamation, "from these useless forms, this useless life, these haunts of intolerance, vice, and folly!" Emancipation, moreover, was now rapidly coming to mean for Southey emigration. "It is not the sally of a momentary fancy that says this; either in six months I fix myself in some honest way of living, or I quit my country, my friends, and every fondest hope I indulge, forever." (May, 1794.) "The visions of futurity are dark and gloomy, and the only ray that enlivens the scene beams on America." (Dec. 22, 1793.)

This thought of fleeing to the new world had not been suggested by Rousseau alone. Immediately upon his return to Bristol in October, Southey had gone back to the perusal of his philosophers. He refers to Plato, and recounts the story of Plotinus's project for an ideal commonwealth. Plotinus requested the emperor, Gallienus, to "give him a ruined city of Campania, which he might rebuild and people with philosophers, governed by the laws of Plato, and from whom the city should be called Platonopolis. . . . The design," says Southey, "would certainly have proved impracticable in that declining and degenerate age — most probably in any age. . . . Yet I cannot help wishing the experiment had been tried; it could not have been productive of evil, and we might at this period have received instruction from the history of Platonopolis. . . . I could rhapsodize most delightfully upon this subject; plan out my city — all *simplex munditiis*." (Oct. 26, 1793.) This idea became at once a favorite subject for meditation and letter-writing. He began speculating as to where one might locate such a city, and immediately planned for the cultivation in its shelter of learning and poetry.

"If this world," he wrote to Horace Bedford, "did but contain ten thousand people of both sexes, visionary as myself, how delightful would we re-people Greece, and turn out the Moslem. I would turn crusader and make a pilgrimage to Parnassus at the head of my republicans (N. B. only lawful head), and there reinstate the Muses in their original splendour. We would build a temple to Eleutherian Jove from the quarries of Paros — replant the grove of Academus; aye, and the garden of Epicurus, where your brother and I would commence teachers; yes, your brother, for if he would not comb out the powder and fling away the poultice to embark in such an expedition, he deserves to be made a German elector or a West India planter. . . . Now could I lay down my whole plan — build my house in the prettiest Doric style — plant out the garden like Wolmer's, and imagine just such a family to walk in it. . . ." (Nov. 13, 1793.)

At the same time Southey came upon a suggestion which made him speak in soberer terms of his dream. In the new world, it might be, perhaps, no dream at all.

"It was the favourite intention of Cowley to retire with books to a cottage in America, and seek that happiness in solitude which he could not find in society. My asylum there would be sought for different reasons (and no prospect in life gives me half the pleasure this visionary one affords); I should be pleased to reside in a country where men's abilities would ensure respect; where society was upon a proper footing, and man was considered as more valuable than money; and where I could till the earth, and provide by honest industry the meat which my wife would dress with pleasing care. . . ."

For further encouragement and even practical suggestion, the poet had not far to go. It is needless to dwell in detail upon the passions and events that in 1793 were turning the eyes of young men upon America, and their wits upon constitution-mongering. Certain books in particular, however, should be mentioned for their influence upon these dreams of Southey's. The register of the Bristol Library Society has fortunately been unearthed [1] and preserves some interesting evidence concerning the young man's reading at this time. On October 28, 1793, he drew out the second volume of Gillies's *History of Greece,* apparently the first book that he borrowed from this library. A few days later (November 1) he took Adam Smith's *Wealth of Nations,*[2] on November 25 Godwin's *Political Justice,* on November 27 Gilpin's *Forest Scenery,* and on December 9 *Political Justice* again. It is plain that the latter book made a great impression upon him; "I read, and all but worshipped." [3] There were two reasons for this interest. One was that he found Godwin's subordination of emotion to logic consistent with the stoicism by which he was himself already trying to cure the effects of that painful sensibility that had been encouraged in him by Rousseau. The other was that Godwin held out a dazzling picture of political equality in such a form as might well tempt one to experimentation. Or in the words of Coleridge to Godwin himself, "When he was young [Southey] just looked enough into your books to believe you taught republicanism and stoicism; ergo, that he was of your opinion and you of his, and that was all. Systems of philosophy were never his taste or his forte." [4] The other book that probably contributed to Southey's enthusiasm for a philosophical colony dealt more immediately with America itself. This was Brissot's *Nou-*

[1] *Books Read by Coleridge and Southey,* James Baker in his *Literary and Biographical Studies,* 1908, 211.

[2] Thomas Poole reports (Sept. 22, 1794) that in August, 1794 Coleridge and Southey referred to Adam Smith in expounding pantisocracy. See Mrs. Sandford, *Thomas Poole and his Friends,* I, 97, 102.

[3] *Life,* I, 247, October 1, 1795.

[4] *Biog. Epis.,* II, 71–72, March 29, 1811.

*veau Voyage dans Les États-Unis de L'Amerique Septentrio-
nale* published in 1791 and translated into English in 1792.
That Southey had read this work[1] before Brissot's execution
as one of the Girondins at the end of October, 1793, is almost
certain, though our belief must be based only on the facts
that, among all the revolutionary leaders, Brissot was his
particular hero and martyr; that the book was conspicuous
at the time of its publication, as is indicated by the long,
favorable review of it in *The Monthly Review;* and finally
that Coleridge quoted at length from it in the first of his
lectures at Bristol in February, 1795,[2] a time when he was
still in close association with Southey.   Brissot[3] had for several years been actively interested in America.   He had hotly

[1] There is no definite evidence that Southey at this time read any
of the fairly numerous works about America that were then beginning
to appear, but he may have seen the following books, or more probably,
he may have seen them reviewed in the *Monthly* or other reviews.

*Letters from an American Farmer; describing certain provincial situa-
tions, manners, and customs, not generally known; and conveying some
idea of the late and present interior circumstances of the British Colonies
in North America* . . . by J. Hector St. John [Crèvecœur], London,
1782; several later editions and translations.

*A Topographical Description of the Western Territory of North America;
containing a Succinct Account of the Climate, Natural History, Population, Agriculture, Manners and Customs* . . . by G. Imlay . . . 1792.
This book cautions settlers from going to America with romantic hopes
of happiness.

*An account of the Progress of Population, Agriculture, Manners,
and Government in Pennsylvania in a letter from Benjamin Rush, M.D.,
and Professor of Medicine in the University of Pennsylvania, to Thomas
Percival, M.D.F.R.S.,* etc., 1792, 2d ed, 1793. This book gives an
interesting description of the best method for settling in the new
country.

*Travels through North and South Carolina, Georgia, East and West
Florida* . . . 1792, 2d ed., 1794, by William Bartram.

[2] Coleridge, *Essays on his Own Times,* ed. by his daughter, Sara
Coleridge, 1850, I, 26–27.

[3] Eloise Ellery, *Brissot de Warville,* 1915; Julia Post Mitchell, *St.
Jean de Crèvecœur,* 1916.

seconded Crèvecœur's defense of the Quakers and attack on negro slavery. He had subsequently joined Crèvecœur and the banker Clavière in founding a "Gallo-Américaine" society, and he had collaborated with Clavière in the publication of a book the purpose of which was to encourage closer relations between France and the United States.[1] The attitude of these men towards republican ideas was romantically enthusiastic, and in 1788 Clavière, together with two other men of wealth, arranged to send Brissot to America to investigate the opportunities in the new country for Frenchmen who might wish to invest money there, to emigrate thither from France, or even to establish somewhere in the regions then open for new settlements a Utopian colony of democratic reformers and philosophers. These hopes and the accompanying theories were summed up by Clavière in the letters of instruction supposedly given by him to Brissot before the latter's setting out, and printed as the introduction to his account of his observations in the new country published on his return. Brissot landed in Boston in July, 1788, with decided prepossessions. The best government was, he felt sure, the least; the least government was a republic; a republic was bound to succeed so long as the people were virtuous; the people would remain virtuous so long as they remained uncorrupted by wealth and great cities. All this was confirmed in Brissot's mind by his journey through Massachusetts, Connecticut, New York, Pennsylvania, Maryland, and Virginia. The Americans were mainly engaged in agriculture, they were virtuous, and they had a republic. Brissot was so enamored

[1] *De La France et des États-Unis, ou de l'importance de la Révolution d'Amerique pour le bonheur de la France,* . . . par Étienne Clavière et. J. P. Brissot de Warville, Londres, 1787; re-imprimé en 1791 au t. III du *Nouveau Voyage dans Les États-Unis de l'Amerique Septentrionale, fait en 1788;* par J. P. Brissot (Warville) Citoyen François, Paris, 1791: trans. into English, London, 1792, 1794, *Month. Rev.*, v. 6 n.s., 531.

of all this that he planned to settle with his wife in Pennsylvania, and sent for his brother-in-law to join him there, but in less than a year, upon news of the calling of the States General, he returned to France. Though all his schemes for emigration were then submerged in the flood of the revolution, the book in which he depicted them so ardently probably added not a little to the confidence and enthusiasm of Southey, possessed of dreams of his own only a little, if at all, more impracticable.

Escape to America, therefore, as all other solutions for his practical problems failed, became indeed an alternative for the young man to consider, and he considered it with his customary precipitancy. Yet it is refreshing to note that the sanity of the man permitted him to laugh a little at his own imaginings.

"Now . . . fancy only me in America;" he writes to Bedford (Dec. 14, 1793), "imagine my ground uncultivated since the creation, and see me wielding the axe, now to cut down the tree, and now the snakes that nestled in it. Then see me grubbing up the roots, and building a nice snug little dairy with them: three rooms in my cottage, and my only companion some poor negro whom I have bought on purpose to emancipate. After a hard day's toil, see me sleep upon rushes, and, in very bad weather, take out my casette and write to you. . . . Do not imagine I shall leave rhyming or philosophizing, so thus your friend will realize the romance of Cowley, and even outdo the seclusion of Rousseau; till at last comes an ill-looking Indian with a tomahawk, and scalps me, — a most melancholy proof that society is very bad, and that I shall have done very little to improve it! So vanity, vanity will come from my lips, and poor Southey will either be cooked for a Cherokee, or oysterized by a tiger."

In such a frame of mind he went back to Balliol to commence Æsculapius or to find that means of honest support which was to be the alternative to the church or emigration. He was also to continue writing poetry, dejected odes, sonnets to Edith, and inscriptions for previous martyrs to the cause of liberty. Now may very well have been written those lines, later made notorious, *For the Apartment in Chepstow-Castle where Henry Marten the Regicide was imprisoned Thirty Years:*

> "Dost thou ask his crime?
> He had rebell'd against the King, and sat
> In judgment on him; for his ardent mind
> Shap'd goodliest plans of happiness on earth,
> And peace and liberty. Wild dreams! But such
> As PLATO lov'd; such as with holy zeal
> Our MILTON worshipp'd. Blessed hopes! awhile
> From man withheld, even to the latter days,
> When CHRIST shall come and all things be fulfill'd" [1]

Southey was once more in a perilous state. Without practical experience in any work save writing, he was not without practical sense. He was engaged to be married, but with nothing to marry upon. What he wanted was a means of immediately removing this difficulty. The Church was impossible; nothing else in his native land seemed to offer; emigration to America, an idea adorned in roseate colors by "philosophy," remained to be made feasible. Southey stayed in Bristol possibly until the very end of March, but then back to Oxford he went, unhappy save for love of Edith and of writing, eager for any course, however wild, that promised to put marriage and a life of lettered retirement within his reach.[2]

[1] *Poems*, 1797.

[2] Baker (see above) reports that Southey drew books regularly from the Bristol Library Society up to March 31, 1794. From that date his name does not appear in the register until July 8, after which it frequently recurs for some time.

COLERIDGE — PANTISOCRACY

I

THE winter of 1794 passed,[1] and what was to become of Robert Southey remained undecided. Then a young man of twenty-one named Coleridge came to Oxford to visit his old school-fellow, Robert Allen, now of the "sober society." Coleridge was also in an unsettled state of mind. The metaphysics of the inspired charity boy had naturally led to deistic religion and Foxite politics, by which he soon talked himself into undergraduate notoriety at Cambridge. This had culminated in championship of the Unitarian and republican Frend upon the latter's expulsion from a Jesus fellowship in the spring of 1793, and in the following December, distraught by debt and unhappy love, Coleridge had run off for six months to the dragoons. When he arrived in Oxford about the second week in June, he had just completed the academic penance exacted for that escapade, and was headed for a walking trip into Wales with a friend. He was still talking upon his old themes, and naturally Allen introduced him to Southey; just as naturally an intimacy at once sprang up between them. Southey immediately wrote to Bedford, "Allen is with us daily, and his friend from Cambridge, Coleridge, whose poems you will oblige me by subscribing to . . . He is of most uncommon merit, — of the strongest genius, the clear-

---

[1] The main facts of this period of Southey's life are to be found in *Life*, I, 209–261.

est judgment, the best heart. My friend he already is, and must hereafter be yours." (June 12, 1794.)[1]

These two new friends soon found several things in common: democracy, deism, poetry, disgust with society, lack of worldly prospects. Southey undoubtedly imparted his dreams of a philosophic colony, and they fell to discussing the principles upon which a group of men like themselves might establish such a community. The relative responsibility for the famous scheme that resulted has been somewhat obscured[2] by the usual tendency of a great reputation like Coleridge's to absorb the exploits of lesser men, and by the failure of Southey's biographers to state candidly his share in the joint project. The facts are clear. Cuthbert Southey says that the idea was originated by Coleridge and communicated to Southey at this time. This statement is incorrect, being based upon Cottle's garbled version of a letter written to him by Southey in 1836. Cottle's version reads, "The scheme of *Pantisocracy* was introduced *by them* [i.e. Coleridge, Hucks, and Allen;] talked of, by no means determined on."[3] Southey really wrote,[4] "The scheme was talked of, but not by any means determined on." The minds of the two youths were thrilling with like enthusiasms, and to seek to prove either to be the sole begetter of pantisocracy would be idle. Yet from what we know of the two men both before and after the event, it is easy to see that Southey must have supplied the initial force, and

---

[1] *Samuel Taylor Coleridge, A Narrative of the Events of his Life*, by James Dykes Campbell, 1894, 30. (Referred to as Campbell, *Coleridge*.)

[2] It has been more correctly stated by A. Turnbull, the editor of the *Biog. Epis.*, I, 41–42. But see G. Mc L. Harper, *William Wordsworth*, I, 279.

[3] *Reminiscences of Samuel Taylor Coleridge and Robert Southey* by Joseph Cottle, New York, 1847 (first edition, London, 1847), 299. The italics are Cottle's. (This work is referred to later as Cottle, *Reminiscences*.)

[4] Campbell, *Coleridge*, 31.

this is confirmed by the description in the *Biographia Literaria* of the impression made by Southey upon Coleridge at their first meeting. Coleridge states that the influence of his new friend upon him was strong and sudden. This effect was not upon his moral and religious principles, but upon his "sense of the duty and dignity of making . . . actions accord with these principles, both in word and deed." Some contribution to the principles of pantisocracy, however, Southey must also have made, for we have it upon Coleridge's own authority[1] that from Southey he first heard of *Political Justice* and that solely from the enthusiasm so suggested, before he had seen the book itself, he had composed his sonnet to the author of that work. Coleridge had run upon one of those straits in his life where the will was hopelessly inadequate to effect a compromise between vague aspirations and circumstances. The first positive force that would relieve the agony of decision would carry him off upon a new tangent, only to drop him, again despairing, when it had spent itself. So Southey, with that aspiring lift of his head, determination in his eye and eagle face, roused his friend's spirit with high talk of new freedom and a new Utopia, and Coleridge swept these suggestions upon rolling periods into a most comprehensive and philosophic system. An ideal society, in which the evils under which men now suffered were to be eliminated, would be based, he agreed, upon the general democratic principles advocated by Southey, whom he denominated (July 6, 1794) a "sturdy Republican"[2] who "dost make the Adamantine gate of Democracy turn on its golden hinges to most sweet music." In view of these principles the new society was called by him "pantisocracy." But this was not all. Property was to be acquired and held in common by the members of the new republic. This system was to be called "aspheterism," and would

[1] *Biog. Epis.*, II, 70, March 29, 1811.   [2] Coleridge, *Letters*, I, 72.

abolish selfishness by abolishing its cause. With this idea Coleridge was particularly enamored; Southey accepted it for the time, but it was the first part of the whole scheme to be repudiated by him. As for formulating a plan for immediately carrying their ideas out into practice, that does not appear now to have concerned them except, perhaps, in the merest outlines. These were, briefly, that a company of young men with their wives should set up a democratic community in which each would share with each his labor and the fruits of it, and devote his leisure, of which an abundance might be expected from the absence of selfishness, to poetry and philosophy. All other human claims were to be relinquished. Here was a dream for Coleridge to descant most eloquently upon, but Southey was the one with the practical motive for seeing the vision realized, and therefore it fell to him during the next few weeks to devise ways and means.

At the end of his visit and at the beginning of the long vacation of 1794, Coleridge set out for Wales on a walking trip with a friend named Joseph Hucks,[1] who had come with him from Cambridge. Southey and George Burnett accompanied them part of the way, and then turned aside to walk down to their own homes in Bristol and Somersetshire. During his journey Coleridge wrote long letters[2] to his new friend, continuing their discussion and describing some of the experiences of his trip. He preached pantisocracy and aspheterism as he went to such effect that wild Welshmen whom he met danced with enthusiasm over his eloquence. "I have positively done nothing," he says,

---

[1] Hucks wrote an account of this tour which I have not examined, *A Pedestrian Tour through North Wales in a Series of Letters*, London; 1795. G. McL. Harper, who has seen it, reports that it contains little with regard to Coleridge, though it expresses democratic and anti-military sentiments, *William Wordsworth*, I, 279.

[2] Coleridge, *Letters*, I, 72–81, July 6 and July 15, 1794.

"but dream of the system of no property every step of the way since I left you." One disturbing interruption came, however, and this too he confided to Southey. The chance sight of Mary Evans from the window of an inn brought back the agony of his disappointed passion. "Her image is in the sanctuary of my heart, and never can it be torn away but with the strings that grapple it to life."

Meanwhile the two other young philosophers were tramping southwards. With the eloquence of his friend a little stilled by separation, though yet ringing in his ears, Southey began to seek in pantisocracy some practicable escape from the difficulties that surrounded him. Now it was, according to his own testimony, that the scheme "was talked into shape by Burnett and myself."[1] This statement is confirmed by one written a few months after the event (October 19, 1794); "My aunt abuses poor Lovell most unmercifully, and attributes the whole scheme to him; you know it was concerted between Burnett and me." Coleridge's speculative mind had enlarged upon the philosophic basis of a communistic democracy in a way that had stirred Southey's feelings to a high pitch of excitement, and the latter's energetic wits now thought of combining pantisocracy with his other vague notion of emigration. The possibility of actually carrying out their ideas in America does not seem to have entered actively into the discussions of the young men up to this point, for it is not mentioned in Coleridge's letters from Wales; it was "aspheterism" that he had been preaching on the road. We have, moreover, Southey's own statement[2] that "the American plan [had] not been formed till after I had left Oxford." That Burnett contributed anything but sympathy and agreement is unlikely. He was an unsteady soul, blown about by gusts of

[1] Letter to Cottle, March 5, 1836; Cottle, *Reminiscences*, 299, in garbled form; Campbell, *Coleridge*, 31, less fully but correctly.

[2] Feb. 11, 1810, *Warter* II, 194.

mistaken pride and back-boneless vanity, much inflated by association with his two brilliant friends. It was Southey who did the "shaping" on this occasion, whoever did the "talking."

They arrived at their journey's end,[1] Burnett going on a little further into Somersetshire to his own home, and the other taking up his quarters with his mother in Bath. Mrs. Southey appears to have opened a lodging-house in that place shortly after her husband's death. Miss Tyler still lived in the College Green, and in Bristol too lived the Frickers and Robert Lovell, now married to Edith's sister, Mary. Southey, therefore, although his aunt at first knew nothing of his plans, went constantly back and forth between the two towns during the next few months. His immediate concern was to devise ways by which to further the new project that promised to make marriage possible. Two things were necessary: more pantisocrats and funds. He set to work at once to obtain both. Edith, Lovell, and Mary were immediately won over, for obvious reasons. His two friends, Robert Allen and Edmund Seward were impressed, if not converted; the latter soon balked, not at democracy but at unitarianism. Eventually (September 20, 1794) some twenty-seven persons were engaged, most of them, evidently, through Southey's efforts; "Lovell, his wife, brother, and two of his sisters; all the Frickers; my mother, Miss Peggy, and brothers; Heath, apothecary, etc.; G. Burnett, S. T. Coleridge, Robert Allen, and Robert Southey." Allen was here included by oversanguine hope, but there were soon to be added Thomas Southey, still but a midshipman in the navy, and probably some obscurer persons. Of Coleridge's converts, except for his two schoolfellows Favell and LeGrice, we have no such account, and probably none could ever have been made.

As for obtaining money, upon this too Southey set to

[1] On July 8 Southey signalized his return by borrowing from the Bristol Library Society Hartley's *Observations on Man*. Baker, *op. cit.*

work.   On July 20 he wrote to Bedford that he had carried
proposals for the publication of *Joan of Arc* to the printer.
This poem he hoped to put forth by the following Michael-
mas providing he could obtain the fifty subscribers that his
proposals were designed to win.   On this account he decided not to return to Oxford for the next term because he
wished to be at hand to overlook the press.   "Many of my
friends will blame me for so bold a step, but as many
encourage me; and I want to raise money enough to settle
myself across the Atlantic."

Meanwhile, in the end of July Coleridge arrived in Bristol,
the new developments in their scheme received his hearty
approval, and the resolution was formed to carry them out.[1]
Coleridge had already welcomed Lovell into their fraternity,
and the next step was to confer with Burnett.   For this
purpose the two brother-philosophers set off at once on
foot for Huntspill, Somersetshire.   They were in high
spirits, and they put no check upon their tongues.   On the
contrary they went through the country preaching pantisocracy to such purpose that scandalous tales about them
lingered in the region for a generation.[2]   At Stowey they
made the acquaintance of Thomas Poole, a man now about
thirty, with a steadier, as well as older, head than the
young enthusiasts.   He was, nevertheless, interested in
them and their schemes.   His cousin, John Poole, on the
other hand, was not so sympathetic.   He was a young
Oxford Don in a powdered wig, and it is to be suspected
that the emancipated undergraduates made him something
of a butt for their radical shafts.   He wrote in his Latin
journal, at any rate, to the following effect: "Uterque vero
rabie Democratica quoad Politiam; et Infidelis quoad Re-
ligionem spectat, turpiter fervet.   Ego maxime indignor."

[1] Cottle, *Reminiscences*, 299;   Campbell, *Coleridge*, 31.

[2] Concerning the whole episode, see Mrs. Sandford, *Thomas Poole
and his Friends*, v. I, 99–105.

Robespierre was the talk of the hour, and the news of his death on July 28 had just reached Stowey. Although Coleridge and Southey both condemned the Jacobins, here was a text and an occasion not to be missed for preaching democracy regardless as to whether or not the good folk of Somerset understood the nice distinctions between parties. Consequently the story could be heard years after that Southey, being told of Robespierre's death, had exclaimed, "I had rather have heard of the death of my own father," and that one of the two had said, "Robespierre was a ministering angel of mercy, sent to slay thousands that he might save millions."

Thomas Poole himself was far more liberal in his temper, and listened attentively to what the young men had to say. In a letter written about a month after this meeting (September 22, 1794) he gives an account of them and their scheme. He was particularly impressed by Coleridge, whom he considered the principal in the undertaking, and who, he says, was "in Religion . . . a Unitarian, if not a Deist; in Politicks a Democrat, to the utmost extent of the word." Of Southey he says that he was a "younger man, without the splendid abilities of Coldridge [sic], though possessing much information, particularly meta-physical, and is more violent in his principles than even Coldridge himself. In Religion, shocking to say in a mere Boy as he is, I fear he wavers between Deism and Atheism." Such was the impression made by the young pantisocrats at the time when their plans were on foot. Poole also gives a detailed account of their scheme, especially interest-ing as the fullest statement from an outsider in any sense contemporaneous. From the glowing periods of Coleridge, he condensed the following points:

"Twelve gentlemen of good education and liberal principles are to embark with twelve ladies in April next. Previous to their leav-ing this country they are to have as much intercourse as possible,

in order to ascertain each others' dispositions, and firmly to settle
every regulation for the government of their future conduct. Their
opinion was that they should fix themselves at — I do not now
recollect the place, but somewhere in a delightful part of the new
back settlements; that each man should labor two or three hours
a day, the produce of which labor would, they imagine, be more
than sufficient to support the colony. As Adam Smith[1] observes
that there is not above one productive man in twenty, they argue
that if each laboured the twentieth part of time, it would produce
enough to satisfy their wants. The produce of their industry is to
be laid up in common for the use of all; and a good library of books
is to be collected, and their leisure hours to be spent in study,
liberal discussions, and the education of their children. A system
for the education of their children is laid down. . . . The regulations relating to the females strike them as the most difficult;
whether the marriage contract shall be dissolved if agreeable to
one or both parties, and many other circumstances, are not yet
determined. The employments of the women are to be the care of
infant children, and other occupations suited to their strength;
at the same time the greatest attention is to be paid to the cultivation of their minds. Every one is to enjoy his own religious and
political opinions, provided they do not encroach on the rules previously made, which rules, it is unnecessary to add, must in some
measure be regulated by the laws of the state which includes the
district in which they settle. They calculate that each gentleman
providing 125 pounds will be sufficient to carry out the scheme
into execution. Finally, every individual is at liberty, whenever
he pleases, to withdraw from the society."[2]

Some months later Coleridge[3] gave a statement of the
pantisocratic plans which, while less definite, confirms

[1] See above.

[2] *Thomas Poole and his Friends*, I, 96–98; see also Coleridge, *The
Friend*, Essay VI, *Works*, p. 203–205.

[3] *Biog. Epis.*, I, 44–45. Letter of Coleridge to Charles Heath of
Monmouth. The date is uncertain, but it was probably sometime
in the fall of 1794. Turnbull states that Charles Heath was one of the
pantisocrats, but it would appear that he was rather the brother of
one, and that Coleridge was trying to interest him in the scheme.

Poole's description. He was writing to a certain Charles Heath, apparently the brother of "Heath apothecary" mentioned by Southey, and states that he and his associates had formed "a small but liberalized party" for emigration and the abolition of property; that they were preparing to print for private circulation among their friends a statement of their principles and of the laws which would govern their community; that all the members of the company were marked by moral rectitude; and that an aggregate sum of £2000 would be needed if, as they hoped, twelve men and their families were to embark on the venture.

Pantisocracy, as thus outlined, led to a number of things. The two leaders, after their conference with Burnett, returned to Bath, where Coleridge seems to have remained for some time as Mrs. Southey's guest. "My mother says I am mad; if so, she is bit by me, for she wishes to go as much as I do." Thus Southey wrote to his brother, the midshipman. "Coleridge was with us nearly five weeks, and made good use of his time. We preached Pantisocracy and Aspheterism everywhere. These, Tom, are two new words, the first signifying the equal government of all, and the other the generalization of individual property; words well understood in the city of Bristol. We are busy in getting our plans and principles ready to distribute privately. . . . The thoughts of the day, and the visions of the night, all centre in America. . . . I hope to see you in January; it will then be time for you to take leave of the navy, and become acquainted with all our brethren, the pantisocrats. You will have no objection to partake of a wedding dinner in February. . . ."

The wedding dinner here referred to may not have been intended for one couple only. Southey, wishing to be married, had become a pantisocrat; Coleridge, having become a pantisocrat, resolved to marry. At Mrs. Southey's lodging house, immediately upon his return with her son from

Somersetshire, he proposed marriage[1] to Sarah Fricker in a burst of enthusiastic consistency, and was accepted. In the same spirit a little later George Burnett is said to have made a similar offer to Martha, the fourth Miss Fricker,[2] and to have been shrewdly rebuffed for his pains. Southey was much astonished at Coleridge's engagement. Only a few weeks previously, before ever the new pantisocratic couple had met, the gentleman had been confiding to him his undying devotion to Mary Evans.

Funds were still as necessary as wives, however, and although the young men hoped to find comrades with means, they immediately set their pens to work in order to earn money for themselves. Coleridge had printed proposals and had obtained some subscribers for his *Specimens of Modern Latin Poets.* Southey, as we know, had *Joan of Arc* and a whole sheaf of smaller pieces in his drawer. Lovell also professed to be a poet, and following perhaps their principle of aspheterism, they sportively set about writing a joint tragedy in three acts upon the death of Robespierre. Each was to produce one act by the next evening. At the appointed time, Coleridge had written part of his, Southey and Lovell the whole of their assignments. Lovell's, not being "in keeping," had to be rewritten by Southey, and Coleridge soon completed the first act. The whole, according to Southey, "was written as fast as newspapers could be put into blank verse," and a dedication to Mrs. Hannah More was concocted. Little need be said of *The Fall of Robespierre.*[3] It is wild boyish rant about liberty, "blood-cemented thrones," and the "emancipated people." Robespierre was a usurping villain whose fall would enable France to fulfill her hopes of free-

---

[1] Campbell, *Coleridge,* 31.

[2] *Memoir of Sara Coleridge,* I, 10–11.

[3] Coleridge, *Poetical and Dramatic Works,* edited by E. H. Coleridge, 495.

dom, and to withstand the despots of Europe leagued against her. The most important result of the work was that, when published, it called down upon Coleridge the remonstrances of his clerical brother.[1]

Meanwhile Southey made an independent effort to embody his principles in dramatic form. It appears that *Wat Tyler* was also written in the summer of 1794, "the work, or rather the sport, of a week."[2] Coleridge avers[3] that the sentiments of this play are opposite to those of the other, but this is now difficult to detect. Merely another crude boyish effort like *Joan*, *Wat Tyler* expresses the same belief that virtue rests in the simple people, that power is righteous when exerted by them in behalf of liberty, but that undue violence is to be deprecated, and that misery and evil proceed from rulers. Wat, the hero, is but a weaker variant of Joan. Needless to say, neither this work nor *The Fall of Robespierre* shows any power save that of whirling words.

A little later in the year, after Coleridge's departure, Southey and Lovell made that visit to Cruttwell, the Bath printer, which has already been described, and arranged for the publication of the volume of poems in the same form as Bowles's sonnets. In the autumn of 1794 the book appeared as *Poems containing The Retrospect, Odes, Elegies, and Sonnets, etc., by Robert Lovell, and Robert Southey, of Balliol College, Oxford*. The date on the title page was 1795, and the circumstances of the authors were glanced at in the motto from Horace, "*Minuentur atrae Carmine Curae.*" At the end of the volume was printed "Proposals for publishing by Subscription, JOAN OF ARC, an Epic Poem, by Robert Southey, of Balliol College, Oxford. To be handsomely printed in One Volume Quarto."

---

[1] Coleridge, *Letters*, I, 103–106.   [2] *Life*, IV, 241.

[3] Coleridge, *Essays on his Own Times*, III, 948. Coleridge here misstates the date of the composition of *Wat Tyler*.

About the first of September Coleridge went up to London; Southey remained in Bath.[1] *The Fall of Robespierre* went up to London too, and was submitted to the publishers there. The trade in Bristol had been too wise to accept the performance, and their brethren in London were not less prudent. It remained unprinted until Coleridge's return to Cambridge, where it appeared (1794)[2] with his name alone on the title page and with a new dedication, both of which changes were probably made to assist the sale.

From London Coleridge sent encouraging news of pantisocracy to Bristol. He met Lamb's simple-hearted George Dyer, who pronounced the system impregnable and assured him that Dr. Priestley, with whom Dyer professed to be intimate, would certainly join them. Three years earlier Priestley had settled at Northumberland in Pennsylvania near the Susquehanna River,[3] and that most liquidly-named

[1] Coleridge, *Letters*, I, 85.

[2] *A Bibliography . . . of Samuel Taylor Coleridge*, by Thomas J. Wise, 1913, 5.

[3] Cottle is the only authority for the statement that Coleridge had no specific information about the Susquehanna region and was attracted to it solely because of the beautiful sound of the word. Cottle, *Reminiscences*, 16.

Professor Harper, in his *William Wordsworth*, I, 268–270, notes that in *The Gentleman's Magazine* for June, 1795, appeared a notice concerning the establishment of a colony of wealthy Frenchmen, former members of the Constituent Assembly, at French Town near the Susquehanna River. By February, 1795, the idea of attempting pantisocracy on the Susquehanna had given way, in Southey's mind at least, to the vague hope of attempting it on a Welsh farm. By June, when the above notice appeared, the whole project was ready to be abandoned as in any sense a workable proposition. Professor Harper states that there can be scarcely any doubt that Coleridge and Southey had their thoughts turned toward America by hearing or reading some account of this French colony. This is not impossible, but there can be no doubt that their thoughts were turned toward America whether they came upon any such account or not.

place was now suggested to Coleridge as a suitable location for his own enterprise.

"Every night," he wrote, "I meet a most intelligent young man, who has spent the last five years of his life in America, and is lately come from thence as an agent to sell land. . . . He says 2000£ will do; that he doubts not we can contract for our passage under 400£; that we shall buy the land a great deal cheaper when we arrive at America than we could do in England; 'or why,' he adds, 'am I sent over here?' That twelve men may *easily* clear 300 acres in four or five months; and that, for 600 dollars, a thousand acres may be cleared, and houses built on them. He recommends the Susquehanna, from its excessive beauty and its security from hostile Indians. Every possible assistance will be given us; we may get credit for the land for ten years or more, as we settle upon. That literary characters make *money* there: etc. etc. He never saw a *bison* in his life, but has heard of them; they are quite backwards. The mosquitoes are not so bad as our gnats; and, after you have been there a little while they don't trouble you much." (Sept. 6, 1794.) [1]

In another letter of the same period Coleridge is even more explicit: "The *minutiae* of topographical information we are daily endeavouring to acquire; at present our plan is, to settle at a distance, but at a convenient distance, from Cooper's Town on the banks of the Susquehanna." [2]

[1] *Life*, I, 218–219.

[2] *Biog. Epis.*, I, 45. In 1787 William Cooper, father of James Fenimore Cooper, had founded the town of Cooperstown on Lake Otsego, the head waters of the Susquehanna River, having acquired a large estate in that region which he proceeded to exploit for a number of years as a great real estate venture. Cooperstown, therefore, became well known even among Europeans, and was visited by not a few notable foreign visitors to the young American republic. It is possible that Coleridge's "intelligent young man" may have been one of Cooper's agents. See *Guide in the Wilderness; or the History of the First Settlements in the Western Counties of New York with useful instructions to future settlers*, by Judge Cooper of Cooperstown, Dublin, 1810. Reprinted with an introduction by James Fenimore Cooper, Rochester, N. Y., 1897.

A little later it would appear that Coleridge had carried his investigation of a possible location for pantisocracy still farther, and that he had come upon a book containing some definite facts that helped at least to stimulate his imagination. "What think you," he writes to Southey on Oct. 21, 1794, "of the differences in the prices of land as stated by Cowper [sic] from those given by the American agents? By all means read, ponder on Cowper, and when I hear your thoughts I will give you the result of my own." The Cowper here referred to is certainly not William Cooper of Cooperstown, but probably Thomas Cooper, a son-in-law of Priestley, a friend of James Watt the inventor, and a sympathizer with the French revolution. He had gone to Paris in 1792, and upon his return to England had written a reply to Burke's *Reflections* for which he was threatened with prosecution. In August, 1793, he visited America, particularly the Susquehanna region, in which his father-in-law had settled, and returned to England in February, 1794. He appears soon after to have published (Dublin, 1794) the book to which Coleridge refers, *Some Information respecting America.* In this he not only expresses his very decided democratic principles, and announces his intention of returning at once to America to establish his home in that land of freedom, but also gives explicit directions and information for any who might be inclined to follow his example. He tells one how to prepare for the voyage, how to avoid seasickness, and what to take by way of money, clothes, and tools. He advises the valley of the Susquehanna, which he describes quite fully, on the grounds of safety, soil, and climate. He then gives statements concerning land and commodity prices, methods of clearing and cultivating the ground, the management of farms, and a mass of similar practical information. Finally he concludes his book by reprinting in its entirety the constitution of the United States. Here was much indeed for Coleridge and

Southey to ponder over. Cooper emigrated to America and had there an interesting and varied career.[1] His book, with its idealism and its strong vein of practicality, gives one a most vivid, concrete sense of the aspirations and possibilities of achievement that were implicit in the hare-brained scheme of pantisocracy.

Coleridge meanwhile (Sept. 18, 1794) was again at Cambridge, his heart still churning with the excitements of the past few months.[2] "America! Southey! Miss Fricker!" he exclaimed in a letter to his friend, and went on to argue that he certainly loved the young woman because he thought of her incessantly with an inward melting away of soul. As for pantisocracy, oh, he would have such a scheme of it. "My head, my heart, are all alive. I have drawn up my arguments in battle array; they shall have the *tactician* excellence of the mathematician with the enthusiasm of the poet. The head shall be the mass; the heart the fiery spirit that fills, informs and agitates the whole." He was as good as his word, and when one whom he called "the most pantisocratic of aristocrats" laughed at him, "Up I arose, terrible in reasoning. He fled from me, because 'he could not answer for his own sanity, sitting so near a madman of genius.'"

While Coleridge was thinking of arguments, more practical considerations were pressing upon his compatriot left with the pantisocratic ladies in Bristol. Not the least of

[1] Thomas Cooper (1759–1840) practised law for a time in Pennsylvania, became involved in 1799 in a controversy with President John Adams who called him "a learned, ingenious, scientific, and talented madcap," held office as land commissioner and judge, served as professor of chemistry in Dickinson College, in the University of Pennsylvania, and finally in South Carolina College, of which institution he was afterwards made president. After his retirement from this position, he collaborated in a revision of the statutes of South Carolina. See *Dictionary of National Biography.*

[2] Coleridge, *Letters*, I, 81–82.

Southey's difficulties was the character of his associate, and here in the first stages of their acquaintance he was to suffer and show that irritation at Coleridge's procrastination which was to reappear constantly in their dealings. Scarcely a month after the engagement to Sarah Fricker we find Southey under the necessity of writing to Coleridge, probably with some asperity, to remind him of his duty towards his future wife, and we find Coleridge replying with promises and excuses of ill-health. He had gone up to London for but a few days on his way to Cambridge. He was to write to Sarah under cover to Southey, to whom he was to send a weekly parcel. A fortnight elapsed, and Coleridge sent no word to Bristol until September 18, the day after his arrival at Cambridge. On the nineteenth he received a letter of remonstrance from Southey, which called forth a highly philosophical flood of explanation in reply. He had intended to write upon reaching Cambridge, had been ill, had postponed departure from London from day to day, had been compelled to write for booksellers to get funds. "Languid, sick at heart, in the back room of an inn! Lofty conjunction of circumstances for me to write to Miss F."[1] As for Southey, he had also written angrily to Coleridge's friend, Favell, concerning the former's silence, and Coleridge felt that this act had been overhasty. He admitted that he had himself been a slave of impulse and child of imbecility, but this had taught him charity toward the failings of others. It was possible, moreover, to suffer from too high a state of moral health; "*virtue* is liable to a *plethora.*" This was Southey's trouble; simplicity of rectitude had made him rapid in decision, and having never erred, he felt more indignation at error than pity for it. There was "phlogiston" in his heart. These were shrewd words, but the little tiff, so ominous of the future, passed by, and pantisocracy bloomed again.

[1] Coleridge, *Letters*, I, 84–86.

On the eighteenth of September Southey wrote, "In March we depart for America," and a month later he exclaimed, "This Pantisocratic scheme has given me new life, new hope, new energy, all the faculties of my mind are dilated; I am weeding out the few lurking prejudices of habit, and looking forward to happiness."

Two clouds, nevertheless, still obscured the sunshine of hope — money and Miss Tyler. Of the first he wrote, "Money is a huge evil which we shall not long have to contend with." As a means of obtaining some of this evil in the interval, however, Lovell was intrusted[1] with two commissions while on a trip to London in October. He was to examine the wills of the Cannon Southey family at Doctors' Commons "to see what is to be done in the reversion way." He was also to seek a publisher for *Wat Tyler*, and for this work, it would appear, the author expected to get ten or twenty pounds. His friend met with no encouragement on the first errand, but a bookseller accepted the manuscript of the play. Lovell found London in a state of political excitement. On October 6 Hardy, Holcroft, and others of the "Society for Constitutional Information" had been indicted for treason. Lovell at once hunted up Holcroft in Newgate, introduced himself, and talked pantisocracy. After Holcroft's release (December 1), the young man wrote (December 11) from Bristol congratulating him and asking for advice on behalf of the pantisocrats. Their minds had, he declares, been illuminated by the writings of Holcroft and Godwin, and they wished their actions to be similarly guided.[2]

Southey's relations with Miss Tyler were coming in the meantime to a sudden climax. She had so far been kept in ignorance of all her nephew's schemes, but concealment

[1] *Life*, IV, 252; *Warter*, III, 66.
[2] *The Life of Thomas Holcroft* in *The Collected Works of William Hazlitt*, edited by Waller and Glover, II, 278–279.

was no longer possible.   On October 17 the whole situation
was made plain to her, and her temper exploded.

"Here's a row! here's a kick-up! here's a pretty commence! we
have had a revolution in the College Green, and I have been turned
out of doors in a wet night.   Lo and behold, even like mine own
brother, I was penniless: it was late in the evening; the wind blew
and the rain fell, and I had walked from Bath in the morning.
Luckily my father's old great coat was at Lovell's.   I clapped it on,
swallowed a glass of brandy, and set off; I met an old drunken
man three miles off, and was obliged to drag him all the way to
Bath, nine miles!   Oh, Patience, Patience, thou hast often helped
poor Robert Southey, but never didst thou stand him in more need
than on Friday the 17th of October, 1794." [1]

His aunt was uncompromising.   Southey's younger brothers
appear to have been quartered with her, but his mother
was loyal to him, and the children were shipped at once to
Bath.   But it was not pantisocracy to which Miss Tyler
objected so much as the alliances that went with it.   Lovell,
the plebeian Quaker, she abused as the author of all the
mischief, but nothing enraged her so much as her nephew's
projected marriage with Edith, the sister of Mrs. Lovell,
and one of the poverty-stricken Frickers.   "My aunt," the
young man wrote to his brother, "has declared she will
never see my face again, or open a letter of my writing, —
so be it; I do my duty, and will continue to do it, be the
consequences what they may.   You are unpleasantly situated, so is my mother, so were we all till this grand scheme
of Pantisocracy flashed upon our minds, and now all is
perfectly delightful."

With Coleridge, however, this was far from being the
case.   At the very time [2] that Southey was coming to an
open break with his aunt, Coleridge's brother, George,
having heard what was in the wind, was sending letters of

---

[1] For another letter relating to the same experience see Coleridge
Letters, I, 107, note 2.   [2] Coleridge, *Letters*, I, 95, 98.

remonstrance and anguish, suggestions that perhaps the young man was deranged; "*Advice* offered with *respect* from a brother; *affected coldness*, an assumed *alienation* mixed with involuntary bursts of *anguish* and disappointed *affection;* questions concerning the mode in which I would have it mentioned to my aged mother — these are the daggers which are plunged into *my* peace." Even Mary Evans wrote,[1] with apologies for "violating the rules of female delicacy," and over the signature "sister," to urge him that he remain true to his friends, his country, and his God.

New difficulties, moreover, soon began to arise in the relations between the two pantisocrats themselves. Coleridge, with no practical responsibility except that of providing for himself, was captivated with the mere idea of pantisocracy, and concerned[2] himself with explaining it and planning a great quarto book upon it. Southey, on the other hand, with a host of poor relations looking to him for help and with the work-a-day wish to marry, busied himself with ways and means. The result was that many of his arrangements, though practical enough, ran counter to the theories which Coleridge was so volubly expounding. Immediately after the latter's departure from Bath at the end of the summer, Southey appears to have written suggesting that his aunt's man-of-all-work, Shadrach Weeks, and wife Sally, together with a Mr. and Mrs. Roberts, persons of similar social rank, be included in their company. Coleridge replied at once in his first letter from Cambridge in a burst of democratic feeling, heavily underscoring "SHAD GOES WITH US. HE IS MY BROTHER." But Southey had planned to have this brother act in the capacity of a servant, and the thought grieved Coleridge intensely. He would not retire from the project if this were done, but "this is *not our plan*, nor can I defend it. . . . The leading idea of pantisocracy is to make men *necessarily* virtuous by

[1] Coleridge, *Letters*, I, 87–88.   [2] *Ibid.*, 103.

removing all motives to evil — all possible temptation."
"Let them dine with us," Southey had written, "and be
treated with as much equality as they would wish, but
perform that part of labour for which their education has
fitted them." Coleridge answered that Southey should not
have written that sentence. He should have bade his
slaves be his equals and his wife to resign the name of
ladyship in retaining the thing. Was every family to
possess one of Southey's "Helot Egalités," or were Shad
and Sally and their few companions to serve all members
of the community? He feared that the inference to be
drawn from the whole discussion of this point was "that
the scheme of pantisocracy is impracticable, but I hope and
believe that it is not a *necessary* inference."[1]

Coleridge was willing to accept Shad as a brother, but
he balked at accepting his future mother-in-law as a sister.
Southey, with an unphilosophical inability to think of
deserting those dependent upon him, proposed to include in
their venture his own mother, his two younger brothers,
Mrs. Fricker, and all her fry not yet provided for. One
night Coleridge defended his system for six hours against
a heterodox divine and a democratic lawyer, whom he
drove to admit that the system was impregnable, "supposing the assigned quantum of virtue and genius in the first
individuals."[2] And then he came home to find Southey's
letter urging that they include servants, women, and children. "I wish, Southey, in the stern severity of judgment,
that the two mothers were *not* to go, and that the children
stayed with them. . . . *That* Mrs. Fricker! We shall have
her teaching the infants *Christianity*, — I mean that mongrel
whelp that goes under its name, — teaching them in some
ague fit of superstition." Perhaps he had even some passing doubts as to Southey himself, for he asked, "Should
not all who mean to become members of our community

[1] Coleridge, *Letters*, I, 89–90.   [2] *Ibid.*, I, 95–103.

be incessantly meliorating their temper and elevating their understandings?" Yet he was still loyal; he would accompany his friend even "on an *imperfect* system."

This loyalty was soon to be further tested. The months went by, and the means for chartering a ship were still as vague as ever. Coleridge, whose movements for the last two months of 1794 are obscure, may have left Cambridge as early as November 8;[1] certainly he was in London on December 11, and was discoursing poetry and necessitarianism in the back parlor of an inn with Lamb, an old intimacy with whom he had now somehow revived. He was still preaching pantisocracy too, for he reports[2] discussing that and other matters with Holcroft, whom he met while dining with the editor and proprietor of *The Morning Chronicle*. He found that Holcroft had misunderstood Lovell, or Lovell Holcroft, and that neither understood "our system." Holcroft fiercely opposed pantisocracy on the ground that it was not virtuous, but his arguments were nonentities, and when he ventured to talk metaphysics and condemn Bowles, Coleridge "*did him over.*"

Yet time was not all spent in talk. The two pantisocrats had been for some time exchanging their poetry. Coleridge had been criticising the pieces that were being prepared for Southey's forthcoming volume (1795), and sent in return many of the things that he was in the act of selling to *The Morning Chronicle*. Among the latter were the notorious lines *To a Young Ass*:

> "Innocent foal! thou poor despis'd forlorn!
> I hail thee *Brother* — spite of the fool's scorn!
> And fain would take thee with me, in the Dell
> Of Peace and mild Equality to dwell." [3]

He also sent to Bristol many of his *Sonnets on Eminent Characters*, among whom were included Burke, Priestley,

[1] Coleridge, *Letters*, I, 97 n.   [2] *Ibid.*, I, 114–115, December 17, 1794.
[3] Coleridge, *Poetical and Dramatic Works*, 74.

Kosciusko, Bowles, Godwin, and Southey. Pantisocracy
itself came in for a sonnet expressing the poet's belief that
he would soon be seeking some "cottag'd dell" across the
ocean where virtue might stray with careless step and the
wizard passions dance a moonlight roundelay. The thought
brings tears of "doubt-mingled joy" to his eyes, like theirs
who start

"From Precipices of distemper'd sleep." [1]

Yet such activity was not enough to mitigate delay, and
Southey was growing restive. About the middle of December Coleridge made a fleeting visit to Bristol, and we find
him writing[2] thence to Southey at Bath in aggrieved indignation at a new suggestion, probably originating with
Wynn, that they try pantisocracy in Wales.[3] "Remember
the principles and proposed consequences of pantisocracy,
and reflect in what degree they are attainable by Coleridge,
Southey, Lovell, Burnett, and Co., some five men *going
partners* together." Yet again he will be loyal at the sacrifice of principle, and consent to a Welsh compromise. He
will even take a reporter's place on *The Telegraph*, and contribute all his surplus earnings to the common cause.
That Southey had grown impatient is shown by the irritation betrayed by Coleridge at the tone of his friend's letters.
"Southey! I must tell you that you appear to me to write
as a man who is aweary of the world because it accords
not with his ideas of perfection. Your sentiments look like
the sickly offspring of disgusted pride."

Wales, nevertheless, seems to have been agreed upon,
America still being the ultimate goal; yet another difficulty
was to ensue.[4] Coleridge heard of the engagement of Mary

[1] Coleridge, *Poetical and Dramatic Works*, 68. First published in
Life, I, 224.   [2] Coleridge, *Letters*, I, 114, 121.

[3] Cottle, *Reminiscences*, 300.

[4] Coleridge, *Letters*, I, 122–126; Cottle, *Reminiscences*, 300; Campbell, *Coleridge*, 38–43.

Evans to another man, and sent her a letter of disappointed passion. Her reply (ca. Dec. 24, 1794) removed his last ray of hope for winning her; nevertheless he wrote at once to Southey that he loved her still, though resigned to his loss. "But to marry another, O Southey," he protested, "bear with my weakness." Yet he concluded with the assurance, "Mark you, Southey! *I will do my duty.*"

It is evident that Sarah Fricker's future brother-in-law had been urging her claims upon Coleridge, not altogether to the latter's comfort. "My friend," he wrote to Southey, "you want but one quality of mind to be a perfect character. Your sensibilities are tempestuous; you feel *indignation* at weakness. Now Indignation is the handsome brother of Anger and Hatred. His looks are 'lovely in terror,' yet still remember *who* are his *relations.* I would ardently that you were a necessitarian, and (believing in an all-loving Omnipotence) an optimist." Finally came the promise "whatever be the consequence, to be at Bath by Saturday." But after such a burst of moral philosophy, Coleridge's subsequent conduct must have been trying indeed to Southey's patience. The letter just referred to was written, probably, on December 24, 1794, and not only did the writer fail to keep his promise of coming to Bath on Saturday, but he sent no word of any sort, and left his pantisocratic comrade and lady ignorant even of his whereabouts. He had established himself at an inn in Newgate Street, where he was deriving comfort for the loss of Mary Evans in the company of Charles Lamb. Southey instituted a search for him, wrote to his school friend Favell, and even thought of going to Cambridge. Favell wrote that Coleridge was to be addressed at "The Cat and Salutation," and thither Southey wrote. He received a reply[1] in which Coleridge set a day when he would arrive by

[1] Cottle, *Reminiscences*, 300, Letter of Southey to Cottle, March 6, 1836.

wagon in Bath. Southey and Lovell walked some score of miles to Marlborough to meet the wagon at the appointed time, but no Coleridge appeared. At last, some time in January,[1] Southey went to London in person, and finding that his friend had left his former hostelry, applied to Favell at Christ's Hospital, and was conducted to "The Angel Inn, Butcher Hall Street."   There he found Coleridge. What passed between the two men at this meeting, we do not know, but friendship was restored, and they returned together to Bristol, pantisocracy, Sarah and Edith Fricker.

Before leaving London, however, Southey had a conference with the bookseller, Ridgeway, to whom Lovell had intrusted the manuscript of *Wat Tyler*. This conference took place in Newgate, where the publisher was then sojourning, but what was said and done, and who were present at the time, became a matter of controversy.[2] Southey said that Ridgeway and one Simonds agreed to print his play, but it does not appear that they paid him any money or that, after leaving them, he ever heard from them with regard to the matter again. Published *Wat Tyler* was in 1817, under far different circumstances, and in the controversy and lawsuit that arose over that publication, there were allegations concerning enthusiastic embraces between the poet and other persons said also to have been present in Ridgeway's Newgate apartment, persons who, however highly they may have been esteemed by the pantisocrat, were distinctly not so esteemed by the poet laureate of 1817.

---

[1] From July 8, 1794, until January 28, 1795, Southey had drawn books from the Bristol Library Society regularly every four or six days. After the latter date there is a break of a month in the entries of his name. J. Baker *Literary and Biographical Studies*, 211.

[2] *Life*, IV, 236–259; *Warter*, III, 59–70; Merivale, *Reports*, II, 435.

II

Early in February[1] the two friends were again together in Bristol. They now realized that any immediate attempt at emigration even to Wales was out of the question. Lovell, perhaps Burnett, could have contributed each his due portion of funds, but the real dependence was upon themselves, and they had learnt what that was worth. Nevertheless their lots were cast together, and they proposed to share fortune and fame, only postponing the foundation of Utopia, and not ceasing to dream and to talk of it. Southey,[2] having surrendered his uncle's assistance upon leaving Oxford, had been living with his mother, but wishing no longer to burden her, now went to live with Coleridge in a rented room at 48 College Street in Bristol where they could, at least, "aspheterize." "There is the strangest mixture of cloud and of sunshine! an outcast in the world! an adventurer! living by his wits! yet happy in the full conviction of rectitude, in integrity, and in the affection of a mild and lovely woman: at once the object of hatred and admiration; wondered at by all; hated by the aristocrats; the very oracle of my own party. . . . Coleridge is writing at the same table; our names are written in the book of destiny, on the same page."

Money was now needed for daily supplies rather than for pantisocracy, and Southey was not behindhand. Adversity was rapidly completing the process of making a writer out of him. He now said of himself that, unable to enter the church or the profession of physic, too notorious for public office, not possessed of the happy art of making or mending shoes, unfitted by education for trade, he must perforce

---

[1] But Coleridge's name does not appear in the register of the Library Society until March 2, after which the two men constantly drew books together, Coleridge sometimes borrowing upon Southey's name, until the succeeding autumn. Baker, *l.c.*   [2] *Warter*, I, 41.

enter the muster roll of authors, and therefore began nego-
tiations with *The Telegraph* in the hope of being its corres-
pondent. It does not appear that the little volume that
he had published with Lovell the preceding fall had done
much to assist his financial condition, but a friend was soon
raised up who relieved the wants of the pantisocratic poets
in more substantial fashion. Joseph Cottle was a young
printer in Bristol. He was not a prudent person; but his
trade must have been fairly prosperous, for he managed
practically to finance Southey and Coleridge for some
months to come. He had a more than Boswellian vanity
which made him take unctuous pleasure in acting the
Mæcenas to poets. When he commenced author himself,
his efforts were not as fortunate. Upon the death of Coleridge he published a volume of reminiscences concerning his
friend, which he enlarged later to include Southey. He is
tasteless, incoherent, and untrustworthy, but we are dependent upon him for some interesting details in this period
of Southey's life.

Cottle reports that at the close[1] of the year 1794 he met
"a clever young man of the Society of Friends, of the name
of Robert Lovell."[2] The latter immediately informed the
bookseller concerning the scheme of pantisocracy, "a Social
Colony, in which there was to be a community of property, and where all that was selfish was to be proscribed."
Lovell promptly invited him to make one of the band.
The head of poor Cottle spun for a moment, but he was
shrewd enough to ask a few questions. Who made up the
party? Coleridge, Southey, Burnett, and Lovell were the

---

[1] Cuthbert Southey (*Life*, I, 216) dates the meeting of Southey and
Cottle in the summer of 1794, but Cottle is probably right, for Southey
would hardly have had Cruttwell publish his *Poems* of 1795, especially
with an announcement concerning the publication of *Joan of Arc*,
after his relations with Cottle had begun.

[2] Cottle, *Reminiscences*, 2–5.

only assured members. How did they go? They would freight a ship with plows and farming implements. When did they sail? Very shortly. Whence came the funds? was the final question; and there was an unconscious irony in the reply, "We all contribute what we can, and I shall introduce all my dear friends to you, immediately on their arrival in Bristol." But these friends were also poets, and Cottle, having meddled with verses himself, looked forward with pride to meeting the young geniuses.

In a few days Lovell introduced Southey: "Tall, dignified, possessing great suavity of manners; an eye piercing, with a countenance full of genius, kindliness, and intelligence, I gave him at once the right hand of fellowship, and to the moment of his decease, that cordiality was never withdrawn. I had read so much of poetry and sympathized so much with poets in all their eccentricities and vicissitudes, that, to see before me the realization of a character, which in the abstract most absorbed my regards, gave me a degree of satisfaction which it would be difficult to express." After considerable delay, the occasion of which has been explained, Lovell at length introduced Coleridge also, and an intimacy rapidly developed between the two poets and their patron bookseller. The latter gloated over his young lions, and assisted in spreading their fame in Bristol.

Cottle says that they were still talking pantisocracy. What they wanted was £100 to £150 a year between them, and they would marry, settle in the country, write and cultivate the soil, until they could raise money enough to go to America — "still the grand object in view" (March 21, 1795). Cottle, meanwhile, alleges that he felt deep concern lest they should heedlessly set sail at once, that he was "haunted day and night with the spectre of the ship! the ship! which was to effect such incalculable mischief."[1] His fears were allayed by a request from Coleridge

[1] Cottle, *Reminiscences*, 8–10.

for the loan of five pounds to help pay their lodging bill. Burnett had joined them, and his arrears even exceeded theirs. Cottle lent the money, and shortly after offered assistance far more gratifying. He urged Coleridge to publish a volume of poems, for which he promised to pay thirty guineas in such installments as Coleridge's necessities demanded. A similar offer was made to Southey, followed by an even better one for the publication of *Joan of Arc*, parts of which had been read to Cottle by the author and greatly approved. The bookseller proposed to print the poem in quarto on fine paper, paying what seemed to the young poet the large sum of fifty guineas as well as fifty copies for the subscribers who might have responded to the proposals that appear to have been published at Bath. With this offer Southey fell in with alacrity. He records later[1] that at this time few books were printed in the country, and Cottle planned to make this the handsomest that had ever appeared in Bristol. A new font of type was sent for, and fine hot-pressed paper. There was no delay in setting to work at the printing, and it was an elated young author who stood by the stove in the center of Bulgin and Rosser's printing office while priggish, powdered Mr. Rosser directed the boy appointed to set up the first page of the great epic.[2] The author, however, was much embarrassed at the defects in his work which he beheld when he saw it in print before him. It stood, except for a few changes made in transcription, exactly as he had written it in those six weeks at Brixton Causeway. For six months now, right up until publication in November, he labored at correcting and rewriting the poem as it passed through the press. Coleridge assisted and contributed to

[1] *Works*, *Preface* to *Joan of Arc*.
[2] Southey had the satisfaction years afterward of receiving an account of this scene from the boy himself. *Correspondence with Caroline Bowles*, 353.

the text considerable portions most of which were carefully noted by Southey in his preface.[1]

There was other poetry on the stocks at the same time. Often, Southey wrote later in life, he walked the streets of Bristol in these months, and went happy and dinnerless to his room to write. "Poetry," he told Bedford, "softens the heart. No man ever tagged rhyme without being the better for it." When he began correcting *Joan of Arc*, he was already at work on *Madoc*, which he thought was to be "the pillar of his fame." He had begun it in the preceding autumn, the subject having been suggested to him at Westminster by Wynn. Now, of course, it had to be laid aside. As for minor pieces, his energies were so engrossed that only a few were composed at this time as compared with the number produced during the year before. He states later that his taste had been ameliorated by Coleridge; they exchanged long letters of criticism on each other's compositions, and doubtless continued such discussions at 48, College Street. Nevertheless the perceptible effect of Coleridge upon Southey's work is small. The former's written criticisms of his friend's poems were mostly verbal, and we know that Southey's poetic tendencies were already fairly well established before the two met. Coleridge may have encouraged the other in the way he had chosen, and doubtless helped in the revision of *Joan of Arc*, but Southey seems, on the whole, to have been far more susceptible to the influence of reading than to that of the talk even of a Coleridge, for talk, consuming, as it did, time that might be used for reading or writing, tended more and more to try his patience. The few shorter poems of these months, therefore, are but obvious continuations of veins already opened. *Written on Sunday Morning* is an ode of strong deistic flavor. Four pieces carry on the

[1] *Joan of Arc*, 1796, *Preface; Works, Preface* to *Joan of Arc;* Coleridge, *Poetic and Dramatic Works*, 1027.

sympathy for the poor which had already been expressed in the *Botany Bay Eclogues*. These consisted of *The Pauper's Funeral*, generously emended by Coleridge;[1] *The Soldier's Funeral; The Soldier's Wife* in dactylics, to which Coleridge contributed a stanza; *The Widow*, a companion piece to the latter in unlucky sapphics made famous by *The Needy Knifegrinder*. After Southey had returned to Bath later in the year, he wrote his only poem of the time that preserves much intrinsic interest. Coleridge himself thought that the lines *On a Landscape of Gasper Poussin* were "worthy to have been published after *Joan of Arc* as proofs of progressive genius."[2] Though pantisocracy was by that time an abandoned hope, the poem shows the desire for a home in retirement which was the abiding aspiration behind that project in the poet's mind.

Joan was Southey's main labor and reliance during 1795, but the pantisocrats turned their wits to finding other means of raising money. They thought of a joint collection of poems in two volumes, and of a periodical, *The Provincial Magazine*, which was to be upon a new plan and to contain all the verses of its two editors. Both these ideas seem to have been held in mind for some time, but were abandoned with the break-up of all joint schemes in the autumn of the year. More certain returns came from the lectures[3] which the two men gave under Cottle's auspices. The friends had become notorious characters in Bristol, and people came, according to Cottle, in fairly large numbers, to hear the young firebrands hold forth. The lectures began in February and continued, in Coleridge's case, into the summer. The year 1795 was a trying time for those who had set their hopes of freedom on the success of the revolution in France. The victories of the

---

[1] Coleridge, *Letters*, I, 108–109.
[2] *Biog. Epis.*, I, 123–124, Jan. 3, 1797.
[3] Cottle, *Reminiscences*, 10–20.

French armies during the first two years of their war with the monarchies of Europe, the threat of French principles, and the excesses of the Jacobins had set the Pitt administration in a panic. Measures one after another had been adopted so repressive that all the old bulwarks of British freedom seemed to be endangered, and these distresses were heightened by economic distress throughout the country. The subjects of discourse for the two young reformers were therefore easily determined. Coleridge lectured upon religion and politics, Southey upon history, but the remarks of both were colored by their attitude toward contemporary events.

Coleridge was, of course, plainly the more successful in these performances. The substance of his first series, which was upon contemporary affairs, appears in his *Conciones ad Populum*.[1] The opening lecture, February 1795, he was compelled to publish[2] in order to disprove the accusation of treason. It maintains the usual thesis that goverment by the people is best, as opposed to the tyranny of kings, prime ministers, and Jacobins, providing that the people are sufficiently "illuminated." Other addresses, *On the Present War* and *The Plot Discovered or an Address to the People against Ministerial Treason*, in the same vein were delivered in quick succession, and the substance of them published later in the same year. Here, however, Coleridge brought his remarks home to the tyranny of Pitt, directed, as it seemed to him, against both the English and the French. How the people should be "illuminated" in order to withstand such tyranny and to rule themselves was a question not avoided by Coleridge. They must be taught

---

[1] Coleridge, *Essays on his Own Times*, I, 1–98.

[2] See letter from Coleridge to George Dyer (dated, 1795), in T. J. Wise, *Bibliography of Coleridge*, 11–13. This lecture was also reprinted in the second edition of *The Friend* in order to prove that Coleridge had never been a Jacobin. Coleridge, *Works*, edited by Shedd, II, 297.

religion. "Preach the gospel to the poor," he magnilo-
quently exclaims, meaning the gospel according to Rousseau, Berkeley, Hartley, and the other apostles of the
religion of nature. Such doctrines constituted the political
principles of freedom, or more specifically of pantisocracy
and aspheterism.

The prospectus of the "theological lectures" in which
these sentiments were delivered, as well as that of a later
political series, and of certain disconnected addresses on the
slave trade and the hair-powder tax, are all preserved by
Cottle.[1] That the speaker was not always undisturbed in
the delivery of his remarks is indicated in a letter written[2]
to George Dyer shortly after the first three lectures in
February. Coleridge there says that so great a furore had
been raised about him by the aristocrats that he doubted
whether he did not do more harm than good. Mobs,
mayors, blockheads, brickbats, placards, and press gangs had
leagued against him and his small, though sturdy, band of
democrats. "Two or three uncouth and unbrained Auto-
mata" had threatened his life, and the mob had in his last
lecture been scarcely restrained from attacking the house
"in which the damn'd Jacobin was jawing away."

Southey's twelve historical lectures made far less stir,
although, as he wrote to his brother, he tried to teach
"what is right by showing what is wrong." His definition
of right and wrong may be gathered from the remark that
"My company, of course, is sought by all who love good
republicans and odd characters." He admitted that his
lectures were "only splendid declamation." The prospectus, preserved by Cottle, though appallingly comprehensive, shows a good grasp of the main divisions of the
subject as a whole. Beginning with Solon and Lycurgus
Southey gave an account of the history of Europe down to
the American Revolution. Tickets for 10s 6d were sold by

---

[1] Cottle, *Reminiscences*, 10–14.   [2] Wise, *l.c.*

Cottle, who testifies that the lectures were well attended and delivered with so much self-possession, grace, and command of reason as to astonish the audience. All were amazed that one so young should be able to tell so much in so short a time.[1]

The notoriety of the pantisocrats may have had the interesting result of bringing about the first meeting of Coleridge and Southey with Wordsworth, who in September of this year came to Bristol to join his sister Dorothy on the way to begin life at Racedown. There is some reason to believe that Wordsworth may have met Cottle too upon this occasion, and begun to negotiate for the publication of *Guilt and Sorrow*.[2] If it were not that the bookseller makes no mention of such a fact, it would be easy to imagine that he somehow brought the three poets together. As it is, we have only Wordsworth's recollection [3] (1845) that in 1795 (September must have been the time because by the next month the two pantisocrats were not on speaking terms), he had met Coleridge, Southey, and Edith Fricker in a lodging in Bristol. Some literary intercourse must have taken place among the three men soon after this meeting, for in the following November Wordsworth included [4] in a translation of some lines of Juvenal, two verses by "Southey, a friend of Coleridge." That anything approaching friendship now took place is unlikely, at least so far as Southey is concerned. In March of the following year Wordsworth wrote [5] that the latter had proved himself a coxcomb by the preface to *Joan of Arc*, and that that poem, though first rate in parts, was on the whole of inferior execution.

For all his labors Southey now had need. Difficulties weighed ever more pressingly upon him, and despondency

[1] Cottle, *Reminiscences*, 19.
[2] J. McL. Harper, *William Wordsworth*, I, 277.
[3] *Letters of the Wordsworth Family*, III, 327.
[4] *Op. cit.*, I, 89.   [5] *Op. cit.*, I, 206.

swept over him from time to time like a wave. As early as February he wrote to Bedford, "Peace and domestic life are the highest blessings I could implore. . . . I am worn and wasted with anxiety; and, if not at rest in a short time, shall be disabled from exertion, and sink to a long repose. Poor Edith! Almighty God protect her!" In June the poet's depression was rendered more acute by the sudden death of his admired friend, Edmund Seward. Yet the immediate cause for the worst of his perplexity was his growing distrust of pantisocracy, even on a small scale, in Wales, and this was due to an increasing lack of confidence in Coleridge. The position was an embarrassing one. In a burst of enthusiasm, Southey had sworn to make one of the company, and to share all equally with Coleridge and the rest, but aways with the hope that the scheme would enable him to meet his family obligations and settle down with his wife. When the scheme failed to materialize, the enthusiasm seemed flaccid and empty. He had sworn fealty to it for practical reasons, and for practical reasons he now wished to withdraw. But such reasons had no weight with Coleridge, and Southey was in the uncomfortable position of appearing a traitor. Neither man enjoyed the process of disillusionment and disintegration which began almost as soon as Coleridge came to Bristol and continued until Southey's departure for Portugal in November.

The greatest discouragement to Southey must have been that while he, feeling the obligations that were upon him, worked industriously at *Madoc*, *Joan of Arc*, his lectures, and other writing, Coleridge procrastinated and talked. Let us remember that they shared the same room. Coleridge should have been preparing copy for the volume of poems which Cottle had agreed to publish, and payment for which was already being received, but, if we can believe Cottle,[1] the printer was put off time after time. Mean-

[1] Cottle, *Reminiscences*, 26–29.

while Coleridge was a conspicuous figure about the town, discoursing everywhere upon his favorite topics, not omitting pantisocracy. To Southey such conduct grew steadily harder to bear, and in a letter written in 1810 he gives an interesting account of its effect upon him at the time and afterwards. He notes the fact that Coleridge, in spite of his passion for close, hard thinking, wrote in a rambling and inconclusive style, while he himself, utterly incapable of the toil of thought in which the other delighted, always wrote perspicuously and to the point. Southey suggests that this characteristic in himself was probably in part due to his having lived with Coleridge at so impressionable a period. The more Coleridge talked and the more he repeated himself, the more Southey was driven to moody silence except when provoked to argue in return, and then, never able to put in more than a few words at a time, he had to take care to make them count. Coleridge, Southey concludes, "goes to work like a hound, nosing his way, turning, and twisting, and winding, and doubling, till you get weary with following the mazy movements. My way is, when I see my object, to dart at it like a greyhound."[1]

Southey's impatience was not lessened, of course, by the fact that, according to his own statement, which there is no reason to doubt, he was contributing four times as much as the other to their joint establishment.[2] Naturally there was something to be said for Coleridge, as Southey's revelations of his own nature indicate. The talker had not been idle when assisting in the revision of his friend's poems and the composition of his lectures. Yet this was but a small part of Coleridge's defense. "The truth is," he told Southey, "you sat down and wrote; I used to saunter about and to think what I should write." This was, of course, the crux of the whole matter; Coleridge was always

[1] *Warter*, II, 188–189.
[2] *Warter*, I, 41; Coleridge, *Letters*, I, 150–151.

thinking, and Southey, who wished to see something done, felt of his friend as he now felt of Godwin, "that he theorizes for another state, not for the rule of conduct in the present" (Oct. 1, 1795). This growing distaste for unending speculation and this insistence upon conduct could not fail to irritate Coleridge; "I am . . . often forced to quarrel with his want of judgment and unthinkingness; which Heaven knows, I never do without pain, and the vexation of a disappointed wish."[1] Finally, there can be no doubt that Southey, in his own "plethora of virtue," made evident his increasing disapproval of his associate's conduct in no graceful or charitable manner; there was always about him something too much the air of showing "what is right by showing what is wrong." Coleridge was learning,[2] as he had said before, that the conscience of a man who has lived free from the common faults of human nature may grow blunt, owing to the infrequency, as that of others may from the frequency, of wrong actions.

Here were shrewd words written by both men after the facts; the facts themselves were beginning to accumulate with disagreeable rapidity. Coleridge, according to an angry letter[3] written when his friend at last deserted the cause in the autumn, had already begun to suspect that Southey was receding in his principles when they began their lectures in February. Cottle reports[4] that, when the time came towards the end of May for Southey's lecture on "The Rise, Progress and Decline of the Roman Empire," Coleridge obtained permission to speak instead on the ground that he had devoted much attention to the subject. If we may trust Cottle,[5] Coleridge omitted to appear at the time of the lecture, and the audience had to be sent away with

[1] To Humphry Davy, Dec. 1808, *Biog. Epis.*, II, 41.
[2] To William Godwin, March 29, 1811, *Biog. Epis.*, II, 72.
[3] Coleridge, *Letters*, I, 139.
[4] Cottle, *Reminiscences*, 19–20.   [5] *Ibid.*, 20–26.

a postponement. On the next day, unfortunately, the bookseller had essayed to drag his "two young friends and their ladies elect" out upon a pleasure party, to which Southey says he would have preferred the luxury of an hour's hanging. They were to visit the Wye and Tintern Abbey. Southey was angry, and at Chepstow, before their excursion was many hours old, his anger burst out in remonstrance with Coleridge. The latter's neglect of the preceding evening seemed to him a matter of great importance, to Coleridge of little. Cottle says that each of the two ladies sided with her gentleman in the dispute, and that he was compelled to pacify them all. The two men shook hands, and the party proceeded, but such episodes could not fail to shake their friendship. There were similar occurrences before very long. On a strawberry party to Ashton,[1] Southey told Burnett that he expected to share only their farm land in Wales with his comrades and to retain his personal property. Burnett carried this to Coleridge, who said (Nov. 13, 1795), "It scorched my throat."

Presently new developments in Southey's own affairs complicated the situation still further. His friend Wynn[2] had promised some years before that upon coming of age he would bestow upon Southey an annuity of £160. Wynn would reach his majority in January, 1796. At the end of 1794 he had been suggesting the trial of pantisocracy in Wales; he may have written to his friend in the meanwhile about the epic on Madoc, a subject suggested by him; at any rate it seems certain that his old promise of the annuity was now renewed[3] with the condition that the recipient study law in order to become independent as soon as pos-

---

[1] Coleridge, *Letters*, I, 140.

[2] De Quincey is the only authority for the statement that Wynn gave the pension out of gratitude for Southey's moral influence at Oxford. De Quincey, *Collected Writings*, edited by Masson, II, 321.

[3] *Warter*, I, 41.

sible. On August 22 Southey wrote to Bedford that he thought in fifteen months to be in London and to enter upon his legal work, not omitting to marry, however, and to continue the trade of author. But at this juncture his uncle, the Reverend Herbert Hill, arrived from Lisbon, and once more took the young man's future under consultation. Southey received a letter from him urging again that he return to Oxford and enter the Church. Here then were two courses which offered feasible escapes from the present difficulties. To surrender either of them for the dubious prospects of pantisocracy and aspheterism with Coleridge was plainly folly, but to admit the folly and to act upon the admission was unpleasant. Nevertheless, when the letter from his uncle arrived, Southey handed it to Coleridge, "and told him I knew not what I ought to do." The old objection to taking orders was still strong. "My uncle urges me to enter the Church; but the gate is perjury, and I am little disposed to pay so heavy a fine at the turnpike of orthodoxy." Coleridge, on the other hand, feared that his friend was considering such perjury as a possibility and meditating ways by which he might gloze over the opinions expressed in *Joan of Arc.*

This was not to be; Southey went to Shurton to confer with his uncle, but returned with the decision to accept Wynn's pension and study law, even though Coleridge thought such a course still more opposite to pantisocratic principles than entering the Church. Southey had thought enough; something had to be done if his ambitions ever were to be furthered. His decision being therefore made, it was also decided, perforce, to dissolve the establishment at 48, College Street. With twenty guineas advanced by Cottle as payment for the copyright of Southey's poems (not published until 1797), the pantisocrats settled their arrears of rent, and parted, Southey going back to his mother's house in Bath, and Coleridge taking another room in the same street. Mr. Hill may have been disappointed, but he was now more immediately concerned with his nephew's principles and with his intended imprudent marriage. In the hope of chilling the ardor for pantisocracy and for Edith Fricker, at the end of October he invited the young man to go with him to Portugal for six months. Reluctantly the invitation was accepted. Southey had still over a year to wait for Wynn's pension, and he was weary of refusing all the importunities of his mother. He had, to be sure, no intention of deserting Edith, but there began to be less cause for his uncle to worry about his principles. Although still believing in natural goodness and social corruption, Southey could now write Bedford (Oct. 1, 1795) that he had learned to confute Godwin, to baffle the atheist, to teach the deist that the arguments in favor of Christianity were not to be despised, and to esteem metaphysics to be mere difficult trifles. It should be noted, however, that with the abandonment of the scheme for emigration to Wales or America Southey did not abandon all the fundamental ideas of pantisocracy. Household customs in Greta Hall, it is reported,[1] were for years colored by the poet's democratic notions, the servants, for instance, never being permitted to use terms of polite address such as Miss or Master to the children. More significant, perhaps, was Southey's continued interest in schemes of emigration and communism of one sort or another throughout the rest of his life. To transplant himself to a new country was sometimes referred[2] to by him as a possible recourse in case of revolution in England, and when he met Robert Owen in 1816, he wrote that the latter was "neither more nor less than such a Pantisocrat as I was in the days of my youth . . . Had we met twenty years ago, the meeting might have influenced both his life and mine in no slight degree."[3]

[1] Information supplied by Mr. Ernest Hartley Coleridge.
[2] *Warter* IV, 121.   [3] *Life* IV 195–197; *Warter* III 45, IV 146–149.

Even so, although Southey had long since learned to distrust such enthusiasm as he saw in Owen, nevertheless he proposed to go to New Lanark on a visit of inspection, corresponded[1] with Rickman at length with regard to this and other coöperative schemes of the day, and in his *Colloquies on the Progress and Prospects of Society*[2] represented himself as discussing various such Utopias with the ghost of Sir Thomas More and advocating the gradual adoption of a kind of Tory socialism in which there should be common ownership of property, but no leveling and no atheism.

In the meantime, as the result of Southey's decision to abandon the immediate pursuit of pantisocracy, the break with Coleridge became open. No quarrel occurred when the former first announced his change of plan and withdrew to his mother's house, but Coleridge wrote letters urging Southey against accepting the advice and assistance of his relatives and friends. Soon afterwards the deserted pantisocrat took on a coldly courteous manner, and began to speak harshly to third persons of his former comrade. Tale-bearers of course went then to Southey. This resulted in a letter from the latter demanding explanation and bringing a reply couched in the tone of high moral philosophy. On October 4, 1795, Coleridge was married to Sarah Fricker on the strength of an offer of Cottle's to pay a guinea and a half for every hundred lines of verse he might produce. A few days later he wrote to Poole that his project for editing a magazine with Southey had been abandoned because he could not be connected with the latter with any comfort to his feelings, and next the two pantisocrats met each other in Redcliff "unsaluted and unsaluting."[3]

The time drew near for Southey's departure for Portugal. On the fourteenth of November he was to leave. On that

[1] *Life*, VI, 50–51, 80–84.   [2] *Colloquies*, I, 132–145.
[3] Coleridge, *Letters*, I, 139–144.

day he received a long letter from Coleridge expressing lofty scorn for his desertion of their noble principles, and defending the conduct of the writer in all their relationships together. On that day, too, Southey corrected the last proof sheet of *Joan of Arc*, went to the church of St. Mary Redcliff, and was married secretly to Edith Fricker. She was to wear her wedding-ring hung from her neck, and to keep her maiden name until the news of the marriage became known. She would live as a "parlour boarder" with Cottle and his sisters, "two women of elegant and accomplished manners," who, Southey says, "make even bigotry amiable." The youthful husband left his wife at the church door and went to take his place on the stage-coach for Falmouth. "She returned the pressure of my hand, and we parted in silence."[1]

III

During the six months of Southey's absence from England the churning passions of 1795 were to subside, and a way of escape from the ills of society was to open for him through study, writing, and a home. The "phlogiston" in his heart would not be quenched, but it would be stopped from consuming the heart that held it, and made to boil the pot. Meanwhile the energies expended upon *Joan* would not have been wasted, for upon his return he would find that that epic of six weeks had roused a reputation for him that would have a certain cash value.

Why an epic should have attracted the attention accorded to *Joan of Arc* is not difficult to understand. In the first place, the form was called for by the grandiose aspirations of the day, and in the state of poetry at the time, Southey's work was not one that could be ignored. The poems of capital pretensions that had appeared since the death of Pope had been conspicuously feeble. There

---

[1] *Works, Preface* to *Joan of Arc*.

had been poetry, of course, as the names of Thomson, Gray, Collins, Johnson, Goldsmith, Cowper, Chatterton, Blake, and Burns signify, not to mention such widely differing men as Macpherson and Churchill, but these writers had left the attempt to compose long, ambitious poems in something like heroic vein to such persons as Wilkie, Glover, Hayley, Rogers, Darwin, and Hole, or to translators such as Hoole and Mickle. There was, moreover, little attempt to express in poetry those thoughts and passions of the eighteenth century that were rising to revolution. Akenside had, it is true, put natural religion and liberal principles into pompous blank verse, but his was a frost-nipt genius that moved only such willing souls as Southey and Coleridge. Burns, it is also true, was to prove a great force for democracy, and Cowper wrote that English hearts would leap when the Bastille fell, but the fame of Burns had not yet gathered way, and Cowper's Calvinism was not the turn of the age. Below Cowper and until we come to Southey there is but such ineptitude as Mason's *English Garden*. Yet the last twenty-five years of the century were seething with aspirations, and the time was more than ripe for these to overflow in verse as in the other activities of the human spirit. This was the opportunity which Southey caught. The more superficial aspects of the new poetry,— its form, technic, decoration, and certain of its subjects,— had already appeared, but in *Joan of Arc* the mood of poetic idealism that had been Spenser's and Milton's was at last fully reopened. Southey had looked in his heart to write; that his promise was greater than his performance may in no small part be due to a certain lack of roots and substance in the religion that was the mainspring of his inspiration. Perhaps no poet could have written an epic out of the eighteenth-century nature-worship.

The tempest over *Joan* was lively enough to make its author notorious. The three reviews that represented at this time various shades of opposition to government all greeted the poem with acclaim, though not without characteristic cavils. *The Monthly Review*[1] regretted the haste of composition, and found it hard to accept Joan as an epic figure after the ribaldries of Voltaire. Nevertheless, Southey's powers were admitted to be "of a very superior kind." In lofty and daring conception, in commanding sentiments and energetic language, the best passages of the poem were said to be unsurpassed, and there were few parts that sank into langour. As for the political principles which it expressed, they were "uniformly noble, liberal, enlightened, and breathing the purest spirit of general benevolence and regard to the rights and claims of humankind." Southey's contemporary allusions gave the reviewer a fine, lip-smacking satisfaction. "We know not where," he exclaims, "the ingenuity of a crown lawyer would stop, were he employed to make out a list of innuendoes."

The notice in *The Critical Review* was even more favorable. The reviewer commended the use of Joan as an epic figure, and particularly praised the mode of her education and her religious principles. To the objection that the subject was not national, he replied that the cause of truth was of higher importance than any particular interest, that national claims might be ill-founded, and that patriotism might be something worse than enthusiasm unless guided by moderation and founded upon justice.

Finally, the lumbering *Analytical*[2] and colorless *Monthly Magazine*[3] added their praise. The latter emitted merely a puff, but the former delivered itself of a labored opinion to the effect that, though it was puzzling to find fifteenth-century personages expressing eighteenth-century politics and metaphysics, nevertheless the noble spirit of freedom,

[1] *Month. Rev.*, April, 1796, n.s.,v. 19, 361–368.
[2] *Analyt. Rev.*, 1796, v. 23, 171–177.
[3] *Month. Mag.*, July, 1796, v. 2, 487.

which was evidently the poet's inspiring muse, was much to be admired.

Hostile criticism was slower in finding its way into print, but by the time of the publication of the second edition in 1798, *The Anti-Jacobin Review* had been established, and then attacked[1] Southey severely for violating the laws of patriotism and criticism. His story was said to have been made ludicrous by Voltaire; it was not national, it was a mere summary of history, and it had no epic machinery. Above all it was "anti-English." Who at this crisis would represent the English as routed by the French without intending treacherous malignity? Southey was admitted to be a man of genius, but unfortunately for him he was inflamed by the fanaticism of liberty, and his poem was but the poem of a party.

The attention that *Joan of Arc* received from certain sections of the reading public is no doubt further indicated[2] in the response that it obtained from that egregious female poetaster, Miss Anna Seward, now in the height of her renown. She did not see the poem until December, 1796, when one of her friends presented her with a copy, but she was then so impressed that she could read but two books in a fortnight. She was drowned in tears, and she recorded her emotions in a notebook kept for such purposes. The author, she said, was another Chatterton, but the more tragic because he was a savage boy of genius defaming the English character and constitution and deifying France in sublime poetry. These sentiments she put into a blank verse *Philippic on a Modern Epic*, and sent (before April 13, 1797) to the editor of *The Morning Chronicle*. They were not published until the following summer, when the editor

[1] *Anti-Jac. Rev.*, May, 1799, v. 3, 120–128.

[2] *The Poetical Works of Anna Seward*, 1810, III, 67; *Letters of Anna Seward*, 1811, IV, 328, 369; *European Magazine*, August, 1797, v. 32, 118.

added a rejoinder which took a less flattering attitude toward the literary merits of the poem.

The effect of criticism was, of course, to advertise the young author's book thoroughly, and the public bought up the first edition, a guinea quarto, in less than two years. It was soon pirated in America, and four more editions in smaller form were required in England before the publication of Southey's collected poems in 1837. After the second edition Cottle sold the copyright of this work, together with that of Southey's *Poems* of 1797, to Longman for £370, his own profit having already amounted to £250 and Southey's to £138. Immediately upon the author's return from Portugal he began his extensive revision for the second edition of his epic. He cut out all those portions that had been contributed by Coleridge, and he removed the entire ninth book, in which Joan made a visionary descent to the lower regions. This was printed separately in the 1799 volume of minor poems and afterwards in the later editions of *Joan of Arc* under the title, *The Vision of the Maid of Orleans*. The notes to the second edition were also increased by many references illustrative of fifteenth-century costume, manners, and methods of warfare from a formidable array of poets, chroniclers, and antiquaries, but Southey had added nothing to his knowledge of the historical characters of his narrative. The revision consisted of certain changes in the diction and a little toning down of the violence of expression without weakening any of the principles of the poem. One episode was added in place of the old ninth book, but without altering the spirit of the whole. In the later editions there were made but a few more changes in diction until the publication of Southey's collected poems in 1837. *Joan of Arc* was then selected because of its fame for the first volume of the collection, and the exuberance of youth was once more toned down, though not as extensively as might have been expected.

CHAPTER IV
1796-1800

PORTUGAL — LAW AND LITERATURE

I

THE young husband,[1] having left his wife at the church door in Bristol, climbed aboard a stagecoach, and after a journey of two wet days arrived in Falmouth. Then for ten days he and his uncle and their companion, Colonel Maber, waited for the packet that was to carry them to Spain. But the drear discomforts of the young man's position were unable to shake the stoic spirit of that parting from his bride, and he wrote at great length to Bedford of his wedding, of his journey, of his poems. He learned that his marriage had become publicly known, but at this he felt no concern, writing to Cottle the real reason for his having taken such a step at this time. So great was the poverty of the Frickers that the support of Edith had already fallen to him. During his absence it might be embarrassing for her to receive money from one not legally her husband, and besides, if through some accident of travel he should lose his life and Edith be left his widow, his relatives would then surely come to her assistance.

The packet sailed, and not later than December 13, 1795, after a stormy passage, landed at Corunna. The next two days were spent by Southey's elders in struggles with Spanish officials, while the young man himself hunted up a bookshop and an English consul who knew Spanish poetry.

[1] The main facts of this period of Southey's life are to be found in *Life*, I, 262–352, II, 1–56 and *Warter*, I, 20–104.

Then the party started on their four-hundred-mile journey[1] by impassable roads and filthy, flea-bitten inns to Madrid. They arrived there on the second of January, and waited ten days before proceeding farther. The king and his court had just set out for the Portuguese border, and the three Englishmen chose not to take the risk of famine and robbery which too close proximity to royalty involved. But on January 12 they ventured forth, barely escaped Carlos, entered Portugal by way of Badajos, and reached Lisbon on the twenty-sixth. It was not an easy or a savory journey for the young man, but important in its effects upon his life.

The hopes of Southey's kindly uncle that this visit would distract his nephew from an imprudent marriage, and direct his attention toward entering the Church were, of course, doomed to disappointment from the start. The statement of Cuthbert Southey, however, that his father returned to England with "the same political bias, and the same romantic feelings as he left it" is misleading. In the stress of love, poetry, and pantisocracy, Southey's tastes and temper had taken their true bent; during this visit to Lisbon, they would be stiffened in the direction they would keep, but with a subtle change which would make that direction not so regrettable as his elders then anticipated. At the end of the six months Mr. Hill wrote that he felt deeply hurt at the misapplication of his nephew's great abilities and high moral qualities. "He has everything you would wish a young man to have excepting common sense and prudence." Yet within the limits of Southey's responsibilities and of his very decided aspirations, practical morality had set the date of his marriage, and a certain prudence was to be his guide from now on.

For the effect upon the recent pantisocrat of first-hand observation of decadent feudalism in Spain and Portugal

---

[1] *Letters written during a Short Residence in Spain and Portugal*, 1–260.

was immediate and profound. Wordsworth caught the revolutionary spirit in France at the same age that Southey completed his recovery from it at Lisbon. In his first letter from Corunna, the latter had described how, when entering the packet, he had found the Spanish mate cutting a cross on the side of his berth, while the sailors were pawing a mess of biscuit, onions, liver, and horse beans out of a bucket. The same cleanliness had appeared in the only meal afforded to the passengers on the trip, and the same spirit of devotion, when the wind blew hard, sent the crew to their prayers. Poverty, filth, ignorance, superstition,— these were the dominant notes in Southey's impressions of the peninsular peoples. The causes of these miseries were the gross incompetence and corruption of the government of Carlos in Spain, and the unbridled sway of the priests in Portugal. The Catholic Church was under the young Englishman's observation in Lisbon, and exercised a fascination of loathing upon him which caused him to revert to it again and again, and colored his whole attitude toward Catholicism. With the royal court of Spain Southey's experience had been almost too intimate for comfort. The household of Carlos, seven thousand strong, was on the road from Madrid to Lisbon just ahead of the party of which he made one. "In England, if his Majesty passes you on the road, you say, 'There goes the King,' and there's an end of it; but here when the court thinks proper to move, all carriages, carts, mules, horses and asses are immediately *embargoed*. Thank God, in an Englishman's Dictionary you can find no explanation of that word." Southey's party traveled for several days through the devastation created by the royal horde. His most Catholic majesty proceeded like the king of the gypsies, stripping the country, robbing the people, burning the trees, and leaving the road strewn with the rotting carcases of horses and mules that had been driven to death.

Such brutal ruin was but an episode in the sodden misery to be observed from end to end of the long road from Corunna. Southey's letters were almost a catalogue of incidents in illustration of it. Near Villa Franca, for instance, where nature seemed a paradise, but where Church and State kept the people in poverty and ignorance, he saw such a sight as Wordsworth had beheld [1] in France, — "a woman carrying a heavy burden of wood on her head, which she had cut herself, and spinning as she went along; a melancholy picture of industrious wretchedness." In Wordsworth such an experience helped to confirm the revolutionary spirit. In Southey it turned loyalty back to England. His indecisions concerning the future were settled; he had a wife in Bristol; the worst of sorrows could be expressed in homesick poems written in dirty Spanish inns; England was clean, comfortable, safe; a man might be comparatively free there, and perhaps an Englishman's hope should be that nothing should disturb the present liberty and order. Comparisons between his own country and Spain were now constantly in Southey's thoughts. He thanks God that the pride of chivalry is extinguished in England, and finds it pleasant that feudal tyranny is there mellowed down, pleasant that, though England may incur the guilt of war, she feels none of its horrors. Noting a case of immorality in Spain, he adds "but in England adultery meets the infamy it deserves." Of Spanish towns he says, "It is not possible to give an Englishman an idea of their extreme poverty and wretchedness." His whole feeling may finally be summed up in a statement made (Jan. 26, 1796) in a letter to Wynn: "I have learned to thank God that I am an Englishman; for though things are not so well there as in Eldorado, they are better than anywhere else."

The change in his thoughts is plainly indicated by these words. As he himself expressed it at a later time, he was

[1] *Prelude*, Book IX.

following the sun as it moved, while others at noon still gazed toward the east. Whether any real change in temper and interest occurred is not so certain. To be sure, he professed still to sympathize with "enthusiasms," but lamented that enthusiasts should turn Quixotes when they might become good husbands and fathers, and that men should be judged upon the Procrustean bed of principle rather than according to their moral character. He had learned to laugh at systems from seeing the mass of wickedness ignored by both pulpit and gallows, "and as for mending the world, Society is an Ass that will kick the man who attempts to ease it of its burthen."[1] Such statements, however, do not indicate any radical change in the temper and sympathies of the former pantisocrat He has gone into harness, he has got a wife, he has something at stake — that is all. The passion for freedom, the sympathy with the enslaved, these remain, though revolution, such as it had become in France, is not desired by him in England or elsewhere. The evidences of this continuity of feeling over the crisis just past in Southey's life are many and striking. He went on writing, for example, inscriptions for martyrs of freedom precisely as before,[2] and, what was more promising for the author's future, he began to make shrewd comments on social wrongs for which he was full of schemes for reform. He quickly caught the main features of the arrested work of Florida Blanca and Pombal in Spain and Portugal, and he analyzed with acuteness and justice the evils that were rooted in the subsidized ignorance of the Portuguese priesthood. Moreover his thought on such subjects now began to be expressed in that lucid and vigorous prose which was to be perhaps his greatest artistic achievement.

[1] *Letters written during a Short Residence in Spain and Portugal*, 234.
[2] *Inscription for a Column at Truxillo*, *op. cit.*, 225; *Inscription for a Bust of Danton*, 270.

One of the most interesting of Southey's youthful sympathies so far displayed had been that for woman in her difficult position in society. *Joan of Arc*, his admiration of Mary Wollstonecraft, a call which he made with Cottle upon Hannah More just before leaving England, — these are evidences of this. The feeling was to suffer no diminution with advancing years. Observing the effects of convents in Lisbon, he said that there was no place in the world where the female mind was not murdered, although woman is a "better animal," purer and more constant, and no less capable of rational education than man. But the problem that came home to Southey with peculiar force was that of finding means of support in English society for the unmarried woman left without the usual provision for maintenance. To make such persons independent he would have them trained for certain industries, such as millinery. This would be feasible, providing that "government consulted the real welfare and morality of the people" or that individuals would "supply the deficiencies of government," neither of which things was to be expected. Of such schemes among Southey's multifarious interests we shall hear more anon.

The months passed at Lisbon were outwardly uneventful. With his uncle the young man took pains to live peaceably. "My uncle and I never molest each other by our different principles." Lisbon itself he had at first no love for; "Lisbon," he dates a letter, "from which place God grant me deliverance." But there he remained during most of his stay, except for an excursion in March to Setuval to see the convent of Arrabida, and except for a sojourn in April at Cintra in the mountains to the north. To the latter place his thoughts were often afterwards to turn with longing. On the slopes of the mountain above the town the English had built their houses, "scattered on the ascent half hid among cork trees, elms, oaks, hazels, walnuts, the tall canes, and the rich green of the lemon gardens." Here, in a secluded place, his uncle had a dwelling surrounded by lemon trees and laurels; there was a little stream running by the door and a prospect of hills tempting one from the sitting room. From the mountain could be seen the bare and melancholy country about Lisbon, a distant convent, a ruined Moorish castle, and the Atlantic. "I cannot . . . describe the ever varying prospects that the many emi-nences of this wild rock present, or the little green lanes over whose bordering lemon gardens the evening wind blows so cool, so rich! . . . I shall always love to think of the lonely house, and the stream that runs beside it, whose murmurs were the last sounds I heard at night, and the first that awoke my attention in the morning." He con-cludes with a quotation from *Anarcharsis;* "C'est un bien pour un voyageur d'avoir acquis un fond d'emotions douces et vives, dont le souvenir se renouvelle pendant tout sa vie."

In spite of homesickness and in spite of the Englishman's dislike of filth, when the time came to leave Lisbon, Southey's heart grew heavy at the thought.[1] For there he had found that retreat from society and himself which he had vainly hoped that pantisocracy would afford. It was in his uncle's library that peace came to his troubled mind. In that generous collection of Spanish and Portuguese lit-erature he came upon a practically inexhaustible new field for learning, and set upon the invasion of it. Immediately upon his arrival at Corunna he had applied himself to the Spanish language, and soon began to understand both poetry and conversation. By the time he had been in Lisbon but a little while he could read Spanish and Portu-guese with no difficulty, call for common necessities, and

[1] For an extensive account of the use made by Southey in his writ-ings, not including his historical works, of his knowledge of Spanish and Portuguese scenery and geography, see Ludwig Pfandl, *Robert Southey und Spanien, Revue Hispaniqne,* 1913, T. 28, 1–315.

converse with the dogs and cats. Reading and some writing, however, occupied far more of his attention than conversation of any sort. In odd moments he wrote long letters home, giving his impressions and experiences in detail so that he could afterwards put together a book on his travels without much additional labor. These letters are hurried and disconnected but graphic and copiously interlarded with information from Spanish chronicles, translations from Spanish poetry, some original verses, and miscellaneous curiosities of learning in his own peculiar vein. A mere list of the erudite references to be found in the little book that he published out of these letters would show how indefatigably he must have labored at the new studies opened before him in his uncle's library. Yet poetry was not forgotten. He was eager for news of *Joan*, which he had not seen out of the press, and he was already anxious for a new edition without Coleridge's additions. He wanted to write a tragedy, but had no leisure for it. The American minister at Lisbon gave him Timothy Dwight's *Conquest of Canaan* to read, and patriotically defended it against the superior claims of Milton. Southey read the book and thought he found some merit in it, but it served chiefly to spur his thoughts of *Madoc*.

II

On the fifth of May, 1796, Southey took ship again for England, and on the fifteenth he leapt ashore at Portsmouth, "the devil a drop of gall . . . left in my bile bag." In two days he was in Bristol with Edith. Yet not even this joy was to be unshadowed by sorrow, for when he arrived, the Fricker family was mourning the death of Robert Lovell, who, less than a fortnight before, had died suddenly of a "fever." His wife was left with no money and a babe in arms. Edith had helped to nurse him, and Southey spent part of his honeymoon trying to publish a volume of his friend's verse in the hope of being able to buy at least a harpsichord for the widow. As for himself and his wife, they had planned to continue living apart until Wynn's pension should commence at Christmas, but the young husband had eighteen pounds remaining from a traveling allowance given him by his uncle, he was still creditor for a little on *Joan's* account, and the faithful Cottle stood ready to make advances on the copyright of a volume of letters from Spain and Portugal. Married life, therefore, began at once in a lodging-house on Oxford Street, Bristol, where the Southeys continued until the arrival of the first payment on their annuity, and with it, the obligation to go to London and begin at the law. In September,[1] meanwhile, Coleridge and his Sara came to live across the street from them, and true to his disclaimer of all rancor, Southey made the first motion toward a reconciliation. He is said to have sent up to Coleridge a slip of paper with the lines from the translation of Schiller's *Conspiracy of Fiesco*: "Fiesco! Fiesco! thou leavest a void in my bosom, which the human race, thrice told, will never fill up."[2] To such an advance of friendship Coleridge could not remain obdurate, and the quarrel was somehow patched up. A few months later, however, although Charles Lamb had told him that they were silly fellows to fall out like boarding-school misses,[3] Coleridge could still write that "the blasted oak puts not forth its buds anew."

It was not long after his return that Southey was again at work. There was the promised volume of poems for Cottle to be prepared, and the new volume of letters. The

---

[1] *Biog. Epis.*, I, 92; Campbell, *Coleridge*, 59.

[2] These lines are also quoted in a review of *Fiesco; or the Genoese Conspiracy; a Tragedy translated from the German of Frederick Schiller* by *G. H. N.* [oehden] *and J. S.* [toddart], (*n.d.*) in *The Critical Review* for February, 1798, 2 ser., v. 22, 201–206. This review is not altogether favorable, but may have been written by Southey himself.

[3] Lamb, *Works*, VI, 52, Oct. 28, 1796.

latter had to be excerpted from communications home, and then to be annotated, no slight labor. Southey had found, besides, a market for his "old rubbish" and for articles on Spanish literature in *The Monthly Magazine,* and always there was *Madoc.* The future was now definitely laid out before him. Willynilly he would be first a "huge lawyer." Wynn was ambitious for him, and in spite of friendly bargaining to the contrary, stipulated for nine hours a day of legal study from his pensioner. This obligation, accepted only with the hope that by meeting it faithfully he could eventually escape from it, was to determine most of Southey's movements during the next four years. But it was an obligation the meeting of which was more and more to be interrupted by better loved pursuits, and at last abandoned with the approval of Wynn himself. During the whole time Blackstone did nothing for the poet but harass his spirit. What Southey wanted was merely a comfortable home in the country with his wife and his books and leisure to write. The law was frankly but a vade mecum. These aspirations were not in any way concealed from Wynn, but they were confided with warmth to Grosvenor Bedford. Southey expected neither amusement, amelioration, nor improvement from the law, but it might get him a little house by the sea and not too far from the post and the bookseller. There he could become a great philanthropist, associating with the dogs, cats, and cabbages and cultivating poetry and potatoes. He invited Grosvenor to a Christmas celebration, when he and Edith should be settled, in order that they might make together a Christmas fire out of the law books. The business of immediate "man-mending," we can here plainly see, was now definitely put aside. To be left to his own devices for his own now clearly distinguished ends, this was all that Southey desired. "The aristocracy," he told Wynn, "have behaved with liberality to *Joan of Arc;* and if they will

favour me by forgetting that I have ever meddled too much
with public concerns, I will take care not to awaken their
memories."

The course thus laid out was not as smooth sailing as
might have been expected. There were certain other responsibilities and certain other ambitions that could not be
surrendered. To meet the former the pension of £160 was
hardly sufficient. In the first place, Southey and Edith
found living in lodgings unbearable; then money had to be
raised to furnish a house, and a house had to be found.
To raise the money a ready pen could write for newspapers
and magazines, but to find a house was more difficult.
London and the law drew them one way, family interests
drew them to Bristol, ill luck and ill health lurked upon
every hand to upset all plans. Few months at a time,
therefore, saw Southey settled in one place until he took
his wife to Keswick in 1803. Meanwhile cares and anxieties
accrued from the other Southeys and the Frickers. Concerning his own family, the law-student's conscience came
near to pricking him, for he was not permitted to forget
that, if he had taken orders, all would now have been well
with them. As it was, his mother struggled on in ill
health, with her lodging-house and with the care of his two
brothers and his consumptive cousin, Margaret Hill. The
boys, Henry and Edward, had soon to be educated, and
Mrs. Southey was in debt, a fact that she characteristically
concealed from her son, and though her house did not pay
its own rent, some persuasion was necessary from him,
when he became apprised of the situation, in order to make
her surrender at a small loss what she could keep only at
a greater. In addition to all this, the needs of the Frickers
were frequently pressing, and when Southey had £10 not
required by his own immediate necessities, he sent them to
Edith's mother. Mr. Hill intervened with assistance now
and then, but if he sent money, it was painstakingly handed

on to Mrs. Southey.   Eventually, of course, the older man's
unfailing kindness and good sense toned down the younger's
pride.

Such were debts of the affections; there were also debts
of ambition which it was no less difficult to forswear.   The
Hymn to the Penates, written immediately after Southey's
return, had been intended as a farewell to the muse as well
as a pantisocratic palinode.   The poet mistakenly thought
that he was going to strike his name from the roll of
authors, though not for very long and not without characteristic regrets, confided as usual to Bedford.   He was
about to leave off writing, just when he had learned what
and how to write.   Was it not a pity that he should give
up his intention to write more verses than Lope de Vega,
more tragedies than Dryden, more epics than Blackmore?
"I have a Helicon kind of dropsy upon me, and *crescit
indulgens sibi.*"   (June 12, 1796.)   To stop poetizing altogether was plainly impossible, of course, and when something had to be given up, either authorship or law or a
country home, it was easy to see which should go.   Nevertheless, for the next four years Southey manfully tried to
reconcile all three aims and to look after his family besides.
The results are evident.   He was constantly on the move
from one place to another.   The old sensitiveness to literary
impulses and the old passion for experiment and imitation
revived with twofold energy under the spur of financial
necessity and the feverish desire to make use of all time
left over from less congenial pursuits.   Lastly the old
"sensibility" showed itself in the manner in which he took
all his personal cares to heart.   The inevitable outcome was
that, at the end of four years of such life, his health began
to show signs of failing under the strain, and a radical
change had to be made that would decide his future with
little more question.

Southey's movements during the years 1796 to 1800 are

somewhat bewildering, but they were all determined by the constant desire to escape from Blackstone, London, and ill health to Edith, the country, and literary work. There was some compensation for him in all this wandering about, for at every turn the poet found friends, two of whom require particular mention at this point. They were Charles Danvers and John May. Just when Southey's acquaintance with the former began it is a little difficult to state, but it was probably during the pantisocracy days at Bristol. The relations between the two men were most affectionate; in his later sojourns in his native city Southey generally stayed at the home of Danvers and his mother. Mrs. Danvers, indeed, came to supply somewhat the place of his own mother to him after Mrs. Southey's death. John May, a little older, was a friend of Mr. Hill's, who had been attracted by the young man at Lisbon. .May was at this time a prosperous merchant, and served as the poet's business adviser, even for a time as an intermediary for him with his uncle.

On the seventh of February, 1797, Southey registered at Gray's Inn, and found two rooms in Newington Butts, where he could miserably spend the few weeks until Edith's arrival. He would study law for nine hours a day, and finish *Madoc* in the evenings, firmly refusing to join a literary club to which he was soon invited. So strict a course, however, was not feasible for the author of *Joan of Arc*. Other literary work and literary society interfered. He began sending verses to *The Oracle* and to *The Telegraph;* he engaged to translate the second volume of Necker's *French Revolution* for twenty-five guineas, Dr. Aiken and son doing the first; and he earned "seven pounds and two pair of breeches in eight months" by writing articles on Spanish and Portuguese poetry as well as by contributing discarded juvenilia to *The Monthly Magazine*. The Godwin set welcomed him, and he dined several times "with Mary Wollstonecraft." She was still the object of Southey's admiration, but her husband he could not endure; though Godwin had noble eyes, language was not vituperatious enough to describe the downward elongation of his nose. Besides, the philosopher loved London, literary society, and talked "nonsense about the collision of mind" (March 13, 1797). The lesser lights of the circle — Mary Hayes, Gilbert Wakefield, George Dyer — made but small impression upon Southey. Of far more importance was the renewal at this time of the poet's acquaintance with Charles Lamb. The two men had met in January, 1795, when Lamb and The Angel Inn had, through Southey's interposition, lost Coleridge to pantisocracy.[1] Since that time Lamb had heard much of Southey. He had greeted *Joan of Arc* with such excessive praise,— deeming the author bound one day to rival no less a poet than Milton,[2] — that Coleridge had had to correct his hasty judgment. Through Lamb Southey continued an acquaintance with Coleridge's pupil, Charles Lloyd, which may have begun in Bath at any time since the preceding October.[3] Lloyd had recently been in London, had confided his troubles to Lamb, and either shortly before or shortly after Southey's arrival in February, returned to Coleridge at Nether Stowey. Lamb, at this time most sympathetic with Lloyd,[4] no doubt had much concerning him to tell Southey. For society in general, however, the latter's distaste was increasing. His sensitiveness and self-absorption told against him, and betrayed him into contempt for the attention accorded to his own now well-known name. He confessed that in company he was a snail popping into his shell or a hedgehog rolling

---

[1] Lamb, *Works* VI, 8, 11 n., ca. June 1, 1796.
[2] Lamb, *Works*, VI, 13, June, 8–10, 1796; 26, June 13, 1796.
[3] Campbell, *Coleridge*, 56.
[4] E. V. Lucas, *Charles Lamb and the Lloyds*, 49–51; *Life of Charles Lamb*, I, 154.

himself up in a rough outside. There had been a short time when high spirits, quick feelings, and enthusiastic principles had made him talkative, but experience had taught the wisdom of self-centering silence. "God never intended that I should make myself agreeable to anybody." (Feb. 16, 1797.)

In May he could flee from London with Edith, and they set out for the Hampshire seacoast. After a trying journey, Southey left his wife ill at Southampton and pushed on afoot through Lyndhurst and Lymington to Burton, a small place near Christ Church. There he found a cottage of three rooms where they could settle down for work and domesticity. The country was a flat plain threaded by many streams from the hills that rose abruptly to the west. The New Forest lay just to the north, and the beach but two miles to the south. There was a fine church with a pile of ruins near by, and a thatched cottage to be seen from their windows. The ensuing summer was full of happiness. Mrs. Southey visited them, and Thomas came to recuperate from a French prison. Friends came, too, among them Cottle with the new volume of poems by Coleridge, Lamb, and Lloyd, and with new plans of publication to be discussed with Southey. Lamb and Lloyd themselves arrived unexpectedly one day. A new phase in the joint relations of all three with Coleridge was about to develop. Lloyd was one in whom mimosa sensibility now and then lapsed into epilepsy and melancholia. His life with Coleridge had been fairly happy for a few months, and by March of this year it had been decided to include some of his poems in the new volume that Cottle was preparing for Coleridge and Lamb.[1] This appeared in June, but by that time Lloyd had felt not a few slights from Coleridge, and had fallen in love with a young woman in Birmingham.[2]

---

[1] Campbell, *Coleridge*, 65.
[2] E. V. Lucas, *Charles Lamb and the Lloyds*, 122.

In his distress he finally came early in August to Lamb for comfort, and the latter, well inclined from his own troubles to help, carried him down to Southey at Burton. Lamb had already spent a week that summer with Coleridge at Nether Stowey, and so had to hasten back to his desk the next morning, but Lloyd remained for the rest of the summer in pleasant companionship with Thomas as well as Robert Southey. The latter could advise him in the writing of "an explicit letter to Sophia," and could sympathize with his grievances against Coleridge.[1]

A friend of far different character and more permanent value was found by Southey at Burton in John Rickman. The latter was a youth who lived at Christ Church close by, "a sensible young man, of rough but mild manners, and very seditious." Rickman's sedition consisted in opposition to Pitt and some notions about man-mending which ultimately resulted in making him the first census-taker. He took the Southeys out in his boat upon the harbor, and the two young men became friends for life.

The retirement of Burton gave welcome opportunity for work. Blackstone came down from London in the luggage, but the law-student commenced writing a tragedy in the stagecoach. Notwithstanding this omen, law was to fill the mornings, and literature, — with a notion of saving the lawyer's reputation under the pseudonym, Walter Tyler, — the rest of the time. The letters from Spain and Portugal had sold so well that Cottle advised a new edition, the volume of poems was being published, *Joan* was ready for another edition, and there was the tragedy on the same subject which had been begun. Besides all this, there was more work for *The Monthly Magazine*, another volume of poems to be hoped for, and always *Madoc*. In addition Cottle had brought a task of purest charity for Southey to share. The kindly Joseph had come upon the sister and

[1] Lamb, *Works*, VI, Lamb to Coleridge, Aug. 24, 1797.

the niece of Chatterton in dire poverty; they had been swindled in 1778 of certain valuable papers of their poet-kinsman by an impecunious, unscrupulous clergyman-baronet named Sir Herbert Croft. All efforts to obtain redress from this person had failed although the stolen material had been utilized in a novel called *Love and Madness* (1779). Southey and Cottle now planned to publish a subscription edition of Chatterton's works for the benefit of the two women, but first attempted again to get some satisfaction from Croft. This took time and was fruitless, so that it was not until November, 1799, that Southey published proposals for the publication in *The Monthly Magazine* together with an explicit account of Croft's rascality. That gentleman replied in *The Gentleman's Magazine* for February, March, and April, 1800, dodging the issue in a whirl of talk about pantisocracy and *Joan of Arc*. The last word necessary was uttered by Southey in the *Monthly* for April of the same year.[1] The number of subscriptions never sufficed to support the printing of the book, but Longman came to the rescue and published it in 1803, allowing some benefit to Mrs. Newton.[2] Cottle did most of the editorial work; Southey probably supervised it and stood sponsor to the public, while Dr. Gregory permitted the republication of his very poor biography of Chatterton.

The idyllic summer at Burton came to an end on September 21, when Southey and his wife went back to Bath to be near Mrs. Southey and more books. Lloyd, still in the thick of sudden intimacy, went with them, and became an inmate of the lodging-house at 8, Westgate Buildings. He had been using recent experience, not to say recent

---

[1] *Month. Mag.*, Nov. 1799, v. 8, 770–772; April, 1800, v. 9, 252. *Gent. Mag.*, v. 70, pt. i, 99, 222, 322, Feb., Mar., Apr., 1800.

[2] *Preface* by Southey to *The Works of Thomas Chatterton* . . . 1803. See *Appendix A*.

friends and their opinions, as material for a novel. This work was done in Southey's company, probably upon Southey's suggestion. The latter had, in the course of his former estrangement from Coleridge, planned (July 31, 1796) a "novel in three volumes of Edmund Oliver." In one of his *Commonplace Books*,[1] furthermore, he made a sketch for a novel with somewhat the same theme as Lloyd's, and with a hero, Oliver Elton, who, like Lloyd's hero, runs away to the army. This note is dated "1798 or 1799" by Warter, but that Southey would have made such a plan after *Edmund Oliver* had been written seems little likely, especially since he added a statement in 1801 that "the soldier part should be omitted." Be that as it may, upon arriving in Bristol, Southey wrote to his brother Tom, "Do you know that Lloyd has written a novel, and that it is going immediately to press?" In the following spring appeared Lloyd's *Edmund Oliver*, published by Cottle and dedicated to Charles Lamb. It is a dull performance except for the fact that the personalities of Coleridge and Southey plainly gave suggestions for the two leading characters. The author's purpose, on the one hand, is to present arguments against unrestrained sensibility and abstract philosophy of the Godwin school of general benevolence, and on the other to plead on behalf of stoicism and private virtue. Edmund Oliver, who shows that abandonment to emotion which Lloyd had seen in Coleridge and from which he had himself suffered, is consumed by unhappy love for a lady of enthusiastic passions who has been convinced and is seduced by an equally enthusiastic democrat, who believes in the Godwin system of morality, has secretly married another woman, and dies in a duel. In his despair at losing the lady, Oliver runs away from his friends, stops eating, lives on nothing but drink and laudanum, and joins a regiment of horse. Fortunately he has a friend, Charles

[1] *Commonplace Book, Series* IV, 9–10.

Maurice, who resides in cottage-seclusion with his wife and children, who preaches and exemplifies the moral influence of nature as opposed to the wickedness of the city, stoicism as opposed to enthusiasm, virtuous conduct in private life as opposed to general benevolence, to democracy, to skepticism, and to metaphysics, and who extricates Oliver from his predicament in the army. There is more to the story after that, but from this point on it merely uses conventional tricks selected and strung together in such a way as to bring the argument to an edifying, if not logical, conclusion. Lloyd denied any intentional reference to Coleridge, but Coleridge naturally saw himself in Edmund Oliver, must have seen his uncomfortably virtuous brother-in-law in Charles Maurice, and was offended.

Meanwhile Lloyd's own love affair was progressing; he now hoped to persuade his lady to a Scotch marriage, and he wrote Lamb that he expected Southey to assist and accompany him in the elopement.[1] This plan was never carried out, but before the end of the year Lloyd went home to Birmingham, where his Sophia lived, and in 1799 he was married to her in quite the usual fashion.

Southey spent the autumn quietly engaged in his usual pursuits. He remained most of the time with his mother at Bath, but visited Danvers for two weeks in Bristol, and renewed his friendship with Joseph Cottle. Now it was, probably, that he found the latter's brother, Amos, making, for Joseph's benefit, a prose translation of the Latin version of the "Poetic Edda." Southey characteristically urged rather the making of a verse translation for publication, for which he offered himself to write an introductory poem.

---

[1] Lamb, *Works*, VI, 120, Coleridge to Lamb [Spring of 1798]. De Quincey distorted these facts (repeated with a question in the *Dictionary of National Biography*) into a story that Lloyd did elope by proxy, and that the proxy was Southey. De Quincey, *Collected Writings*, ed. by Masson, II, 389.

The suggestion was adopted, the book[1] appeared shortly after, and Southey, although he thought lightly[2] of the merits of Amos Cottle's work except as a convenient source of information, contributed twelve pages of blank verse to the volume dealing with the general subject of northern poetry. Meanwhile the time came for him to eat another set of dinners at London, and thither he went with Edith some time before Christmas of 1797. Law there again harassed him, but he found happiness in routing the spiders from an old library that offered material for many learned notes to the second edition of *Joan*. He had recently engaged to write for *The Critical Review*, and now he contracted to supply *The Morning Post* with verses at the rate of a guinea a week in the hope of raising enough money to furnish a house. But he again complained of "swarms of acquaintances who buzz about me and sadly waste my time," and early in February ill health again drove him and his wife back to Bath. Though Lloyd had come to London at about the same time as they, he had been little with them during their stay in town. He was living in a boarding-house, and had got, says Southey, "a vast number of new acquaintances, a false tail, a barber to powder him every morning, and is I believe as happy as he wishes to be." The misunderstanding with Coleridge had, at the same time, grown apace. In November the latter's Higginbotham *Sonnets in the Manner of Contemporary Writers* had appeared in *The Monthly Magazine;* they were good-humoredly directed at Lamb, Lloyd, and Coleridge himself, but the friends[3] took the third as being intended for

---

[1] *Icelandic Poetry, or the Edda of Saemund Translated into English Verse*, by A. S. Cottle, Bristol, 1797; see also F. E. Farley, *Scandinavian Influences in the English Romantic Movement*.

[2] *Taylor*, I, 246–247.

[3] Lamb, *Works*, VI, 119–121; Lucas, *Charles Lamb and the Lloyds*, 61–80.

Southey, and all three felt offended, Lloyd the most and Lamb the least so. In the following March (1798), Coleridge, then deep in his intimacy with the Wordsworths, sent a sarcastic message in reply to Lloyd's request to Cottle that his contributions be omitted from the next edition of Coleridge's poems. Shortly afterwards Lloyd gave the next cut in the publication of *Edmund Oliver*, and in the summer, probably egged on by Lloyd's tattle, Lamb sent his old friend the famous *Theses quaedam Theologicae*, not neglecting to supply Southey with a copy for his enjoyment. In September Coleridge departed for Germany with Wordsworth, and the eclipse was complete. The most interesting result was that Southey became established for a time in Coleridge's place in Lamb's correspondence, though not in his most intimate feeling.

One of Southey's concerns upon reaching Bath was the education of his fourteen-year-old brother, Henry. The lad had shortly before been sent up to Yarmouth to be tutored by George Burnett, now a Unitarian minister in that place. Pantisocracy had not been happy in its effect upon Burnett. In the break-up of that affair he had sided against Southey, and, deprived of his father's support, had joined Coleridge for a time at Clevedon to serve as an incapable assistant in the ill-fated *Watchman* of 1796. After that he had obtained his present position, and a sufficient reconciliation with Southey must in the meantime have taken place to render him eligible for the supervision of Henry. Thus it came about that in May, 1798, Southey went up to Norfolk for a consultation concerning his brother, and was introduced to William Taylor of Norwich.[1] The latter had

---

[1] *Taylor*, I, 211–212, *et passim*. See also O. F. Emerson, *The Earliest English Translations of Bürger's Lenore;* Emerson states (p. 63) that Southey's interest in Taylor's translation of *Lenore* led to a correspondence and eventually to a meeting between the two men. I have encountered no evidence that indicates that such was the order of these events.

now settled down to his comfortable bachelor existence, associating with Dr. Sayers and with the dissenters and "literary circle" of Norwich. He lived in studious, conversational, tobacco-smoking, letter-writing ease, described in characteristic fashion by Borrow in *Lavengro*, and he contributed occasional articles in an extraordinary style upon a variety of curious subjects to *The Monthly Review*. At the age of seventeen (1781–1782) Taylor had spent a little over a year in Germany, and as a result became master of more knowledge of the language and literature of that country than any modern Englishman had up to that time possessed. This knowledge he sought to disseminate, and had already won some renown by the translation (1790) of Bürger's *Lenore*, published in *The Monthly Magazine* for March, 1796. Southey had read this piece with great interest, and attributed it to the hand of Sayers. The latter's acquaintance he now also made, but it was the racier personality of Taylor that attracted him. There was much for the two men to talk of together, and Southey's debt to Taylor for suggestion and criticism in literary matters as well as for thoughtful kindness towards his brother Henry was very great. As they grew older, the intimacy between the two men would have kept warmer if their religious opinions had not tended in opposite directions.

Upon his return home from Norfolk about June first, another revolution took place in Southey's living arrangements. His mother had given up her house in Bath, and with her niece Margaret now joined her son in a little house at Westbury, a pretty village about two miles from Bristol. At the end of June Southey wrote to his brother Tom, describing some of the agony of settling. After hesitating over the appropriate names of Rat Hall, Mouse Mansion, Vermin Villa, Cockroach Castle, and Spider Lodge, the Southeys dubbed the place Martin Hall from the birds that had built and bemired upon it. This was to be the home of the whole family for the next twelve months. Books, poetry, and friends, all were there to be had, and the poet was very happy. A certain amount of law, supposedly, was to be read, but he was beginning to take that obligation less and less seriously, and we hear chiefly of literary work. "I have never," Southey wrote in 1837, "before or since, produced so much poetry in the same space of time." In the late summer of 1798 he published second editions of his *Joan of Arc* and of the *Letters written during a Short Residence in Spain and Portugal*, and at the end of the same year another book of poems (*Poems* 1799). For the last-named volume, for an *Annual Anthology* undertaken upon Taylor's suggestion, and for *The Morning Post*, he composed a whole host of minor pieces, — eclogues, ballads, lyrics, and occasional verses of many sorts. He continued at the same time to review for the *Critical*, he went steadily on with *Madoc*, and his prolific mind swarmed with ideas for still more works. Among these dreams were a tragedy that never was written, and "an Arabian poem of the wildest nature; . . . *The Destruction of the Dom Danyel*," which became *Thalaba*.

Some of the poet's new friends contributed much to the encouragement of all this work. He corresponded with Lamb for one, from whom came characteristic comments on his ballads, eclogues, and other minor pieces as well as extracts from *John Woodvil*. In return, although the letters are apparently not preserved, Southey evidently stimulated Lamb's literary and antiquarian interests, putting him upon the track of such favorites as Quarles and Wither.[1] Southey's intimacy with Lloyd, meanwhile, had met the fate of many of Lloyd's attachments; "I never knew a man," the former wrote, "so delighted with the exteriors of friendship. . . . I believe he now sincerely regards me, though the only person who has

[1] Lamb *Works*, VI 124–149.

ever upon all occasions advised, and at times reproved him, in unpalliated terms. . . . I love him, but I cannot esteem him, and so I told him." In spite of this frankness, Lloyd wrote one poem of friendship to Southey in 1800[1] and another in 1815 dedicating to him a translation of Alfieri;[2] Southey, on his part, visited Lloyd at Old Brathay for a few days in 1804.[3] A man of another calibre was William Taylor, whom the poet now began to consult with regard to many personal and literary matters; other friends nearer home were Danvers, an appreciative companion for a long walk such as Southey took into Herefordshire in August of this year, and Humphry Davy, a dazzling inspiration, who, though barely twenty-one, had just been made assistant to Thomas Beddoes at a "Pneumatic Institution" which the latter had established in Bristol. There, in the course of experiments for the discovery of a cure for consumption, Davy was beginning his notable career in chemistry. Southey was so fascinated that he set to work reading Davy's scientific treatises, and Coleridge a little later tried to set up a chemical laboratory of his own at Keswick. But Davy had written verses before becoming a chemist, and often did one or the other of the two youths walk the two miles between Martin Hall and the Pneumatic Institution in order to exchange chemistry and poetry. "Miraculous," "extraordinary," were the adjectives that Southey applied to his new friend. The disease that Davy was seeking to understand came closely home to him, for his cousin and mother were both strangely ailing under his own roof, and now he himself was beginning to suffer seizures about the head and heart with a cough and a pain in the

---

[1] Charles Lloyd, *Nugae Canorae*, Third ed. 1819.

[2] Lloyd, *The Tragedies of Alfieri*, 1815.

[3] *Warter* I 284, *Taylor* I 520. The statement in the article on Lloyd in the *Dictionary of National Biography* that Southey visited Lloyd at Old Brathay upon returning from Portugal is apparently an error.

side which gave him serious alarm.   He was willing, therefore, to permit himself to be experimented upon, more so
than to have the ordinary practitioners treat him.   Davy
set him to breathing nitrous oxide which he had just discovered, and they studied the effects together; "Oh, Tom!
such a gas has Davy discovered, the gaseous oxide!   Oh,
Tom! I have had some; it made me laugh and tingle in
every toe and finger tip.   Davy has actually invented a new
pleasure, for which language has no name.   Oh, Tom! I am
going for more this evening; it makes one strong, and so
happy! so gloriously happy! and without any after-debility,
but, instead of it, increased strength of mind and body.   Oh,
excellent air-bag!   Tom, I am sure the air in heaven must
be this wonder-working gas of delight!"   In return for these
drafts of paradise, Davy received drafts of *Madoc* upon his
visits to Martin Hall.   Section by section, the poem was read
to him as it was composed, and received his cordial approba-
tion.   These were roseate days for both.

So the winter of 1798–1799 passed swiftly by, and when
May returned, Southey dutifully, though with sinking
heart, went up alone to London for another term of dinners.
The result was the same as before; — too much confinement, too many acquaintances, too much law to read,
homesickness, and no joy but in hunting the bookstalls,
even though he lodged at Brixton with Bedford.   At the
end of the month, therefore, Southey fled back to Edith,
and found that another removal of his household had become necessary.   The lease of Martin Hall could not be
renewed, and the whole family had to return to Bristol,
Robert and Edith finding shelter under the kindly roof of
Danvers.

House-hunting was again the order of the day, and
Southey went down to Burton, most of the way a-foot, to
look for a place.   There he found that their former genial
neighbor, Biddelcomb, was willing to throw two adjoining

cottages into one so as to make a small house with spare room, sitting-room, and above all, a book room. It was not pretentious but for the Southeys it would be a "palace." Possession not being possible until October, the poet and his wife would go on a journey in the interval. Late in July they set out for Devonshire,[1] and arrived on the twenty-fifth, both wet and Edith ill, at Minehead. Southey walked on alone to Lynmouth and Ilfracombe, finding the former second only to Cintra. The wild beauty of the Valley of Stones also impressed him deeply, but the barren moors repelled him. The south of Devon was to be their next stage, but on the way they turned aside to visit the Coleridges at Nether Stowey. For another reconciliation, made easier, no doubt, by Lloyd's elimination of himself from the situation, had now taken place, this time upon Coleridge's initiative. The latter had returned from Germany some time in July, and had written[2] at once to Southey entreating an explanation and a renewal of old ties. His words strikingly suggest certain traits of the man to whom they were written; after entreating Southey that, if they should be thrown together in the future, they should meet with kindness, he concludes, "We are few of us good enough to know our own hearts, and as to the hearts of others, let us struggle to hope that they are better than we think them, and resign the rest to our common Maker." Southey appears to have replied to this letter by citing the slanders that Lloyd had reported. Coleridge, in return, disavowed everything, and referred to Lamb, Wordsworth, Poole, even Lloyd himself as witnesses to prove that he had never accused Southey of any offense against himself except enmity. Finally a letter of August 8 from Thomas Poole was delivered to Southey at Minehead by special messenger, clinching Coleridge's statements and effecting the recon-

---

[1] *Commonplace Book, Series* IV, 517-524.
[2] Coleridge, *Letters*, I, 303-304; Campbell, *Coleridge*, 103.

ciliation.   Shortly afterwards the two families were together at Nether Stowey, and on August twentieth Southey was writing at the same table again with his old associate: "Here I am, and have been some days wholly immersed in conversation. . . . The hours slip away, and the ink dries upon the pen in my hand." From Stowey they went together to Ottery, where all the small literary men and radicals came forth to meet them, and where Southey made the acquaintance of Coleridge's family, and heard deaf old Mrs. Coleridge long for the presence of Samuel's father to set him right in an argument. A few weeks of rambling in south Devon followed, and ended by the Southeys settling down in September at Exeter until their new house should be ready. For part of the time the Coleridges were their guests.

It was during Southey's visit at Stowey that the famous squib, *The Devil's Thoughts*, or, as it was afterwards called, *The Devil's Walk*, was composed by the two men.

> "There, while the one was shaving,
>   Would he the song begin;
> And the other, when he heard it at breakfast,
>   In ready accord join in." [1]

The one who was shaving was undoubtedly Southey, and the spark of the *jeu d'esprit* was suggested by William Taylor, who had sent him his translation of Voss's *The Devil in Ban*.[2] Southey had been delighted with the idea contained in this piece; "A meeting of devils might make fine confessions of whom they had been visiting." Out of this suggestion rose *The Devil's Thoughts*, and an odd history the verses had. They were published anonymously in *The Morning Post* on September 6, 1799, and became imme-

[1] *Works*, 179.

[2] *Taylor*, I, 228, 233; *Month. Mag.*, v. 7, 139; *Historic Survey of German Literature*, II, 64.

diately popular.[1] A story obtained wide circulation that
they had been composed by Dr. Porson at an evening party
which took place, according to Porson's nephew, at a
Dr. Deloe's, and according to Southey himself, at Dr. Vincent's. Illustrations were drawn for later editions by
Landseer and by Cruikshank, and changes were rung upon
the theme by Byron, Shelley, and lesser hands. The fabri-
cations concerning the authorship were put at rest in 1827
by Southey's publication of the piece expanded to fifty-
seven verses instead of the original fourteen, and including
a description of its origin and a reference to Dr. Porson's
supposed authorship.

The Devil's Thoughts was not the only literary work that
Southey engaged in during these months of moving about.
He complained at the time that his health demanded so
many hours of exercise that none were left for more serious
pursuits, but the mass of writing that he was carrying on
under such circumstances makes one suspect that the study
of law was the only labor serious enough to be sacrificed.
At any rate, we find him writing on July 12, 1799, "Yesterday I finished *Madoc*, thank God! and thoroughly to my
own satisfaction," and immediately he decided on the theme
and metrical form of his next long poem, *Thalaba*. He
went to work upon this at once. It was to be printed
promptly, and unlike *Madoc*, was expected to prove popular and profitable. By September 22 the author wrote,
"*Thalaba the Destroyer* is progressive," and by the end
of October he had begun the fifth book while he gutted
the libraries and book shops of Exeter for notes.

But the law-student had many other literary irons in
the fire during these summer rambles in search of health.
A throng of epic figures filled his imagination; "it seems
as though all I have yet done is the mere apprenticeship

[1] Coleridge, *Poetical and Dramatic Works;* T. J. Wise, *Bibliography
of Coleridge.*

of poetry, the rude work which has taught me only how to manage my tools." On his way through Devonshire Southey read the *Koran*, and Taylor,[1] after the cue of his German poets, had been suggesting the use of hexameters in English. Consequently, on his visit to Stowey, Southey easily persuaded Coleridge to join him in an hexameter epic on Mohammed. Both men made beginnings, and Southey expected to finish without Coleridge, but neither left anything but fragments. At the same time Southey was borrowing from Taylor[2] a copy of Bodmer's *Noachide*, and thinking of making his way through it by dint of patience, curiosity, and the "dark-lanthorn glimmer of grammar and dictionary." In similar fashion he was attacking Dutch for the sake of Jacob Cats's poem on the deluge. This, he agreed with Taylor, was the noblest epic subject afforded by the "Christian system" or "perhaps any system." If he had but leisure, what a plan he would mold of the idea. But there was also Zoroaster, and on the third of September Southey received a copy of the *Zend-Avesta* from John May. By the twenty-seventh of October he had "extracted the kernel"; "the outline of the mythology is fine, and well adapted for poetry, because the system is comprehensible." In this respect he compares it favorably with the Hindoo fables, which he thought were rendered unpoetical by their intricacy. The most magnificent system of all, however, was the Edda, and he will one day "graft a story upon it, to contrast with the oriental picture of *Thalaba*."[3] All these schemes were topped on September 22, when he announced that he had determined to undertake one great historical work, — a history of Portugal in two, probably three, volumes in quarto that would easily surpass Gibbon in its success.

One might suppose that something of Coleridge's impractical expansiveness had infected Southey, if it were not

[1] *Taylor*, I, 277.   [2] *Ibid.*, I, 276–280.   [3] *Ibid.*, I, 304.

that he was still sending the usual number of somehow finished products to the press. The first volume of the *Annual Anthology*[1] appeared during the summer. It had been undertaken on Taylor's suggestion, and was made up of pieces of Southey's own that had been saved from the newspapers or the flames, and of a few dragooned from his friends. He admitted that there was barely enough cork in the book to float the lead; Taylor heartily agreed with this judgment, Coleridge regretted he should so waste his time, Lamb mildly jeered, and nobody bought. Nevertheless the editor went on with his plans for another volume, and Coleridge wrote him a long letter of criticism, suggesting a better principle of classification, and discussing the bestowal on the volume of *Christabel* "if finished." In addition to this unpromising venture, Southey published a new volume of poems during the year (1799), and went on reviewing for the *Critical*, writing articles on the American Indians for *The Morning Post*, and still planning a moneymaking tragedy.

In October, after a season of such activity, he finally carried his household of wife, mother, and cousin down to the new "palace" at Burton, hoping there to find peace both for his chosen and his necessary labors, but in vain. Hardly were the rooms swept, when the strain under which he had been working made itself felt in a "nervous fever." The new home was abandoned at the end of a month, and Southey and Edith moved back to lodgings with Danvers in order to have the advice of Beddoes and Davy. Enforced rest and the miraculous gas-bags, the latter taken not without misgivings, effected some improvement, but several causes — the anxieties of the past few years, too much sedentary labor, and an unsettled way of living — had contributed seriously to weaken Southey's health. He

---

[1] Taylor, I, 291–300; Coleridge, *Letters*, I, 312–314; Lamb, *Works*, VI, 177.

was evidently dyspeptic, he was afraid of heart or lung trouble, and, worst of all, he was in an alarmingly disturbed not to say unbalanced state of nerves. The last-named affliction he attributed in later years largely to the excitement incidental to poetic composition. Writing in 1811 to Landor[1] with the experiences of this period in mind, he said, "I could not stand the continuous excitement which you have gone through in your tragedy. In me it would not work itself off in tears; the tears would flow while [I was] in the act of composition, and they would leave behind a throbbing head, and a whole system in a state of irritability, which would soon induce disease in one of its most fearful forms." Such apprehension of insanity occurred not infrequently to Southey, and had its influence in the efforts that he made in later life to control his sensibilities. At this time, as is stated in another part of the letter just referred to, he decided that the only permanent cure both for himself and his wife, who had been ailing ever since her marriage, was to be found in a sojourn abroad in a milder climate. He began at once to make plans and to seek ways and means for such a course. His first hope was that Coleridge with his family might join them at some Mediterranean place. How the two men cursed the war for closing France to them, and then discussed the possibility of taking their families to Italy, Constantinople, the Greek islands, Trieste! All this was futile, for Coleridge expected that duty to the Wedgwoods would cause him to finish his *Life of Lessing*, and so keep him in England. Early in February, therefore, Southey, still suffering from his complaint, which seems to have been merely the scholar's dyspepsia, aggravated by fear of heart-trouble or consumption, wrote to his uncle in Lisbon for advice. In spite of fears that this would not be what he

---

[1] From an unpublished letter in the Forster Library in the South Kensington Museum.

wished, he nevertheless went ahead with plans for work in Portugal, and in a couple of months reply came from Mr. Hill in the form of an invitation to Lisbon and Cintra. Preparations for the Southeys' leaving England began at once.

But before escape could be consummated, certain necessities had to be provided. The project for going abroad had to be explained to Wynn, who was not inclined to be obdurate upon this point, though still quite firm upon another. For Southey also attempted, unsuccessfully, to mitigate his friend's generous ambition, and proposed to go into chancery instead of common law, on the ground that the former would be less uncongenial, no less certain of profit, and free of the possibility of causing him to argue against a man's life. As for ambition, the poet confessed in good round terms that he had none of it. To Bedford he wrote (Dec. 21, 1799), as usual, with even less reserve, "Reading law is laborious indolence — it is thrashing straw. I have read, and read, and read; but the devil a bit can I remember. I have given all possible attention, and attempted to command volition. No! the eye read, the lips pronounced, I understood and reread it; it was very clear; I remembered the page, the sentence, — but close the book, and all was gone!"

The question of money for the journey was, of course, particularly pressing. Illness had kept Southey from reviewing for three months, and newspaper work had been given up before that. He would keep up his connection with the *Critical* by writing a few reviews of Spanish and Portuguese books while abroad, but he was sure to lose £100 from this source alone. He thought of finishing *Thalaba* in a hurry, but changed his mind, especially since his old schoolmate, Peter Elmsley, sent him £100 in the emergency through the kindness of Wynn. Great comfort, moreover, must have been derived by Southey from the reports that Coleridge, now in London writing for Stuart in *The Morning Post*, sent[1] concerning the sale of *Joan* and the *Poems* of 1797. For the copyright of these two volumes Longman had paid Cottle £370 after the latter had already obtained profit from them to the amount of £250. Southey's return had been £138 12s. "You are a strong swimmer," wrote Coleridge, "and have borne up poor Joey with all his leaden weights about him, his own and other people's." The name of Southey had thus come to have a financial value, and Coleridge was full of schemes for his friend to turn it into cash in the present need. He was prepared to ask £200 on the author's behalf for *Thalaba*, concerning which Longman was already solicitous, and Southey, encouraged, determined to ask not less than £100 for the first edition alone. Coleridge had other plans besides. One was the composition of a "History of the Levelling Principle," to be written by skimming through Brücker, Lardner, Russell, and Andrews. Southey could do this, Coleridge argued, instead of torturing himself for Stuart, merely by writing a sheet of letter paper full a day for twelve weeks. He would himself contribute "a philosophical introduction that shall enlighten without offending." The profit was to be sixty or seventy guineas. If it could be done anonymously, Southey was ready to consider the idea, but to this the booksellers would not consent. Coleridge, undaunted, had another project, — that his friend should write a history of poetry for the use of schools,— but was again met with refusal, because Southey felt that he knew too little German, French, and Italian, and would not set his name to work that did not satisfy his own judgment. But a novel was what Coleridge, upon Longman's suggestion, urged above all other things as a means of making money, especially, he added, if four hundred pounds could be got by no more pains than were

[1] Coleridge, *Letters*, I, 319–330.

required for a *St. Leon*. If he and Southey were together, they might easily "toss up" such a work. Though the latter offered no encouragement to this notion either, he had a few alternatives. Again he thought of a drama, but Coleridge in his turn disapproved of this as of a periodical with signed articles. Southey concluded that the only certain thing was still the trip to Portugal. "My eyes and ears are sufficiently open and quick, and I shall certainly pick up a hundred pounds' worth of matter upon my way." Beyond that were the hopes involved in his grander projects, *Madoc*, *Thalaba*, and the *History of Portugal*.

Early in April, therefore, Southey made bold to fix the day of his departure, having carefully arranged for the disposition of his affairs in case of accident. *Madoc* was left with Danvers. The written books of *Thalaba* were left with Wynn. The second volume of *The Annual Anthology* having appeared — no more prosperously than the first — just before his departure, the editor delegated Davy and Danvers, unless Coleridge would take it, to manage the third. Coleridge was named, too, as his literary executor, John May being appointed to care for his other interests. All he had was to be used for Edith, his brothers, and his mother, unless she went to live with Miss Tyler at the College Green. Having thus carefully stewarded his small estate, Southey was ready for the voyage, no little undertaking in those days for a man prone to be seasick.

III

The welter of emotional excitement through which Southey had passed in the years from 1796 to 1798, however characteristic of the man and the age, had not been a comfortable experience. Pantisocracy, to Coleridge a system of thought, had been to Southey a rule of conduct, and when it failed as such, there resulted a chaos from which it became his chief concern to escape into tranquillity.

Coleridge might go on building ever new foundations for ever new philosophies, but Southey longed "for a repose that ever is the same." Such was always the end of mimosa sensibility in common minds with a strong sense of moral responsibility. Southey and Wordsworth both found that the fever of excitement engendered by new ideas prevented the fulfillment of old duties. Therefore they sought escape from the fever by denying the new ideas, by a surrender to mysticism, intolerance, and self-isolation. They took a view of life as their rule of conduct and as the faith upon which their minds did indeed repose which was in both fundamentally the same. They adopted that form of idealism which was embodied in the religion of nature, but they adopted it as an end of speculation, as the quietus to emotions otherwise engendered, and finally, having lost confidence in the natural goodness of the great mass of the population, as an antidote to popular revolution and as an adequate sanction for the existing constitution of Church and State. Their political apostle, in other words, was no longer Rousseau, no longer Godwin, but Burke. Enough has been said to show that Southey, a Quixote rather than a monastic by nature, was never able to surrender himself completely to the quietism which such a faith encouraged in Wordsworth. Nevertheless, it is plain that, at the end of his early troubled years, emotional calm was the thing he desired, even at the cost of intelligence. He owned[1] now (Mar. 12, 1799) to a dislike of all strong emotion; a book like *Werther* gave him unmingled pain, and he proposed to dwell in his own poetry rather on that which affects than on that which agitates. He said (Sept. 22, 1797), with great relief, that his mind held no more hopes and fears, no doubts, no enthusiasms, — that it was quiet and repelled all feelings that might disturb. He forswore metaphysics (June 12, 1796), and thought he could

[1] *Taylor*, I, 261–262.

prove that "all the material and necessarian controversies [were] 'much ado about nothing.'" Hence it would be that the children in Southey's household would be named for no series of philosophers-ascendant; rather would he bless the hour he "'scaped the wrangling crew," dodge the issues of the mind under cover of religion and common sense, and give Coleridge just grounds for complaining of his "unthinkingness." His religion had, of course, not yet adopted the Church, but he could now easily have refuted the charge of atheism, not so easily that of Socinianism. Nevertheless the true direction of his feelings is shown by the statement made at this time that he would have given every intellectual gift he had for the implicit faith that would have made it possible for him to enter the Church.

As it was, he henceforth devoted most of his poetry to the expression of the worship of nature in various forms.[1] Here, of course, he was upon the same ground with Wordsworth, and we shall see that he paralleled upon a lower level all the striking peculiarities of the latter's theory and practice. Some of his most charming poems, for instance, are blank verse pieces that read not unlike the less lofty parts of the *Prelude*.

> "To you the beauties of the autumnal year
>   Make mournful emblems, and you think of man
>   Doom'd to the grave's long winter, spirit-broken,
>   Bending beneath the burden of his years,
>   Sense-dull'd and fretful, 'full of aches and pains,'
>   Yet clinging still to life.   To me they show
>   The calm decay of nature when the mind
>   Retains its strength, and in the languid eye
>   Religion's holy hopes kindle a joy
>   That makes old age look lovely.   All to you

---

[1] For a discussion of certain aspects of Southey's poems on nature, see, J. Schmidt, *Robert Southey, sein Natürgefühl in seinen Dichtungen*, Leipzig, 1904.

Is dark and cheerless; you in this fair world
See some destroying principle abroad,
Air, earth, and water full of living things,
Each on the other preying; and the ways
Of man, a strange, perplexing labyrinth,
Where crimes and miseries, each producing each,
Render life loathsome, and destroy the hope
That should in death bring comfort. Oh, my friend,
That thy faith were as mine! that thou couldst see
Death still producing life, and evil still
Working its own destruction; couldst behold
The strifes and troubles of this troubled world
With the strong eye that sees the promised day
Dawn through this night of tempest! All things, then,
Would minister to joy; then should thine heart
Be heal'd and harmoniz'd, and thou wouldst feel
God, always, everywhere, and all in all" [1]

Similarly, in his most intimate letters, Southey dwells upon this mystic apprehension of deity in nature. He records[2] (May 25, 1797) that to lie and contemplate an ancient tree filled him with feelings of indefinable and inexpressible delight, feelings that made him a happier and better man. The same thought occurs in a striking letter (Sept. 10, 1797) to John May, in which Southey says that the imagination peoples the air with intelligent spirits and animates every herb with sensation.

"Wherever there is the possibility of happiness, infinite power and infinite benevolence will produce it. The belief of a creating intelligence is to me a feeling like that of my own existence, an intuitive truth: it were as easy to open my eyes and not see, as to meditate upon this subject and not believe. — The recollection of scenery that I love recalls to me those theistic feelings which the beauties of nature are best fitted to awaken."

[1] *Works*, 149–150, Westbury, 1798.
[2] See also *In a Forest, Metrical Tales; Works*, 182, Westbury, 1797.

Akenside's notion of finding in the Greek gods symbols of the God of nature was, of course, as we see in such sentiments, actively shared by Southey. In the letter just quoted he had said, in words reminding one of Wordsworth's wish to be "a pagan suckled in a creed outworn" for sake of seeing Proteus and old Triton, that he almost wished that he believed in the local divinities of the pagans, and he writes in the *Hymn to the Penates*, a poem plainly suggested by Akenside's *Hymn to the Naiads*, that the ancient poets did not dream idly in suggesting that earth was peopled with deities, because dryads, oreads, and river gods, — in other words, nature, — were infallible teachers of reverence, holiness, and purity of thought.[1]

All the usual romantic concomitants of such a faith were also to be found in Southey. The world was checkered by the dualism of good and evil, peopled by beings naturally good but capable of evil. Good was to be found and fostered in the retirement of nature; evil grew rank in society. God made the country; God made man; but man made the town, and the town rotted. Therefore Southey expresses repeatedly in his letters "an unspeakable loathing" for London. His heart sank within him whenever he approached the place, and all the ideas that he associated with it were painful. Only in the country or in the outskirts of Bristol, where within half an hour one could be among rocks and woods with no company except the owls and jackdaws, could a man be virtuous and happy. Rousseau might be buried in Paris, but his spirit remained at Ermenonville, whence a traveler was sure to return purified of heart.[2] The city, consequently, became for Southey one of his symbols of all evil, a veritable wood of error out of which the good spirit sought to escape. Long after pantisocracy was a vanished dream, he constantly played with

[1] *Hymn to the Penates, Poems,* 1797; *Works,* 156, Bristol, 1796.
[2] *Poems,* 1797; *Works,* 181, Bristol, 1796.

the idea of a flight that would carry him far beyond the
bounds, not only of London, but of Britain and all the
pollution of society. He fancied a fairy ship, a new ark,
that would bear him and his family to some island in the
sea where they might stand upon the shore, congratulating
themselves that no mariner would ever reach their quiet
coast, and where life would pass away like one long childhood without a care.[1] These were dreams; in reality he
found two ways of escape, which bulk as largely in his
work as the worship of nature and the fear of society.

> "Type of the wise who soar but never roam,
> True to the kindred points of heaven and home,"

he cherished most warmly the love of home and the expectation of heaven. The desire for a household of his own
has, of course, been amply in evidence in the troubled years
of moving about that we have just reviewed. It is the
burden of most of Southey's letters during the whole period;
a home is to give him the relief that pantisocracy failed to
afford. The first poem that he composed after his return
to Edith, — planned indeed on board the vessel from
Lisbon, — was a *Hymn to the Penates*. Here he records
that, whether amid scenes of intemperance at college he
mused on man redeemed and perfected or whether he
wandered abroad or in cities "an unfit man to mingle
with the world," still he had loathed human converse,
and had pined to possess household gods of his own,
even if they had to be sought far beyond the Atlantic.[2]
Home, however, and those friendships which Southey
always associated with it, were both subject to sorrows
such as he already well knew. Losses by death in the
circle of his friends and family had been and would be but
too frequent. Heaven, therefore, was the ultimate haven

[1] *Metrical Letter written from London*, *Poems*, 1799; *Works*, 149,
London, 1798.   [2] *Poems*, 1797; *Works*, 156, Bristol, 1796.

of the former pantisocrat. There he would be reunited with those loved ones he had lost, a notion that recurs with tragic insistency throughout the rest of his life. One of his most charming poems is a blank verse epistle in which he expresses the hope of returning to his kindred from the "Vanity-town" of London; failing in that, he would expect to find in heaven those he had loved on earth.[1]

Here then was the philosophy that was to be Southey's guide during the rest of his life. He would shun evil, both its effects upon him from without and its growth within, by fleeing like Rousseau from the general society of the city to the retirement of his home in the country where he might worship the principle of good displayed in nature, and devote himself to the affections and pursuits that accorded with domestic happiness and the fulfillment of private duties. The part of Epictetus in all this is plain, but Epictetus was not all. The self-sufficiency of the soul that has committed itself to an ideal is the theme of those romances that Southey read so eagerly in his youth and of Spenser, whom he well-nigh worshiped. His stoicism, therefore, is but the spiritual independence of the perfect knight of *The Faerie Queene* and of Wordsworth's *Happy Warrior;* Epictetus, while confirming much, contributed nothing new to this view of life.

A fortune-teller once promised Southey "a gloomy capability of walking through desolation," and the noblest side of the man is displayed in the manner in which he confirmed that prophecy. He proposed now to govern and to judge his own conduct, his own work, solely by his own ideals. But pride was the besetting sin of his race, and Southey's strength of soul was not to escape that pride which, though spiritual, is yet pride and yet unlovely. The weakness, the strength, and the inner kinship with

[1] *Metrical Letter written from London, Poems,* 1799; *Works,* 149, London, 1798.

Wordsworth as well, are expressed in the poem written at Westbury in 1798 *To a Friend, Inquiring if I would live over my youth again,* and in the writer's constant vaunt that he feels no regret for any action of his past. The happy warrior of Wordsworth, it will be recalled, was one who

"wrought
Upon the plan that pleased his boyish thought,"

and whatever resulted from this plan, remained content in the expectation of heaven's applause. So Southey writes that he is satisfied with what he is and has been, and that he looks to the future with cheerful hope that happiness will be his reward hereafter.[1] Here was more than a suggestion that self-sufficiency in virtue might well degenerate into the complacent self-righteousness, into that incapability of changing their minds or apprehending new ideas which not a few contemporaries found to be such irritating characteristics of the lake poets.

Southey's political feelings were consistent with such a view of life. We have already noted that he had no relish now for any personal share in revolution. He wished to be left alone to wreak his energies upon the pursuits — domestic, studious, and literary — that he had chosen. Yet his feelings with regard to public affairs were none the less positive. Political goodness resided in the people when left to themselves and to nature. They were now, however, generally corrupted by the evils arising from contact with the great and the rich, from association in towns and cities, and from the oppressions of rulers, who were depraved by the nature of their position. Mobs and tyrants, in short, were the dragons and Orgoglios of humanity. The old government of France Southey therefore still condemned, and to that extent approved the revolution by which the people, with natural right upon their side, overthrew it. When the

[1] *Metrical Tales,* 1805; *Works,* 141, Westbury, 1798.

tyranny of the Paris mob, however, finally developed into
the dictatorship of Napoleon, the poet's old feeling of distrust for cities, rulers, and warriors was merely confirmed.
The French might have done much, but they lacked morality and were weak as children. The English were, after all,
the only men, and though Southey had little respect even
for them, he was ready to die in order to make them what
they ought to be. Yet he no longer trusted in "the per-
suadability of man," nor felt "the mania of man-mending."
"The ablest physician can do little in the great lazar house
of society; it is a pest-house that infects all within its
atmosphere. He acts the wisest part who retires from the
contagion; nor is that part either a selfish or a cowardly
one; it is ascending the ark, like Noah, to preserve a
remnant which may become the whole." (June 26, 1797.)

This disclaimer of the passion for "man-mending," and
this desire to "retire from the contagion" did not, however,
prevent Southey from taking active interest in certain
efforts, humanitarian rather than political, to improve the
"lazar house" in which he lived. He denied himself sugar,
for instance, in the hope of discouraging the slave trade,
and he tried to persuade others to do the same. More
interesting were certain schemes suggested to him by some
of his new friends. With May and another he drew up a
plan to establish a farm and asylum to which poor conva-
lescents might go when dismissed from the hospitals, and
support themselves by light labor in gardening or manufacture. For about a year this idea seems to have been
kept under discussion, but nothing appears to have come
of it. There were other schemes as well. At Bath, in the
spring of 1798, Southey investigated an old charity for John
May, and discovered that thirteen paupers were supported
like paupers upon a foundation that had increased in value
to £100,000, and that well-nigh £5000 a year went to no
one knew who. John May himself was at the same time

opening an office in London, where he might receive beggars and learn their histories.

Still another idea, and one that promised more tangible results, was worked out in some detail with John Rickman, of whom Lamb said that he was very intimate with Southey, but never read his poetry. Rickman's chief interest was in political economy, and out of this his new proposal to Southey arose. He admitted that poetry was one of those human superfluities that we should feel awkward without, but he had been surprised that Southey did not use his facility in writing to some more useful purpose. He therefore suggested (Jan. 4, 1800) that his friend take as his subject the economic amelioration of woman, investigate the Béguinages of Holland and Flanders, and write a book proposing similar institutions for the benefit of women in England. Rickman himself would furnish the "dry deductions on the head of political economy," but he longed to see Southey in prose, believing that he had both the conscience and the imagination necessary for this work. "You like women better than I do; therefore I think it likely that you may take as much trouble to benefit the sex, as I to benefit the community by their means." Southey responded to all this with great interest, and they went so far as to plan for Rickman's coming to Bristol so that they could be together for the work. But before anything could be decided, Southey was off to Portugal, and after that both men were otherwise too occupied ever to carry out the scheme, although both frequently referred to it with interest.

As it was, by far the largest portion of Southey's time during the four years from 1796 to 1800 was devoted to poetry in one form or another. *Madoc* was now put together, to be taken apart again and rewritten later. *Thalaba* was planned and begun. Lastly, most of those smaller pieces were composed which have given Southey his best claim to popularity as a poet. The reason for writing these was the need of bread. They appeared in *The Monthly Magazine, The Morning Post, The Oracle*, in the two volumes of poems published in 1797 and 1799, and in the two volumes of *The Annual Anthology* for 1799 and 1800. The poet's purpose from now on was for the most part didactic. Dreary as the immediate prospects of society appeared, and vain though the hope might be of his doing anything to help mankind personally, he declared, "I will at least leave something behind me to strengthen those feelings and excite those reflections in others, from whence virtue must spring. In writing poetry with this end, I hope I am not uselessly employing my leisure hours." (June 26, 1797.)

This added stress upon the function of the poet as moral teacher was, of course, but the natural development of the juvenile homilectics of *Joan*, and in all other respects Southey now followed up the veins that had been opened before pantisocracy. Postponing consideration for the present of the more ambitious pieces, we find in the shorter ones the same sensitiveness as before to new literary tendencies, and the same facility at imitating the devices suggested by others. The themes were supplied by the studies to which Southey was more and more turning his attention, and by the moral convictions with which experience was stiffening his spirit. Nature being the great source of happiness and of virtue, the burden of many of the blank verse reflective poems, of the sonnets, inscriptions, and other lyrics, is that "the world is too much with us," that man were better if he would but retire to a country home away from the corruptions of society. Nature again, as the great source of good, is also the great source of moral instruction, and in such poems as *The Oak of our Fathers, The Holly Tree, The Ebb Tide, Autumn, Recollections of a Day's Journey in Spain*, the moral lessons

are read in·varying degrees of directness, not with Wordsworth's power, but very much in Wordsworth's manner and
spirit. Similarly the lessons to be derived from simple folk,
children, and lower animals are expressed in *The Old Man's
Comforts, To a Bee, To a Spider, The Battle of Blenheim,
The Sailor, The Victory, The Cross Roads, Jasper, The Com-
plaints of the Poor,* and especially in the *English Eclogues.*
As compared with the best that Wordsworth was writing
at the same time, these things are but crude and pedestrian.
Southey had neither the genius nor the leisure to express
the most intense moods of mysticism, but he was aiming at
precisely the same effects. At best he achieved but a
secondary success like *The Holly Tree* or a household immortality that at least equals *We Are Seven* in *The Battle
of Blenheim;* yet in some lesser known pieces his resemblance and even his approach to Wordsworth are still more
striking. *The Victory,* for instance, is in theme and treatment almost purely Wordsworthian. A sailor on Thomas
Southey's ship was married to a woman whom he had first
seduced and then, in a revulsion of good feeling, married
and treated honorably. Pressed into the navy, he showed
sufficient address, though almost illiterate, to rise to midshipman's rank, and sent most of his pay to his wife and
family. In a successful engagement with a French vessel
he was killed. Southey, struck by the nobility of the man,
not only wrote a poem about him, but tried to raise a few
pounds for his widow. If he had been a dalesman of Cumberland, he might have found a place in *The Excursion.*

> "He was one
> Whose uncorrupted heart could keenly feel
> A husband's love, a father's anxiousness;
> That from the wages of his toil he fed
> The distant dear ones, and would talk of them
> At midnight when he trod the silent deck
> With him he valued, — talk of them, of joys

That he had known, — oh God! and of the hour
When they should meet again, till his full heart,
His manly heart, at last would overflow,
Even like a child's with very tenderness." [1]

The *English Eclogues* deal in the same vein for the most part with the darker side of the life of the country people, with murders, ruined damsels, mothers desolated by the pressgang, witch superstition, the evil influence of wealth, and the other corruptions of human nature in society. All this is couched in a simplicity of language which apes the simplicity of the country-folk themselves. In some cases Southey even attempted to throw over his subjects an air of literal veracity, prefixing to several pieces, quite as Wordsworth did, solemn asseverations of accuracy. *The Sailor who had served in the slave trade*, for instance, opens as follows: "In September, 1798, a Dissenting Minister of Bristol discovered a sailor in the neighborhood of that city, groaning and praying in a hovel. The circumstance that occasioned his agony of mind is detailed in the annexed Ballad, without the slightest addition or alteration. By presenting it as a Poem, the story is made more public; and such stories ought to be made as public as possible." [2]

For suggestions concerning two of his new experiments in form Southey was indebted to his friend, William Taylor. Upon their first meeting at Norwich in the spring of 1798, the poet had listened avidly to all that Taylor had to tell of German literature, and he read with equal interest what Taylor wrote on the same subject in his letters and in his articles for *The Monthly Review*. "You have made me hunger and thirst after German poetry." [3] In one of their conversations at Norwich he had thus heard of German

[1] *Poems*, 1799; *Works*, 150 Westbury, 1798.

[2] *Poems*, 1799; *Works*, 111, Westbury, 1798. In *Works* Southey emended the word "hovel" to "cow-house."

[3] *Taylor*, I, 255.

attempts in the so-called eclogue form, notably by Goethe and Voss, and was delighted with a translation of Goethe's *Der Wandrer*. Southey was reminded of his own *Botany Bay Eclogues*, and in the first letter to Taylor, written after his return from Norfolk, he said that the German eclogues had revived some forgotten plans of his own for writing similar pieces that should be strictly English, but like the German, aim at "domestic interest."[1] There followed upon this, for Taylor's perusal, *The Old Mansion House*. Taylor replied with encouragement, and turned Southey's attention to Voss's *Luise*, which had lately been reviewed in *The Critical Review*. This was the beginning of Southey's experiments with this form. He wrote[2] nine such pieces in all, the last in 1803, in each attempting to display common life of the lower classes with didactic purpose, but never learning to make his peasants as eloquent and striking exponents of his view of life as Wordsworth did in *Michael* and similar poems. As for German, Southey made several endeavors to learn the language, the most serious with his boy Herbert in 1815, but his interest turned aside to German drama, which he was contented to read in English translation, and he never advanced much further than that.

Taylor's other notable suggestion to Southey came at first through his translation of two ballads of Bürger. In *The Monthly Magazine* for March, 1796, had appeared Taylor's *Lenora, a Ballad from Bürger*, followed the next month by his translation of the same author's *Des Pfarrers Tochter von Taubenheim* with the title, *The Lass of Fair Wone*. Southey had read both of these poems soon after their appearance, and had asked (July 31, 1796), "Who is this Taylor? I suspected they were by Sayers." It was

[1] *Taylor*, I, 213.
[2] For notes for other poems of the same sort, see *Commonplace Book*, *Series* IV, p. 195, where there is a note for an eclogue upon the same theme as that of Wordsworth's *Michael*.

not long before he learned who Taylor was, and in even less time he tried his own hand at a ballad. *Mary the Maid of the Inn, Donica,* and *Rudiger* were all composed at Bristol in 1796, the meter of *Mary,* however, being taken from Lewis's *Alonzo and Imogene.* In the following year *King Charlemain* was the poet's only new attempt in this form, but in the great year of 1798 and 1799 at Westbury, encouraged now by actual correspondence with the translator of *Lenore,* Southey composed nearly all his popular successes in the ballad form, such as *St. Romauld, The Well of St. Keyne, Bishop Bruno, Lord William,* and *The Old Woman of Berkeley.* "I shall hardly be satisfied," he wrote to Wynn in January, 1799, "'till I have got a ballad as good as *Lenora.*"

Some of the traits that were chiefly sought in these poems are suggested by Taylor in his praise of *The Old Woman of Berkeley,*[1] a subject that he and Sayers had each also attempted. Taylor wrote (Dec. 23, 1798) that Southey had treated the story in the best possible way; "it is everything that a ballad should be — old in the costume of the ideas, as well as of the style and meter — in the very spirit of the superstitions of the days of yore — perpetually climbing in interest, and indeed the best original English ballad we know of." This statement, however, only partially summarized the ideal that Southey aimed at in the poems that he called ballads. The meters that he used ranged all the way from the usual ballad stanza to blank verse and his own irregular rimed stanza. Confessedly a versifier rather than a melodist, — he admitted that his ear was easily satisfied, — he experimented with rough lines in imitation of the old ballads, and he defended against the conventional strictures of Wynn the substitution of two or even more syllables "for the dilated sound of one" in such lines as "I have made candles of infant's fat." This feature of the

[1] *Poems,* 1799; *Works,* 472, Hereford, 1798.   [2] *Taylor,* I, 235.

meter of *Christabel*, indeed, is as much Southey's rediscovery as Coleridge's.

Taylor's statement also fails to take cognizance of the variety of themes which Southey treated in the ballad form and of the didactic purpose which he generally displayed. In the first place, the popular origin of the old ballads, thoroughly accepted though widely misunderstood, reënforced the faith of men like Southey and Wordsworth in the virtue of simple human nature when uncontaminated by society, and encouraged them to seek for the moral lesson implicit in the poetry as well as the experiences of the folk. When, therefore, they set themselves to revive, as they thought, the writing of ballads, nothing seemed more logical than to present in this form what Southey, in a different connection, called stories "sermoni propriora . . . very proper for a sermon." Consequently the line between pieces of the type of *Bishop Bruno* and others of the type of *The Battle of Blenheim*, or between *We Are Seven* and *Peter Bell* on the one hand and *The Rime of the Ancient Mariner* on the other, was in the minds of Southey and Wordsworth somewhat confused. Southey classified all such pieces as "Metrical Tales"; Wordsworth, with Coleridge, called them "Lyrical Ballads." In order, moreover, to add weight to the sermon from nature, Southey, like Wordsworth again, as has already been intimated, was in most of his ballads careful to cite the exact source of his story. In *Mary the Maid of the Inn*, for instance, where we have a poor maiden ill-requited for her love by a corrupted lover, there is a prefatory note to the effect that "The story of the following ballad was related to me, when a schoolboy, as a fact which had really happened in the North of England."[1] It is to be noted that Southey is in general less optimistic than Wordsworth, and such a character as Jasper in the ballad of that name, instead of reforming like Peter

[1] *Poems*, 1797; *Works*, 435, Bristol, 1796.

Bell, whom he somewhat resembles, and so showing the way to grace, is made to serve as a warning by going mad in the end of his sin. In *The Cross Roads*, however, theme, didactic purpose, and manner so closely resemble Wordsworth at his worst that the reader may well wonder whether he has not stumbled upon a fugitive number from the *Lyrical Ballads*. This poem was written at Westbury in 1798, and has the inevitable note stating that "the circumstance related in the following Ballad happened about forty years ago in a village adjacent to Bristol. A person who was present at the funeral told me the story and the particulars of the interment, as I have versified them." The poem then begins in the veritable "lake" style.

> "There was an old man breaking stones
> To mend the turnpike way,
> He sat him down beside a brook
> And out his bread and cheese he took,
> For now it was mid-day.
>
> "He lent his back against a post,
> His feet the brook ran by;
> And there were water-cresses growing,
> And pleasant was the water's flowing
> For he was hot and dry.
>
> "A soldier with his knapsack on
> Came travelling o'er the down,
> The sun was strong and he was tired,
> And he of the old man inquired
> How far to Bristol town.
>
> "Half an hour's walk for a young man
> By lanes, and fields, and stiles.
> But you the foot-path do not know,
> And if along the road you go
> Why, then, 'tis three good miles.

"The soldier took his knapsack off
For he was hot and dry;
And out his bread and cheese he took
And he sat down beside the brook
To dine in company." [1]

It is needless to quote further. The old man relates the story of a maiden who has been betrayed by a wealthy sinner, has hanged herself for shame, and is buried at the crossroads with a stake through her breast, the very stake against which the soldier leans as he eats his bread and cheese. The resemblances to Wordsworth, — in the tone, the style, the subject, the use of the figure of the old man met upon the road and of the concrete object to center the attention, — is painfully unmistakable. This particular poem was, indeed, written at Westbury in 1798 after Southey had undoubtedly read the *Lyrical Ballads*. It may show that he had been encouraged, perhaps in spite of himself, by that volume to continue his earlier attempts in this vein and to qualify as a member of the "lake school."

The study, however, and not, as with Wordsworth, the highway, was to be Southey's chief Parnassus, and most of his ballads are derived, not from his own experience, but from books. He gives[2] a characteristic picture of himself on the hunt for grist to be made into such poems. While in Hereford in August, 1798, he had sought for admission to the cathedral library, and was locked up several mornings in the room where the books were kept in chains. Some of the volumes on the upper shelves had but short tethers, and the only way by which he could get at them was by piling up other books to serve as a support for that he wished to peruse while he stood upon a chair to read. Thus he found *The Old Woman of Berkeley* in Matthew of Westminster. Whatever their source, however, it is im-

---

[1] *Poems*, 1799; *Works*, 445, Westbury, 1798.
[2] *Preface* to *Ballads and Metrical Tales*, Vol. I, *Works*.

portant to note that the intention in Southey's ballads is always moral and didactic. Even though the supernatural is constantly introduced, this is done, as Wordsworth would have had it in *The Ancient Mariner*, generally to strengthen the arm of righteousness. Thus the drowned boy rises to drag Lord William into the flood, the miraculous rats devour the wicked bishop in his tower on the Rhine, and the devil gets the old woman of Berkeley in spite of her witchcraft and the merits of the monk her son and her daughter the nun. Southey's faithfulness to his serious purpose is all the more noteworthy because he was turning these things out as pot-boilers. Yet the circumstances under which they were composed account for the fact that it is difficult to take them as anything more than grotesquerie and diablerie. "If you should meet with a ghost, a witch, or a devil, pray send them to me," he wrote to Wynn. The diablerie, and in the case of *The Well of St. Keyne* and *St. Romauld*, a pleasing though simple kind of humor, as well as a concreteness and vigorous directness in the narrative, combined to make these poems popular and to throw into the shade their didactic purpose. For Southey's ballads, after all, fail to convince us that they have a vital bearing upon human experience, and for all their terrors, they therefore lack sublimity, unless it be the German sort that their author himself attributed to *The Ancient Mariner*. That attempt of Coleridge's at the same kind of thing far surpassed anything of Southey's, because, although begun by Wordsworth and Coleridge with the same purpose of making the supernatural natural, of making witchcraft, that is, help morality, and although therefore supplied by Wordsworth with a moral tag, it does arrest us with the eye of a genuine old man who had beheld with human sight unearthly things alone upon the sea. Coleridge, transcending the bounds of parables and homilies about cruelty to animals, penetrated the true sublime of human character.

Southey, for all his facile skill at turning a story, never did.

To William Taylor Southey was also indebted for one of his book-making ideas, and not a very lucky one at that. In September, 1798, Taylor had expressed[1] surprise that some English poet had not undertaken an "Almanack of the Muses" such as had been popular in France and, under the editorship of Voss, Schiller, and others, in Germany.[2] Eager for any means of turning a literary penny, Southey took up with Taylor's suggestion, and in the two years following edited, and in large part wrote, the two volumes of *The Annual Anthology* (1799, 1800), to which reference has already been made. Something more than half of the first volume and about a fourth of the second was his own composition over a variety of signatures. Other contributors in 1799 were Taylor, Lloyd, Bedford, and his brother Horace, George Dyer, Mrs. Opie, Joseph and Amos Cottle, Davy, Beddoes, Lamb, Lovell posthumously, and several obscurer persons. In 1800 the greatest addition to this list was Coleridge. Among other pieces of his, *Lewti, This Lime-tree Bower, Fire, Famine, and Slaughter*, here found a berth, and *Christabel* missed such a fate partly because it had first to be finished. Southey's own pieces were most of them salvaged from the newspapers and the wastebasket; some of them were deservedly never republished, and the rest re-appeared in 1805 as *Metrical Tales and Other Poems*.

One other form of Southey's literary activity in these busy years remains to be mentioned. Friends who were anxious that he should make money, notably Wynn and

[1] *Taylor*, I, 228.

[2] *Almanac des Muses*, 1765; *Göttinger Musenalmanach für das Jahr 1770*, founded by H. C. Boie and F. W. Gotter in imitation of *Almanac des Muses*, continued by Voss in 1775, by Göcking in 1776–1778, and Bürger, 1779; *Anthologie auf das Jahr 1782*, edited by Schiller.

May, urged him to write a tragedy, and we find him, from the time of his first trip to Portugal until his departure on the second, planning and occasionally attempting to write such a work. It is not strange that he did not succeed, for the romantic optimism that avoided conflict in the thought of the omnipotence of benevolence was even less capable of achieving drama than epic. As time went on Southey relinquished his purpose, and when his energies finally turned upon *Thalaba*, thought no more of his dramatic schemes. Nevertheless he took them quite seriously for a number of years. His immediate inspiration and models were, of course, derived through translation from Schiller and Kotzebue. His acquaintance with the former may have been due to Coleridge, who, in 1794, after the first summer of pantisocracy, had sat up one night until after one to read *The Robbers*, and had then seized pen to write, "My God, Southey, who is this Schiller, this convulser of the heart?" It is not strange, therefore, that after Southey's return from Portugal in 1796 it should have been a quotation from *Fiesco* that he sent up as a peace-offering to his offended friend, and that among his many plans of the same year (July 31) we should find mentioned no less than three "tragedies of the Banditti" by some one or all of which he hoped to raise money to furnish a house. A year or so later, however, Kotzebue made a more vivid impression upon him, probably owing to the suggestions of Taylor, and Southey, though surprised that the anti-Jacobins should permit the performance of such plays undisturbed, declares the German to be of "unsurpassed and unsurpassable genius." A few of his own themes for tragedies are described in letters to May and Wynn. He said that the most noble character he could conceive was that of a martyr, "firm to the defiance of death in avowing the truth, and patient under all oppression, without enthusiasm, supported by the calm conviction that this is his duty." Of one such story, at least, he thought seriously enough to plan a complete plot and to write a first act,[1] but that was all. Like Joanna Baillie, whom he greatly admired, and like Coleridge, Southey was possessed, not by any dramatic sense, but, as he says, by a notion of "delineating the progress of the hero's mind." It was as well that more knowing friends than Wynn and May warned him away from the drama.

Much of the poetry of Southey that we have been discussing seems now flat and jejune. To contemporary readers it possessed qualities that were striking if not altogether praiseworthy. When they compared it with the poetry of the preceding generation, they found some startling advances and departures. There was, above all, a spirit of enthusiasm for some of the new ideas that were disturbing Europe. There was also a free and daring use of new forms, together with the turning to nature, to country scenes and country people, and the use of a greater range as well as greater simplicity of language. Such qualities were quickly perceived, and it was not long before critics and partisans took up the task of marking out Southey and other such innovators for praise and censure. There arose in consequence a notion that certain new poets were working more or less in collusion, and some of them finally came to be lumped together as all belonging to a "school," variously described but finally dubbed the "lake school." Each of the three leaders of this group, especially Southey, disclaimed the existence of it or his own membership in it, and later critics have tended to accept their disclaimer and to suppose that the so-called school owed its existence only to the accident that three of its members went to live in the lake country. Southey, in particular, because of certain peculiar developments in his work, has frequently been dissociated from the others. Such versions

[1] This fragment is not extant.

of the facts are, however, misleading. Before 1800 the associations and friendships that existed among these young men, and certain accidents of publication as well as certain common characteristics in their writings, warranted contemporaries in supposing that there was at least agreement among them, and possibly collusion. Hence it came that, before any of the lake poets had settled at the lakes, the popular notion that a new "school" was being attempted was well defined, and Southey was at first taken to be the leader of it.

That such an idea should arise in political partisanship was not surprising in the ten years subsequent to 1793. Political questions were so all-absorbing that political considerations were the determining elements in many questions and reputations. Poetry was no exception to this rule. We have seen that to politics *Joan of Arc* owed its popular success; with politics, therefore, Southey's name was at once widely associated by those who looked upon revolutionary ideas with interest. In spite of the diminution of youthful heat the impression made by *Joan* was not removed by its author's immediately subsequent work. Finally Southey's connection both with *The Morning Post* and with *The Critical Review* made certain that his writings would continue to be read in some circles with a touch of partisan interest. By 1798 he had become the most conspicuous poet opposing the ministry and the war with France. Coleridge was associated with him from the first; they had made themselves notorious together at Bristol, Coleridge's contributions to *Joan of Arc* had been publicly acknowledged by Southey in his preface, and so also had been his stanza in *The Soldier's Wife*,[1] companion piece to the unlucky sapphics. Consequently, upon the publication of Coleridge's *Poems on Various Subjects*, in 1796, *The Monthly Review* immediately classified[2] him with Southey, and praised his work in terms similar to those

[1] *Poems*, 1797.   [2] *Month. Rev.*, June, 1796, n. s.,v. 20, 194.

used in praise of Southey, asserting that Coleridge had written his *Monody on the Death of Chatterton* because he too had been born in Bristol. In this volume, as in the *Ode on the Departing Year* (1796), in the second edition of his *Poems* (1797), and in *Fears in Solitude* (1798), there was nothing as violent, or, on the whole, as striking to the readers of the day, as in Southey's work of the same years, although the *Lines to a Young Ass* (*Morning Chronicle* Dec. 30, 1794) and *Fire, Famine, and Slaughter* (*Morning Post*, Jan. 8, 1789) came in for the clamorous condemnation which they courted. It should be noted in passing that nearly all of the poets of the new school indulged in joint publication with each other, and that most of their first volumes, including the *Lyrical Ballads* itself, emanated from the press of Cottle at Bristol. Thus Southey published with Lovell and collaborated publicly with Coleridge; Coleridge also published with Lamb and Lloyd; the two latter joined in a volume independently printed; and the *Lyrical Ballads*, therefore, but followed the established custom among Coleridge's associates, a custom, again, which could not help suggesting to the public the existence of a veritable "school." [1]

It is plain that Southey was at first supposed to be the

[1] Southey's early volumes, except *Poems*, 1795, were all either published or printed by Cottle at Bristol. (See *Appendix A*.) Coleridge's *Poems on Various Subjects*, 1796, was printed for C. G. and J. Robinson in London and for J. Cottle, Bookseller, in Bristol. In this volume there were four sonnets by Lamb signed C. L. and acknowledged in the preface to have been written by Charles Lamb of the India House. In the same place Coleridge also acknowledged that one of his "Effusions" had been developed from a "rough sketch" by Favell, and that the "first half" of another was by "the author of *Joan of Arc*." Coleridge's *Ode on the Departing Year* was published in 1796 at Bristol, but although printed by "N. Biggs," Cottle's printer, Cottle's name was not on the title page, and only that of "J. Parsons, Paternoster Row, London" appeared as publisher. In the same year, 1796, came out *Poems on the Death of Priscilla Farmer by her Grandson Charles Lloyd, Bristol, Printed by N. Biggs, and sold by James Phillips, George*

most important member of this group; the sheer bulk as well as the boyish brilliance of *Joan* would start such an impression. Consequently he found it necessary to deny the authorship of *Fire, Famine, and Slaughter*, and complained that strangers were always confounding him with Coleridge. Wordsworth, of course, was almost entirely unknown, and his reputation was not rapidly enhanced by the anonymous *Lyrical Ballads*. When Canning, Frere, Ellis, and the government wits, therefore, began *The Anti-Jacobin* in November, 1797, as a way of casting weekly scorn on the opposition, it was inevitable that Southey should

Yard, Lombard-Street, London. This volume also contained an introductory sonnet by Coleridge and included Lamb's *The Grandame*, with a complimentary acknowledgment of his authorship. In 1797 was published *Poems by S. T. Coleridge, Second Edition to which are now added Poems by Charles Lamb and Charles Lloyd. Printed by N. Biggs, for J. Cottle, Bristol, and Messrs Robinson, London.* This volume, of course, placed the three authors in conspicuous association with each other, a fact signallized by a Latin motto on the title page invented for the occasion by Coleridge. It also reprinted from the 1796 edition the effusion or sonnet half of which was written by Southey, and made acknowledgment in a footnote. In 1798 appeared *Blank Verse by Charles Lloyd and Charles Lamb*, printed not in Bristol, but in London by T. Bensley for John and Arthur Arch. Lloyd's *Edmund Oliver*, with a dedication to Lamb, was also published in this year through Cottle at Bristol, but Coleridge broke away from the latter at the same time with his *Fears in Solitude*, which was printed in London for J. Johnson in St. Paul's Churchyard. Finally the *Lyrical Ballads* was printed by Biggs for Cottle in the same format as Southey's 1797 and 1799 *Poems*, the second and later editions of his *Joan of Arc*, and *The Annual Anthology*, 1799, 1800; Coleridge's 1796 and 1797 *Poems;* and Lloyd's *Edmund Oliver*. When Cottle sold his interest in the *Lyrical Ballads* his name disappeared from the title page, and that of J. and A. Arch, Gracechurch-Street, London, appeared instead, though a few copies are known to have been sold under Cottle's name. I have noted above Southey's acknowledgment of contributions by Coleridge to *Joan of Arc* and *Poems*, 1797. For the whole subject see T. J. Wise, *Bibliography of Coleridge*, Lamb's *Works*, V, edited by E. V. Lucas, and *Appendix A*.

be the poet to receive their immediate attention. In the introduction to the first number (Nov. 20, 1797) of their paper they proclaimed the existence of a school of "Jacobin poets," and proceeded to define the "springs and principles of this species of poetry."[1] These were said to consist of a proneness to all kinds of exaggeration, and "the direct inversion of the sentiments and passions, which have in all ages animated the breast of the favourite of the Muses, and distinguished him from the 'vulgar throng'"; that is, the Jacobin poets exaggerated the poet's usual scorn for riches and grandeur into hatred for the rich and great, and they inverted the love of country into love of the French, the praise of military glory into rejoicings for the victories of England's enemies. The application of all this to *Joan* is plain. *The Anti-Jacobin* went on to announce that "we shall select from time to time, from among those effusions of the *Jacobin* Muse which happen to fall in our way, such pieces as may serve to illustrate some one of the principles on which the poetical, as well as the political, doctrine of the *New School* is established." The editors were immediately as good as their word. Southey's 1797 volume of poems was in their hands fresh from the press, and in their first number they reprinted in full his *Inscription for the Apartment in Chepstow Castle, where Henry Marten, the Regicide, was imprisoned thirty years,* followed by a parody entitled *Inscription for the Door of the Cell in Newgate, where Mrs. Brownrigg, the Prenticecide, was confined previous to her Execution.* In the very next number (Nov. 27, 1797) Southey was again singled out for attack, and those *Sapphics* entitled *The Widow* were immortally parodied in *The Friend of Humanity and the Needy Knife-Grinder.* A few weeks later (Dec. 11, 1797), Southey's *Dactyllics* were twice parodied, but less brilliantly, in *Come, Little*

[1] *The Anti-Jacobin or Weekly Examiner — Fourth Edition — 1799; Poetry of the Anti-Jacobin, Fourth Edition, 1801,* 3–4.

Drummer Boy (Dec. 11, 1797) and *Wearisome Sonneteer* (Dec. 18, 1797). After that no other references to Southey were made and no names were added to the "new school" until July 9, 1798, when Canning, Frere and Ellis contributed *The New Morality*. In the course of this satire the new poets were accused with other "Jacobins" of worshiping that rather mild deist, the "theophilanthrope," Lépaux.

"*Couriers* and *Stars*, Sedition's Evening Host,
   Thou *Morning Chronicle*, and *Morning Post*,
   Whether ye make the lights of Man your theme,
   Your Country libel, and your God blaspheme,
   Or dirt on private worth and virtue throw,
   Still blasphemous or blackguard, praise Lepaux.
   And ye five other wandering Bards, that move
   In sweet accord of harmony and love,
   C[oleri]dge and S[ou]th[e]y, L[loy]d, and L[am]be and Co.
   Tune all your mystic harps to praise Lepaux!" [1]

The injustice of making all these poets do homage to Lépaux, of whom they knew next to nothing, did not affect the popularity of *The Anti-Jacobin*, which was both immediate and wide. The influence upon Southey's reputation was important. Tory satire assisted anti-ministerial criticism in making his name better known than ever, identifying it more than ever with democratic notions, and fixing the idea that there was a definite group of new poets with radical principles in poetry as well as in politics. The later strictures against the lake school, and the anathemas heaped upon Southey by Byron, Hazlitt, and others for turncoating were all in part the result of the satire of *The Anti-Jacobin*. It is to be especially noted that, in the opinion of satirists and reviewers, so far as there was any new school at all, Southey was at first the most conspicuous member of it. This idea was now to grow with the public while *Thalaba* was being written.

[1] *Poetry of the Anti-Jacobin*, 250.

CHAPTER V

1800–1803

"THALABA" — A SCHOOL OF POETS

I

SOUTHEY watched[1] the weathercock at Falmouth for a week before his departure on his second trip to Portugal. He had with him a volume of Coleridge's poems, the 1798 *Lyrical Ballads*, Burns, and *Gebir*. The last-named had become matter for daily reading. "I like Gebir more and more; if you ever meet its author, tell him I took it with me on a voyage" (Apr. 1, 1800). For other pastime he walked the beach, caught soldier-crabs, watched the sea-anemones, and wrote half a book of *Thalaba*. Then on Apr. 2, 1800, he embarked with his wife in the Lisbon packet, and after a short voyage of five days and a half, during which both Southey and Edith were wretchedly sea-sick and upon one occasion much alarmed at the approach of a Guernsey cutter, which their captain at first took to be French, the ship put into Lisbon. The old thrill of admiration returned to the poet. "Convents and Quintas, gray olive yards, green orange-groves, and greener vineyards; the shore more populous every moment as we advanced, and finer buildings opening upon us; the river, bright as the blue sky which illuminated it, swarming with boats of every size and shape, with sails of every imaginable variety; innumerable ships riding at anchor far as the eye could reach; and the city extending along the shore, and covering the hills to the farthest point of sight."

[1] The main facts of this period of Southey's life are to be found in *Life*, II, 57–234 and in *Warter*, I, 104–237.

They landed on the eighth of April, and went at once to a small house that Southey's uncle had engaged for them. It was very small and thoroughly Portuguese, little rooms all doors and windows but cool, with a view across the river to the hills of Alentejo. The domestic arrangements were clean and English only as far as Edith could extend her personal sway. Ceremonial calls and letters once disposed of, Southey went busily to work until the time for retreating to Cintra. This was not to be until June, for he delayed departure in order to see a bull-fight and the processions of Corpus Christi, of St. Anthony, and of the Heart of Jesus. With careful prudence he described his impressions in detailed letters home, so that material would be at hand for another volume similar to that which had been the fruit of his first visit. There was little new to record; he found the same filth, misgovernment, corruption, ignorance, and fascinating picturesqueness as before. His letters are, perhaps, more graphic and spirited, but they express merely the old sense of charm and the Englishman's revulsion at squalor and popery. At the end of June he and Edith set out joyfully for Cintra, with its olive hillsides and running streams. There they remained until the end of October, when they returned to Lisbon. On the whole it was a tranquil time of happy industry. Under the influence of constant "ass-back-riding," the health of both recovered almost immediately, and they found some pleasant English acquaintances, especially a Miss Barker, who was to continue a friend and, settling later at Keswick, found a place in *The Doctor* as the Bhow Begum. There were, besides, fortunately, no casual or idle visitors to invade the peace of Cintra. Though the Southeys longed for bread and butter, and for gooseberry pie, they feasted contentedly upon grapes, olives, oranges, and excellent wine. Rumors of pestilence and the alarm of war disturbed them somewhat, but neither came so close as to cause real danger.

In February, 1801, after they had returned to Lisbon, they set out upon a three weeks' journey on mules to Coimbra and back over some three hundred and fifty miles of the execrable roads of the country. An Englishman named Waterhouse and, much to the marvel of the natives, a carriage with three ladies, in addition to Edith, went along upon the journey. Luckily the carriage and two of the ladies did not persist very far, and the historian of Portugal could travel comparatively unhampered. The party returned in the highest spirits and the best of health, so that in April Southey was moved to set forth again, but this time with Waterhouse alone, for an expedition to the south through Alentejo and Algarve. He came back boasting that he had then seen all of the country except the northern provinces.

Southey looked upon the approach of the twelvemonth's end and his return to England with regret. He wished to continue his travels, and he was loath to suspend his labors of study and writing. But the state of the country was unsettled, his wife longed for home, and the English, his uncle among them, were preparing to flee before the French invasion. In June, therefore, he and Edith returned to England, both seasick for the whole two weeks of the passage. The year of Southey's second sojourn in Portugal came nearer to realizing the ideal existence he had conceived for himself than any similar period he had ever passed before or would soon pass again. Here was the life he had desired, — retirement, a home, the beauty of nature out at Cintra, poetry, and historical study. *Thalaba* and the history of Portugal consumed all his thoughts and nearly all his time. Of the former he had written six books in January, 1800; in the succeeding month two more were added, and in spite of the distractions of ill-health and travel, ten were complete by the middle of June. Finally, on July 23, Southey wrote to Wynn that the whole twelve

books were finished, and were being corrected. This took
some time, but by September, 1800, the poem was ready to
be submitted for publication. Rickman, who, though he
did not read his friend's poetry, evidently could be trusted
to sell it, was selected to be his plenipotentiary with Longman, and secured an agreement that Southey was to receive
£115 for an edition of one thousand copies. This poem
was not as important in its author's mind as *Madoc* or the
great history, but it was expected to be popular, or at least
to furnish funds to buy chairs and tables for the house he
hoped to secure upon his return.   If it succeeded, he planned
to follow it up with a series of similar works that would
carry out his old intention of illustrating the mythologies
of the world. "It is a good job done, and so I have
thought of another, and another, and another" (July 25,
1800).

In the same letter to Wynn that announced the completion of *Thalaba* Southey also wrote that he had a distant view of manufacturing a Hindoo romance, wild as
Thalaba, and a nearer one of a Persian story.   In the latter,
to be based upon the *Zend-Avesta*, the powers of darkness
were to persecute a prince, but every evil they inflicted was
to cause the development in him of some virtue which prosperity had smothered. The outcome of the whole would
be that the prince would be exalted into an Athenian
citizen, and the French revolution be forgotten in the
thought of Attic republicanism. For some reason this
scheme went no further, but from a distant view of the
Hindoo romance Southey plunged at once into the manufacture of *The Curse of Kehama*, or, as it was originally
called, *of Keradon*. By April, 1801, this had "matured into
a very good and very extraordinary plan,[1] which has become
a favorite with me;" before the author's departure its
"ground-plan" had been "completely sketched," and the

[1] *Commonplace Book, Series* IV, 12–15.

composition already begun. This was halted, however, pending the returns from *Thalaba*, and owing to some scruples concerning the use of rime as well as to the desire to employ all the time in Portugal for work that could be done only there.

For Southey had come to Lisbon filled with the intention to write the history of Portugal, which he felt that he could do as it should be done. There was, he thought, a wholeness and unity in the story, splendid actions, and an important lesson. He wished to know well the entire country, and he intended to do what he said had never been done, that is, to include a narrative of the manners of the people. Though it seemed a task that involved terrifying labor, yet he had now the inclination and leisure to attempt it. Great help could be expected from Mr. Hill, whose estimation of his nephew had risen greatly, partly because the young man had, in his own chosen way, made no inconsiderable figure in the world. Southey's historical investigation interested his uncle greatly, and the good gentleman had been adding industriously to his already well-stocked library. In this collection and in such public collections as might be accessible in Lisbon, supplemented by his own purchases, Southey expected to find his materials. His workmanlike plan was to go through the chronicles, make a skeleton of the narrative, and fill in details at leisure. By August he could say that he had the main facts and personages well in mind, that he could speak the language fluently if not correctly, that he knew its history, and that he was almost as well acquainted with Portuguese literature as with English. "It is not worth much," he adds (Aug. 25, 1800), "but it is not from the rose and the violet only that the bee sucks honey." When completed the intended book would consist of three parts, a section on the literature, another on the history of the country proper, and a third on that of the colonial enterprises. The first of these and a volume of the second Southey was ready to put together for publication immediately upon his return to England, but he would have to return to Portugal before he could complete the whole. The style that he planned to use and the expectations that he entertained of success were both characteristic of the man. It was to be a plain Doric building in a compressed, perspicuous manner, with abundant notes to "drain off all quaintness"; it would surely endure. With half the success of Gibbon or Roscoe, the author's profits would be important, and he knew that his work would be of more permanent reputation. Such was the state of the great history when Southey set out again for home. "I have stewed down many a folio into essential sauce." He would now hope and struggle for leisure, and for an opportunity to come back for more materials to Lisbon. All this would be in vain, however, although at least two bulky historical works and one epic would be the off-shoots of his lifelong studies.

II

Thalaba was the epitome of Southey's youth and the clearest augury of his manhood. It was the fullest expression that he had yet attained of his passionate, self-confident idealism. It was his boldest experiment in style, versification, and subject matter. It was at once his first mature effort to garner in poetry the results of his wide reading, and the first member of the series of epics which he had planned illustrating the mythologies of the world.[1] Lastly, in the figure of Thalaba, — a hero of single purpose, of complete faith in himself, of implicit adherence to the

[1] Southey was at this time also planning an epic on Noah, a sketch for which may be seen in *Commonplace Book, Series* IV, 2–3. This poem was to express the same ideals put forth in Southey's other poems, but the story of events before the flood was to express the poet's attitude toward the French revolution.

line of duty made plain by his faith and purpose, — here was the moral character of Southey himself.

I have already dwelt upon the fact that Southey and Wordsworth both emerged from the fever of the revolution with substantially the same view of life, and that in their early poems they adopted similar methods of expressing their idealism. After that, as *Thalaba* first conspicuously shows, Southey took other ways, which appeared to differ from those of Wordsworth more than was really the case. The latter continued substantially in the way of the *Lyrical Ballads*. He surrendered himself to the mystical contemplation of the ideal as he beheld it in nature, and he made poetry a vehicle for the delineation of the moral influence of that ideal upon those who live in close communion with nature. His faith was so unquestioning that he joyfully gave up his life to such poetry; gave up, indeed, much that he should have kept, — reading, study, travel, friends new and old, the habit of thought, catholicity of spirit, almost the very power of poetic expression itself. Southey, with interesting individual differences, was to go through essentially the same process. The turn for mystic contemplation, however, although not absent, as we have seen in some of his earlier work, was not as strong in him as in Wordsworth. The latter could consistently present nature as a calm power in whose world there was no strife, for the faith of the idealist has always been that there can be no opposition, no hate, in the presence of perfection, that evil, by definition, is but the absence of good; the arm of Artegal falls powerless before the might of Britomart's awful loveliness. To reap "the harvest of a quiet eye" and behold that loveliness, not to present the strivings of imperfection nor even the omnipotence of its opposite, was Wordsworth's purpose. Southey, on the other hand, though forever straining after peace in his own soul and sternly guiding conduct to that end, never had time for undisturbed contemplation. Rather, with his passion for action, for committing himself, for getting things done, he found himself always preoccupied with the presence of evil, and always impatient to banish it headlong before perfection.

Mrs. Piozzi once wrote of him, "Oh, how I delight to see him trample on his enemies!" "And that," said Southey when he had been shown the lady's letter, "was worth all the panegyric in the world."[1] Good trampling evil, perfection banishing wrong by its mere presence, — in short, Joan driving the English from Orleans, Thalaba destroying the Dom-Daniel, and both acting, not as ordinary human agents, but as "missioned" maid or hero appointed from on high and with arm made omnipotent by faith in the eternal good, — this was Southey's perennial theme, and in his own eyes he was himself, when he began Quixotically tilting at windmills of immorality in his own day, not the least potent of his own heroes. "Is there not," asked William Taylor, "in your ethic drawing . . . a perpetual tendency to copy a favorite ideal perfection? " To this Southey replied, "There is that moral mannerism which you have detected; Thalaba is a male Joan of Arc."[2]

This "favorite ideal perfection" is precisely stated for us in Wordsworth's *The Character of a Happy Warrior*. That, however, is a contemplative man's reflection upon life. Southey's instinct, as well as his problem, was to depict his warrior in action, and Thalaba's story is built accordingly. The Arabian youth begins as "a generous spirit" to whom God has given a plan "to please his boyish thought," and whose task in real life is indeed to work upon this plan. Fear, bloodshed, pain, — difficulties that the poet seeks to make concretely terrible, — face him, but he

> "Turns his necessity to glorious gain;
> In face of these doth exercise a power

[1] *Warter*, III, 474.   [2] *Taylor*, II, 81–82.

> Which is our human nature's highest dower;
> Controls them, and subdues, transmutes, bereaves
> Of their bad influence, and their good receives,"

or in the words of Southey's hero, as he receives a magic
ring which was originally a tool of the unrighteous,

> "In God's name, and the Prophet's! be its power
> Good, let it serve the righteous; if for evil,
> God and my trust in him shall hallow it." [1]

Thenceforth Thalaba goes through his trials keeping "the
law in calmness made," seeing as he goes "what he foresaw," irresistibly playing

> "in the many games of life, that one
> Where what he most doth value must be won."

Thus persevering, finding "comfort in himself and in his
cause," Thalaba achieves his plan, overthrows evil by con-
fronting it with faith in good, and finally, as his reward,
draws breath, not merely in the "confidence of Heaven's
applause," but in heaven itself.

Such was the central theme of Thalaba, derived not from
Wordsworth, but from its author's acknowledged master,
Spenser. It would be easy to press too far the search for
resemblances between Southey's poem and *The Faerie
Queene*, but it will be enough to point out that, aside from
his use of the figure of an appointed hero fighting evil with
faith, Southey shows an interesting resemblance to Spenser
in the scope of his scheme for a series of epics or romances
on mythologies each of which was, no doubt, to present the
same recurring hero under various names forever fighting,
like the knights from the Faerie Queene's court, the same
battles over again. From Spenser to Southey no poet had
conceived quite so elaborate a scheme, and none had so
nearly achieved it. The younger man's failure to approach

[1] *Thalaba*, III, 116.

the older's success was largely due, of course, to a difference in the power of sheer poetic expression, but also to a difference in the manner of presenting the underlying thought. There are two ways of showing the triumph of good over evil in narrative, both to be found in *The Faerie Queene*, seldom but the one in *Thalaba*. Evil may be displayed as the crass, hideous, unmitigated negation of perfection, and therefore, granted the faith of the hero, easily to be overthrown by his good right arm. On the other hand it may be represented far more subtly as consisting in impulses disguised, glozed over, adorned with show of truth, such as exist in all minds, tend toward evil, and threaten, by taking faith in the rear, to overthrow it in the citadel of the soul. The struggle against evil, when turned into story, then becomes an allegory of our innermost mental processes instead of a mere glorified Jack-and-the-Giant nursery tale. Spenser uses both methods; he has his dragons, his Corflambos, his Blatant Beasts, but he has also his Duessa, his false Florimell, his Despair, and a host of figures that betray often amazingly subtle perceptions of the workings of the mind. The trouble with Southey's poem is that evil for him is always either a transparent scoundrel or a blatant beast. He has no notion of projecting the soul into narrative. Thalaba, it is true, does upon one occasion deviate from the path of virtue, but he is so quickly righted that the impression of impeccability is not disturbed, and though an enchantress shortly afterwards tricks him into her power, she does so through no fault of his, and is helpless to do anything with him save show her own impotence. Southey's hero represents no experience easily recognizable as human, but an ideal phrased in terms so remote as to be uninteresting, and the opposing evil too hideous to have any semblance of reality. Wickedness in his hands becomes a thing only to scare children, a mere abstraction tricked out in horrors not felt but read in old books, the

bloody hocus-pocus of witchcraft, and mumbo-jumbo of
dead men's bones. It is all a bad dream out of the reign
of terror and the *Arabian Nights,* and there is something
pathetic in the childish satisfaction which the poet takes
in belaboring his bugaboos in their Dom-Daniel house of
cards.

The origin of Southey's plot is plain.[1] To display a single
virtue wreaking its perfection on the unrighteous, he wove,
like Spenser again, a story out of the fluid themes of romance. In boyhood he had attempted new *Faerie Queenes*
and new *Orlandos; Thalaba* was the man's effort to fulfill
the boy's dream. In a general way the story resembles
any story of the quest of an other-world castle. Thalaba's
youth is that of the boy whose father and kindred have
been slain by evil enemies, and who has been driven into
exile with his mother. The enchanters who are his foes
have their headquarters in a cavern under the roots of the
sea, and there they keep the charmed sword of the hero's
father, by which they are themselves to be overthrown
when the youth shall have penetrated to their strong-
hold and regained the weapon. To find the Dom-Daniel
caverns, to win the sword, and to avenge his father is the
plan and purpose of the boy's life. Bereft of his mother,
under strange circumstances that permit Southey to describe the fabled garden of Iram, Thalaba grows up with
simple people in the desert. These are a noble Arab and
his daughter, who perform the same function for him that
was performed for Joan by the hermit and Theodore in
the forest. Like Joan, too, Thalaba is reared in virtue by
the influence of nature and solitude, and like Joan he is
finally apprised by miraculous means of his mission.
Thereupon he departs for Babylon to begin his quest, but

---

[1] For Southey's extensive preliminary notes for the poem, together
with suggestions for giving the story certain allegorical significance,
see, *Commonplace Book, Series* IV, pp. 97–195 *passim.*

not without regret on the part of the maid, Oneiza, for a pure and tender love has grown up between them. This simple story is wrapped up in a bewildering apparatus of charms and talismans and special providences. Although communion with nature has taught Thalaba such faith that Allah has a bee or a simoon ready at any time to save him, yet the youth is supposed to possess a magic ring as a protection against enchanters, and he must be told by Haruth and Maruth in their cavern under the ruins of Babylon, whither he is unwittingly guided by the forces of evil themselves, that he also possesses that faith which is talisman sufficient to daunt the unfaithful. To obtain this knowledge is simple enough, for he has but to follow his unknown enemy into the cavern, throw him into an abyss, and shout aloud in the name of Allah. After that is accomplished, and the talisman learned, the poet's problem was the one with which all who tell this story are confronted, namely to supply his hero with suitable adventures to consume the time until he should proceed to the end of his quest. Southey solved it in the usual way by transporting Thalaba to a bower of bliss. The machinery is not strange to romance; there is an enchanted steed, a valley in the mountains, iron gates to be set open by the blowing of massy horns, then lissome harlots in filmy lawn dancing lewdly by a fountain in the forest. Thalaba and Southey hasten swiftly by, for it is really a long time since the age of Spenser. Oneiza appears upon the scene, fleeing like Angelica from the embraces of lust, and the hero rescues her. Then, of course, he destroys the sorcerer who rules the place, and passes out with his beloved through riven enchantments to meet the sultan marching to overthrow the iniquities that have just been disposed of.

The youth and the maid are carried in triumph to Bagdad to be luxuriously rewarded. But now, like one of Spenser's knights, Thalaba is tempted to err, for such is the influence

of wealth, of cities, and of kings. He proposes to marry
Oneiza, and deceives himself with the thought that his
mission is done. The maiden, however, is claimed by the
angel of death in the bridal chamber, and thereafter for a
short time Thalaba is betrayed by the devices of witchcraft
until Oneiza's father comes to him with fresh faith from
the desert, and sets him free to continue his quest. He is
again ensnared, but this time through no fault of his own,
and is wafted to an island of all unrighteousness, whence
he escapes partly by the aid of a repentant witch, and
partly by wickedness overreaching itself. This is the
weakest part of the poem, for it is difficult to see why
Thalaba should be even temporarily overcome. But be
that as it may, he is now directed toward his goal by a
dervish and by the Simorg, and encounters another enchanter, who tries to trick him into believing that it is his
destiny to slay an innocent maid, the enchanter's own
daughter. Thalaba knows better, though Azrael himself
stands by demanding the fulfillment of fate; in the scuffle
that ensues, destiny receives its due, but by the knife of
the wicked father, who is not so wicked as not to mourn
his loss. Thalaba pities the old man's grief, and goes on,
guided by a green bird which is the maiden's soul. The
finest descriptive passages of the poem now occur. The
difficulties that remain in the hero's path are ice and cold
and perilous seas in fairy lands forlorn, but he is at last
safely ferried over the waters that in romance forever flow
between our world and the other-world where the castles
lie in which the Percivals and the Galahads and the Thala-
bas finally achieve the quest. Southey's hero relieves
another youth, who has failed at the very threshold of
success, makes his way past Afreets and Teraphim to the
innermost caverns of the Dom-Daniel, regains the magic
sword, destroys the seats of the wicked, pities and forgives
his father's murderer like the good Christian that he really

is, and is translated to Heaven for his pains. The respectable Englishman does not forsake him, even in paradise, for he is met by but one Houri, and that Oneiza, to whom the poet had taken pains previously to marry him, and who has been patiently reserving her charms to reward him alone.

If the reader of to-day reads *Thalaba* at all, he generally does so without having in mind the nature of Southey's earlier work, and it may seem surprising that this poem should at any time have been thought to possess traits in common, not only with *Joan of Arc*, but also with its author's shorter pieces published in 1797 and 1799, and even with the *Lyrical Ballads*. Yet such was the case, and we must not neglect to observe what just basis Jeffrey was to have for making this poem the text of his first diatribe against the lake school.

"My aim has been," wrote Southey, "to diffuse through my poems a sense of the beautiful and good."[1] This was true of all his serious work, both before and after *Thalaba*. The next mythological poem, for instance, was intended to be founded on the system of Zoroaster, in the hope that the fables of false religion might be made subservient to the true. Yet, besides being written with the same general moral purpose, *Thalaba* also expresses the peculiar beliefs which Southey shared with Wordsworth, and for which "the lake poets" were conspicuous. The most striking of these, of course, is the belief in the beneficent influence of nature and solitude. Thalaba grows up in the Arabian desert precisely as he would have done upon the shores of Windermere. We are told that his lot was cast by heaven in a lonely tent in order that his soul might there develop its energies of faith and virtue, and his heart remain un-contaminated by the world.[2] In addition to this Southey emphasizes, characteristically, the influence of domesticity.

[1] *Life*, III, 351.   [2] Bk. III, 130.

The home in the Arab's tent, the firelight at evening, the sweet family picture of the old man intoning the holy book or placidly smoking at the tent door, the maiden at her loom or with her goats and birds, the boy with his basket-weaving or his bows and arrows, — these too have their moral influence. But the power of nature, — the mornings in the desert, the winds, the rains, the broad-leaved syca-mores, the moon, — chiefly mold his character.

> "When the winter torrent rolls
> Down the deep-channelled rain-course, foamingly,
>   Dark with its mountain spoils,
>   With bare feet pressing the wet sand
>   There wanders Thalaba,
>   The rushing flow, the flowing roar,
>   Filling his yielded faculties;
> A vague, a dizzy, a tumultuous joy.
>   . . . Or lingers it a vernal brook
>   Gleaming o'er yellow sands?
>   Beneath the lofty bank reclined,
> With idle eye he views its little waves,
> Quietly listening to the quiet flow;
> While in the breathings of the stirring gale
>   The tall canes bend above,
>   Floating like streamers in the wind
>   Their lank uplifted leaves." [1]

What matters it if the old Arab intones the *Koran* beneath no lamp-illumined dome or marble walls bedecked with flourished truth, azure and gold! To Thalaba and the maid her father is their priest, the stars their points of prayer, and the blue sky a temple in which they feel the deity.[2]

The wisdom thus learned by the child suffices the man during the rest of his career. So when Thalaba wavers in

---

[1] *Thalaba*, Bk. III, 135. There is in these lines, perhaps, an echo of *Tintern Abbey*, admiration for which Southey had expressed a year before in his review of the *Lyrical Ballads* in *The Critical Review*.

[2] Bk. III, 145–147.

his purpose, owing to the influence of life in Bagdad, it is
Oneiza and her father, with safer instinct, who recall him
to virtue by recalling him to nature and the desert solitude.
Knowledge is otherwise to be learned only through league
with the powers of hell. Metaphysics, it will be remembered, had become anathema to Southey, and the evil
sorcerers in his poem are metaphysicians of the school of
Locke, but Thalaba stanchly defends revelation and innate
truth. Lobaba argues that Solomon grew wise by observation and reflection, but Thalaba maintains that wisdom is
God's special gift, the guerdon of early virtue; providence
at once intervenes to aid him and prove the point. This is
the faith that renders him invincible, and he acts throughout merely as the unreasoning instrument of omnipotence.
He cries out that the wicked blindly work the righteous
will of heaven, casts the protection of magic embodied in
the ring into the abyss, pitches his enemy after it, and
attains his purpose by the aid of God alone.

It is needless, though it would be easy, to dwell more
particularly upon the fidelity with which *Thalaba* expresses
the philosophy of the lake poets. The cardinal sins of
obscurity of thought and mystical enthusiasm are obvious.
Affected simplicity, trivial and vulgar subject matter, prosaic style, — these, on the other hand, have been obscured
by the Arabian machinery and ignored by later readers
owing to that inattention which has been the meed of
Southey's poetry. To be sure the author himself said of
the poem, "Simplicity would be out of character; I must
build a Saracenic mosque, not a Quaker meeting-house."[1]
Nevertheless the notorious faults of the new sect of poets
were present in sufficient abundance to justify the critics.
One of the passages which, with its footnote, was particularly obnoxious to Jeffrey occurs in the opening book, and
gives uncomfortable premonitions of *Peter Bell*. What more

[1] *Taylor*, I, 272.

"lakish" in tone, diction, subject matter, and thought could
be found than the following lines:

> "It chanced my father went the way of man,
>   He perished in his sins.
>   The funeral rites were duly paid,
>   We bound a camel to his grave
>   And left it there to die,
>   So if the resurrection came
>   Together they might rise.
>   I past my father's grave,
>   I heard the Camel moan.
>   She was his favorite beast,
>   One that carried me in infancy,
>   The first that by myself I learnt to mount.
>   Her limbs were lean with famine, and her eyes
>   Looked ghastlily with want.
>   She knew me as I past,
>   She stared me in the face." [1]

To the last line of this passage Southey added a note,
saying that it had been taken from one of the most beautiful passages in one of the most beautiful of "our old
ballads." Never having seen this poem in print, he quotes
ten stanzas of a piece called *Old Poulter's Mare*, an imperfect copy of which he has with difficulty "procured . . .
from memory." It is the story of an old beast turned out
to die by her owner, who, repenting a little, sends one to
find her and bring her home again.

> "He went a little farther
>   And turned his head aside,
>   And just by goodman Whitfield's gate
>   Oh there the Mare he spied.
>   He asked her how she did,
>   *She stared him in the face,*
>   *Then down she laid her head again, —*
>   *She was in wretched case.*" [2]

[1] Bk. I, 28–29.   [2] Bk. I, 29–32. The italics are Southey's.

Southey's story did not supply many opportunities for such passages, but this one alone sufficed to evoke Jeffrey's ridicule and Taylor's condemnation.

The charge of obscurity of style can even more easily be maintained against *Thalaba*. The narrative was drawn from romances, but the manner of presenting it from far different sources. It is told, not directly and flowingly, but by implication, imprecation, and ejaculation. The action is suggested lyrically by the exclamations of the poet at interesting points in his hero's career. Whence Southey learned this method has already been suggested. It is the style of Sayers's choruses and of Gray's odes. It is somewhat the manner, also, of Landor's *Gebir*, which Southey was reading with enthusiastic interest at the time of composing *Thalaba*. It is the style of *Ossian*, and also, especially in its constant use of parallelism of thought and image, of the poetic narratives of the Old Testament. Finally, it was suggested by the abruptness of the ballads, leaping like them from pinnacle to pinnacle of the action, but never achieving their dramatic movement and concreteness. At best certain passages of *Thalaba* equal Gray and surpass Macpherson, but taken as a whole the narrative style is not good, for simple as the plot is, only the willing and attentive reader can follow and remember it.

But the most conspicuous poetical innovation of *Thalaba* was its meter. Southey's interest in versification and his love of experimenting with verse forms have already been described. They had very early made him subject for ridicule, for the attacks of the *Anti-Jacobin* upon him in 1797 had been in part due to his attempts in the use of accentual Sapphics and Dactyllics. His early interest in the ode, especially as developed by Gray, Collins, and Mason, and his particular interest in the rimeless form used by Sayers have also been discussed. Now when he undertook the project, which Sayers had ventured so timidly upon, of "illustrating" the mythologies of the world, Southey turned to the meter of the *Dramatic Sketches* as his proper vehicle. Yet he took some months in deciding the question. He began by resolving against blank verse in order to avoid mannerism and feebleness, and he planned at first to use irregular rimed stanzas, possibly with blank verse at dramatic moments in the narrative.[1] But in August, 1799, he had composed the first book and a half in the irregular unrimed stanzas. In this he met encouragement from William Taylor,[2] who cited Klopstock's choral dramas, Stolberg's odes, and Cesarotti's translation of *Ossian* into Italian. Sayers, however, was constantly acknowledged by Southey to be his model.

The metrical beauties of *Thalaba* can easily be overstated. There were so many faults that Southey might so easily have committed but foresaw and avoided, that we are apt to praise the verse of the poem as a positive success. The lines, undistinguished as they are by rime, and irregular as they are in length, do not run into insignificant prose. On the other hand, the pauses are managed with such skill that one gets no impression that one is reading the conventional blank verse unconventionally printed. The absence of rime is not an annoyance to the ear, largely because the mind is constantly satisfied by the use of parallelism. What Southey prided himself particularly upon was his skill in constantly varying the beat of the rhythm and the time-length of the verses to fit the changing sentiments expressed.

> "The Arabian youth knelt down,
> And bowed his forehead to the ground
>   And made his evening prayer.
> When he arose the stars were bright in heaven,
>   The sky was blue, and the cold Moon
>   Shone over the cold snow.
>   A speck in the air!

[1] *Taylor*, I, 272.   [2] *Ibid.*, 284.

> Is it his guide that approaches?
> For it moves with the motion of life!
> Lo! she returns and scatters from her pinions
> Odours diviner than the gales of morning
>   Waft from Sabea." [1]

Yet Southey's facility in thus varying the verse, — and the passage just quoted is taken almost at random, — was so great as to outreach itself. The tune shifts so often that the reader gets no sense of harmony, and the poem is like an opera that is all aria; while the singer curvets through trills and runs, the listener loses himself, the story, and the music in sheer admiration of dexterity. Consequently there is no enchantment of tone and overtone in the verse of *Thalaba;* all, even in such fine passages as the opening lines upon night or those upon the wedding and death of Oneiza, conveys at best the suspicion of legerdemain, and consequently there is some justification, aside from the rimelessness and the general resemblance to a prose-printed thing like *Ossian,* for the accusation of the critics that the poem was but "prose run mad."[2] There is one curious result of the meter of *Thalaba* in the fact that it is a very difficult poem to remember. The style and the bewilderment of machinery have much to do with this, but the shifts of the verse play their part also. Southey himself called it "the Arabesque ornament of an Arabian tale," but he neglected to observe that even Arabesque must have some pattern to avoid confusion.

Finally we must note that one strong reason for Southey's using a novel meter, aside from his sense of its appropriateness and his desire to experiment, was his unconquerable impulse for committing himself, for challenge and controversy. English versification was in a bad way; why not reform it at once and with a flourish that would put the whole matter out of question! He coolly expected that the

---

[1] Bk. XI, 268–269.   [2] *Crit. Rev.,* 3rd. Ser., v. 4, 118.

meter of *Thalaba* would have many imitators;[1] that it did not do so he attributed in later years to the fact that it was not so easy a form to practice as it looked.[2] Meanwhile, in the preface to the first edition of the poem, he delivered himself of the judgment that his verse could be read with a "prose mouth," but could not be distorted into discord, and furthermore that English taste in verse had been corrupted by the "regular Jew's-harp twing-twang of what had been foolishly called heroic measure." As if to make sure that this challenge to the conservatives should not go unregarded, Southey placed upon his title page a Greek motto from Lucian to the effect that poetry is free, and the poet a law unto himself.

Besides experimenting with style and meter, Southey also had the temerity in this poem to attempt an experiment in subject. *Joan of Arc* purported to deal with the Europe of the fifteenth century, but although some learned notes were attached to the first edition, and more were added to the second, in order to enforce that impression, the poem palpably referred mainly to contemporary affairs. *Thalaba,* on the other hand, seriously set out to illustrate not only Arabian mythology, but also the Arabian people and the scenery of their country. Southey is, therefore, frequently associated with Scott as one who attempted to use eastern material as the other did the history of his own country and of the rest of Europe. We shall see that this resemblance is only upon the surface, and that in the broadest sense Scott was a finer scholar as he was a finer artist than Southey.

The latter was not, of course, the first Englishman to write an Oriental tale,[3] though he was the first to profess, —

[1] *Taylor,* I, 292, August, 1799.

[2] *Quar. Rev.* v. 35, 214. *Correspondence with Caroline Bowles,* 51, 53–54, 58–59.

[3] See Martha Pike Conant: *The Oriental Tale in England.* 1908.

unfortunately it was only profession, — seriously to "illustrate" Oriental things in English poetry. From the first translation of the *Arabian Nights* out of Galland's French early in the eighteenth century, eastern material had been used in some form or other by many writers in English for a variety of purposes. That famous work was followed by the translation out of French of similar collections which had been drawn from the original languages or spuriously concocted. Eastern costume and machinery were speedily used on the continent and in England as a vehicle for satire and, as is often the case with romantic material, for moral and philosophical didacticism. In this field the Oriental tale achieved its greatest strictly literary distinction in such hands as those of Addison, Steele, Montesquieu, Voltaire, Johnson, Goldsmith, and others. Eastern names and scenery had also been used in poetry for purely decorative purposes by such men as Parnell, Collins, and Chatterton, but their performances had attained no popularity to compare with that of the Oriental tale pure and simple or with the Oriental apologue. None of these attempts, moreover, had ostensibly enlisted all the apparatus of scholarship in order to "illustrate" the Orient for western minds; satire, moral or philosophical instruction, and pure entertainment had been the sole objects. The growing importance for England of India, to be sure, was fostering an interest in the east which became truly scholarly in the work of Sir William Jones, but Beckford's *Vathek* (1786) was the first attempt to employ the results of such learning in new work. Yet even so, the Oriental learning in *Vathek*, although it appears that Beckford himself was not ignorant of the matter, was supplied chiefly in the footnotes by Henley, who was the prime instigator in the composition of the story, and who translated it from the original French. Henley pretended that he obtained the story from the Arabic, but he quoted freely from Sale and D'Herbelot, and although *Vathek* has been declared worthy to stand beside the *Arabian Nights* themselves, it cannot be said that it is free from the touch of eighteenth-century Europe. The voice of Voltaire is evident in its cynicism, and the famous conclusion, for all its power, is plainly that of the moralizing European, magic and deviltry being presented, not with the naïve gusto of the *Arabian Nights*, but solely as instruments for the punishment of sin.

The resemblance in moral purpose between *Vathek* and *Thalaba* is obvious; each is preoccupied with the question of retribution. Beckford's hero attains to the caverns of evil enchantment by stupid persistence in evil, and finds success to be its own punishment. *Thalaba* achieves a similar quest by means of faith in good and by the very efforts of the unrighteous to oppose him. For that reason Southey could say, "The poem compares more fairly with *Vathek* than with any existing work, and I think may stand by its side for invention."[1] But it was Henley's annotations that particularly impressed the poet, for he wrote that the translator of Beckford's tale had "added some of the most learned notes that ever appeared in any book whatever!"[2] William Taylor probably knew that his friend would be pleased to read in his *Critical Review* article upon *Thalaba* that the notes to that poem were "worthy of the commentator of *Vathek*."[3]

As a matter of fact, however, Henley was far outdone by Southey.[4] What Gray and Sayers had attempted to do for "northern antiquities," what Scott was to do for Scotland and England, Southey essayed to do for the Orient. To be sure, he knew no eastern language, he had never visited an eastern country, nor was he at all intimately acquainted with anyone who could supply these lacks, but he was

[1] *Taylor*, I, 371. [2] *Warter*, I, 303. [3] *Crit. Rev.*, 2d ser., v. 39, 378.
[4] See *Appendix B* for a list of the books and authors probably referred to by Southey in connection with *Thalaba*.

intoxicated by the vistas that investigation and travel were beginning to suggest, and he deluded himself into supposing that the mirage that he could project across any one of them out of his own Englishman's book-learning and insular imagination would long be taken for a picture of the truth. Under the circumstances, from the little he could know he constructed a setting for his poem which seems and never is Oriental, and which is carefully authenticated in notes that represent many days of labor and that nearly equal in bulk the poem itself.

To the *Arabian Nights* and all its numerous progeny Southey probably owed much of the atmosphere and nomenclature of his poem, but most of his specific information concerning Mohammedanism was derived from Sale's recent translation of the *Koran*, with its long "Preliminary Discourse," from the Latin translation of the *Koran* and refutation of its heresies by a seventeenth-century Italian named Maracci, from Sir William Jones's various translations and essays on Oriental literature, from an English translation with notes of a Persian romance called *The Bahar-Danush*, and from the *Old Testament* and the *Apocrypha*. This probably was the extent of the Oriental literature that was available to Southey. He supplemented these sources with such publications as D'Herbelot's *Bibliothèque Orientale*, Knolles's *General Historie of the Turks*, Marigny's *Histoire des Arabes*, Pococke's *Description of the East*, and Morgan's *History of Algiers*. Far more important, however, were volumes of voyages and travels, which had steadily grown in number through the eighteenth century. With these Southey had a wide acquaintance, and some, indeed, he may have reviewed for the *Critical* in the few years before the composition of *Thalaba*. In his notes he goes back as far as to Hakluyt and Purchas, and he refers frequently to later seventeenth-century writers, such as Olearius, Chardin with the profuse illustrations to his book on Persia, and

Tavernier. Of more modern books, there was great abundance; Shaw, Volney, Chénier, Carsten Niebuhr, Mungo Park, La Pérouse, are some of the men to whom Southey was most indebted for local color. Finally he makes careful acknowledgement for much of his witch-lore and some of his imagery to a mass of curious and out-of-the-way sources that need not be detailed here.

There was a pedantic look about all this learned apparatus that was not lessened by the printing of the author's references illustrating camels, simoons, Arabian cookery, and the like as footnotes to the pages of the first edition. The opportunity for ridicule thus afforded was quickly seized. Jeffrey said that, when Southey had filled his commonplace book, he began to write, and that the pattern of his work had only the merit of those patch-work draperies to be met with in "the mansions of the industrious, where a blue tree overshadows a shell-fish, and a gigantic butterfly seems ready to swallow up Palemon and Lavinia."[1]

Southey felt that this criticism was unjust because most of his poem was distinctly original in design and execution. Certainly it was a remarkable achievement for him to fuse the details of his background into so smoothly-running a piece of machinery. Nevertheless, the reader to-day is inclined to admit the truth of the criticism. As a representation of the Orient, *Thalaba* is a *tour-de-force*, dazzling but hollow because Southey made no advance, except in the bulk of his learning, upon Sayers. The great innovation of Scott was that in far larger measure he succeeded in showing, not merely the costume, manners, scenery, and mythology of strange times and places, but life itself regardless of all strangeness of time and place. For life in all its forms he had no contempt, but abundant love and that imaginative sympathy which enabled him to reveal it as he saw it. Never do we find Scott, upon the basis of

[1] *Edin. Rev.*, v. I, 77–78.

some meager second-hand information, damning a whole
civilization, expressing a wish that it might be entirely
swept away, and at the same time utilizing it as "machinery" for the explication of a totally foreign moral doctrine
of his own.   Yet that was what Southey did in *Thalaba*,
and the criticism that would associate him with Scott shows
but scant understanding of the latter's greatness of soul
and scope of mind.

Enough has been said to show that, in spite of the
handicaps under which he labored, Southey's knowledge of
the Orient was considerable.   Upon this point it is difficult
to be just to him.   His limitations, as betrayed in *Thalaba*,
are so positive and so concrete, so conspicuously those of
his race as well as of his time, that we are apt to allow too
little credit to his unceasing activity in seeking and spreading information.   This labor not only strengthened the
soundest things in his mind, but it constituted what was
probably his greatest service to his generation, a service
no less great for being difficult to measure.   Yet the limitations must be stated.   With the same theory of life to
expound as Wordsworth, Southey distorted Mohammedanism, as the other "lake poet" distorted nature, to prove
his point.   Neither was wholly true to the facts of his
subject; yet each made a parade of veracity.   Of the true
spirit of the east Southey remained as ignorant as Wordsworth did of the true science of nature.   All his reading
was done, like all the observation of the other, not to en-
large his own spirit, but merely to confirm his preconcep-
tions about life, and to condemn what disagreed with them.
In short, he traveled to the Orient in the same spirit in
which he had gone to Spain, — to congratulate himself at
every step that he was an Englishman.   He wore his
Arabian plumage precisely as the English ladies wore the
rich Indian shawls sent home by kinsmen free-booting in
the train of Warren Hastings.   The attitude of the home-

loving, middle-class Englishman was that you had better
stay in England if you were able to afford it, but if you
went out to India, you had better garner all the wealth
you could as rapidly as possible, and hurry back to be a
Nabob before it should be too late. This was the spirit
with which Southey approached his subject. "Somebody
should do for the Hindoo gods," he wrote to Taylor, when
he had read Sir William Jones and a French translation of
the *Zend-Avesta*, "what Dr. Sayers has done for Odin; we
know enough of them now for a poetical system."[1] Enough
forsooth! Enough for an Englishman, but for the Hindoos
and the Hindoo gods how little!

In July, 1799, Southey read Sale's translation of the
Koran, and found it dull and repetitious. When he came
to make the characters of his poem talk,[2] he therefore used
the language of the *Old Testament*, because, he said, the
tame language of the *Koran* can hardly be remembered by
the few who have toiled through its tautologies. By Mohammed himself Southey was puzzled. The prophet might
have been an "enthusiast," but the fact that he had a
verse of the *Koran* revealed in order that he might marry
the wife of Zeid stamped him as an impostor. In spite of
this lack of sympathy, the author of *Thalaba* was at about
the same time planning to make this scoundrel the theme
of an epic all to himself, keeping, of course, "the mob of
his wives . . . out of sight."

To the spirit of Mohammed's religion Southey's own
spirit bore only the resemblance that it bore to all religious
systems in which the passion of faith is particularly stressed.
"I began with the religion of the *Koran*," he said of his
projected mythological series, "and consequently founded
the interest of the story upon that resignation, which is the
only virtue it has produced."[3] *Thalaba* is not, however,

---

[1] *Taylor*, I, 262–263.   [2] *Thalaba*, Bk. I, 3–4.
[3] *Thalaba*, 2d ed. Note to Bk. I, p. 29; *Life*, III, 352.

an expression of Mohammedan fatalism. Southey's faith in his own ideals had steeled him to resignation, and this steeling is the theme of his poem. What faith had not done was to change his resignation to that indifference which is fatalism. Any other religion, therefore, which gives opportunity for the celebration of faith would have served equally well as "machinery," and indeed Southey found himself turning to faith as the theme of all his epics and romances. As for the art and literature of the Orient, the author of *Thalaba* takes an early occasion in the notes to his poem to deliver a round condemnation of both, stating that all the work of eastern artists is characterized by waste of ornament and labor. He had seen Persian illuminated manuscripts which were to him nonsensically absurd because they showed, not representations of life and manners, but curves and lines like those of a Turkey carpet. The little Oriental literature that had reached Europe he pronounced equally worthless, and said that to call Ferdusi,[1] whom he admitted to have seen only in a bad rimed translation, the Oriental Homer is sacrilege. This unscholarly attitude toward his subject matter is even more strikingly illustrated in the same note. The *Arabian Tales*, by which he may refer to the *Arabian Nights* or more probably to the spurious *Continuation*, "certainly abound with genius; they have lost their metaphorical rubbish in passing through the filter of a French translation." How Southey could have had any just notion of the metaphorical rubbish of an Arabian work that he knew only in filtration, it is a little difficult to see, unless he supposed that the style of the *Bahar-Danush*, a Persian story which he saw in either or both of two English translations, was characteristic of all Arabian literature. Finally, we must observe that Occidental imperialism intrudes even into the very text

[1] Sir William Jones, *On the Poetry of the Eastern Nations* in his *Poems*, 2d ed., 1777; *Thalaba*, Bk. I, 9–10.

of *Thalaba*. When his hero arrives at Bagdad, the poet indulges in a little independent elegy and prophecy. He regrets the ignorance and servitude that in his time obtained in the city, but expresses the hope that one day the Crescent may be plucked from the Mosques by wisdom when the enlightened arm of Europe conquers to redeem the East.[1]

In view of all that has just been said, there is a certain irony in the fact that the acknowledged source of the immediate suggestion for the story of *Thalaba* came from a piece of spurious Orientalism. In his original preface Southey says that "In the continuation of the Arabian Tales, the Dom-Daniel is mentioned; a Seminary for evil Magicians under the Roots of the Sea. From this seed the present Romance has grown." The work here referred to was *La Suite des Mille et Une Nuits, Contes Arabes*, published as a part of the *Cabinet des Fées* (1788–1799), and purporting to be translated from the Arabic by a certain Dom Chavis and M. Cazotte. Chavis was an Arab and Cazotte was a clever cleric, but these tales were at most but very free versions of originals which, if they ever existed, were scanty and have disappeared. In 1792 the book was translated into English by Robert Heron with the title, *Arabian Tales, or, A Continuation of the Arabian Nights Entertainments*. More than the mere conception of a seminary for evil magicians may have been suggested to Southey by this collection. One of its four volumes is entirely given up to the story of a wicked enchanter named Maugraby. He and his equally wicked parents "were the founders of the formidable Dom-Daniel of Tunis, that school of magic whose rulers tyrannize over all the wicked spirits that desolate the earth, and which is the den where those monsters are engendered that have overrun the country of Africa." The master of all this is, of course,

[1] Bk. V, 262–267.

Zatanai, or Satan himself, and his servant, Maugraby, makes it his chief business to lure kings to give him their first-born sons, whom he educates, or in the event of their proving unworthy pupils in the black arts, tortures in the Dom-Daniel caverns, "the chief roots of which lie concealed under the waters of the ocean." In the course of time a prince of Syria is introduced as one of Maugraby's victims. He, gaining superior knowledge of magic, destroys the enchanter's power, breaks the charms of the Dom-Daniel, and releases all its victims. The place itself, however, he is unable to overthrow. "That great work," it is said, "is reserved for the powers of Mahomet," and the Dom-Daniel is to be "burnt and destroyed with all its contents" by a hero named Zanate Kalifé.

This theme Southey developed rather under the influence of Ariosto and Spenser than of the *Arabian Tales* or of the *Arabian Nights*, but there are certain other bits of resemblance to his immediate source which are worthy of mention. The first is a resemblance in spirit. In that respect in which Cazotte, — for he seems to have been the responsible party to the joint authorship, — differed most from the *Mille et Une Nuits* Southey most resembled him. One of the eternal charms of the *Arabian Nights*, at least to a reader of the present day, is their expression of that naïve love of power which most men and nations at some time feel. To wave a wand, to cry "Sesame," to push a button, to say a word into a telephone, and be wafted through space by magic or by taxi, which of us has ever quite outgrown such small-boyishness? Here is one of the charms of the *Arabian Nights*. Magic may be bad or good, as the exigencies of the story demand, but we are not interested in it for its badness or its goodness; we are interested because it is magic and will do things. Not so with the eighteenth-century European. In the tale of Maugraby, magic is all bad; it exists, not to be enjoyed, but destroyed.

In *Thalaba* it is the same. Cazotte's hero, therefore, shatters the hideous idol of the Dom-Daniel standing poised against him to strike if his courage or his knowledge should fail, and burns all the instruments of magic, especially an immunizing ring like that of Thalaba. Finally Cazotte dwells upon the idea that the wicked are always hoist with their own petard, and makes Maugraby the author of his own overthrow. The resemblances to all this in *Thalaba* are obvious, and it must be said that the earlier tale is by no means an unworthy predecessor of the later.

The *Arabian Tales* provided the central situation; the sources for the leading episodes in Southey's plot are suggested in a letter to Taylor in January, 1799,[1] as well as in the notes to the poem itself. The story of the boy who has lost his father by murder, who is exiled with his mother in childhood, and who grows up to return and take vengeance upon his father's foe is obviously but a stock theme from romance in general. Southey decorated it with the Mohammedan tradition of the garden of Iram of which he read in the *Koran*, Sale, and D'Herbelot. From the same sources came Haruth and Maruth, and hence, too, as well as from the *Arabian Nights*, *Arabian Tales*, and much reading in demonology and other curious literature, came the enchanters with all their apparatus. The bowers of Aloadin were suggested by the account of the paradise of Aladeules which Purchas gives from Marco Polo. Finally the Arctic and marine landscape into which Southey transported the Dom-Daniel from its original Tunis was suggested to him by the French traveler La Pérouse.

Southey's opinion of his own work was not uncertain, and he would have added, not unduly flattering. In this connection he made a distinction between two faculties of the poet's mind which somewhat suggests that which Coleridge and Wordsworth made between fancy and imagination.

[1] *Taylor*, I, 247.

Joan and *Madoc*, he felt, were more closely related to truth and to human nature. They represented Robert Southey, the man; *Thalaba* was a romance, displaying not truth or character or Robert Southey; — it was a work, rather, of the fancy, indeed of pure imagination, using the word in the contrary sense to that in which the other two poets used it. With this limitation, *Thalaba* was, nevertheless, in its author's judgment, a great achievement. He knew no poem that deserved a place between it and the *Orlando*, and was even ready, if he cared to speak out, to assert that it might stand comparison with Ariosto's work; certainly it could be weighed with Wieland's *Oberon*. Speak out he did in another place where he asserted that there was no poem of equal originality save *The Faerie Queene*, "which I regard almost with a religious love and veneration."

The reasons why the world has not accepted the poet's rating of his own work are not far to seek. It cannot be denied that Southey possessed eloquence, descriptive power, rhetorical effectiveness, skill in versification, and above all a genuinely sincere ideal, but neither can it be denied that he never displayed any of these qualities with more than second-rate ability. He remained always in the tragic position of the man who, within his limitations, has left nothing undone that he can do to be a very great poet, and lacks nothing necessary for being one except genius. The fact that he lost while playing gallantly for the highest stakes should not detract from our personal respect for him. *Thalaba*, although it made some stir in the world, fell lukewarm from the press, and has lain so ever since. The explanation for this failure to achieve even popularity was supplied to the author by William Taylor both in letters and in the review which he wrote for the *Critical*.[1]   Taylor maintained that the fundamental fault was the "moral

[1] *Crit. Rev.*, Dec. 1803, 2d ser., v. 39, 369–379.

improbability," the lack of recognizable human motive in
the story and character of the hero. He "is a talismanic
statue, of whose joints capricious destiny pulls the strings,
who with a forgiving temper undertakes a work of vengeance, and who is moved here and there one knows not
why or wherefore."[1] This is Taylor's central contention,
but he also notes the bewildering effect of the whirling
witchcraft and the ever-shifting style.

"The ballad lends its affecting simplicity, the heroic poem its
learned solemnity, the drama its dialogue form, and the ode its
versatility of metre. All the fountains of expression are brought
together, and gush with sousing vehemence and drifting rapidity
on the reader: who admires, but not at ease, and feels tossed as in
the pool of a cataract, not gliding as in a frequented stream."[2]
And of the confusions of the magic he says, "There is in Thalaba a
sort of pantomimic scene-shifting; harlequin touches the landscape
with his wand, and it becomes a palace of flame or a desert of snow,
but *cui bono?*"[3]

This criticism was sufficiently severe, although much of it
had been previously expressed in letters, to make Taylor
suffer some apprehension lest Southey should feel sore at the
publication of such sentiments. The poet was·man enough
to take the whole article in good part, and to be grateful
for the generous modicum of praise which Taylor also gave,
expecting, indeed, that this review would help the sale of
the poem. As for adopting any of the criticisms, that was
out of the question. The second edition did eliminate
some of the demonology from the ninth book, relegated
the notes to a less conspicuous place, and made minor
changes in the diction and versification, but more thoroughgoing reformation was impossible.

There has never been any danger that public taste would
not confirm Taylor's judgment. The habit of disparage-
ment that has persisted about Southey has assessed his

[1] *Taylor*, I, 373–374.   [2] *Crit. Rev., l. c.*   [3] *Taylor*, I, 390.

faults at their full value. However often we read it, *Thalaba* is still a bewildering poem that slips from the memory before we are aware. The moral that it teaches we prefer to obtain in the naked vigor of the *Happy Warrior*, or in the magic verse and with all the subtle implications of Spenser. The glamor of other times and places still comes to us in more lifelike terms and without the smell of the scholar's farthing candle in the true wizardry of Scott. Finally, and this may be Southey's greatest praise, the mystery of strange seas and continents comes to us with more convincing power from Shelley, who made the scenery of *Thalaba* his own in *Alastor*. Yet many a poem of far less worth has received larger meed of amiable praise from critics. *Thalaba* failed of its high purpose, true, but the theme was of the noblest, the intent courageous, labor not lacking, and the performance so near to success that the reader is surprised to find the poem more beautiful than he had expected or remembered. Unfortunately Southey has not quite succeeded in that conspicuous kind of poetry wherein anything short of supreme success meets but little charity. *Thalaba* is almost a great poem; yet almost to achieve immortality is to be but mortal after all.

III

Joan of Arc inaugurated its author's reputation; *Thalaba* now settled his position before the public, for upon the appearance of this work the still more or less vaguely expressed notion that the younger poets were making a concerted effort at innovation in the style and subject matter of poetry was crystallized and proclaimed in the pages of the first number of *The Edinburgh Review*. The poem had been sent from Lisbon to London in October, 1800, and accepted by Longman for an edition of a thousand octavo copies at a price to the author of £115. Davy and Danvers were to overlook the press; they did so very badly. The peculiarities of Southey's meter were rendered more conspicuous by obscure punctuation, and the page arrangement was spoilt by the manner of printing the voluminous notes. These were strung along the bottoms of the pages in such a way that in many places the reader was forced to suspend from a single line of text solid blocks of fine print on Oriental geography, mythology, and history. Before Southey's return from Portugal in June this damage was done, and the book had appeared. The sale was slow from the first; only three hundred copies had been sold by November 20, 1801. Not until October, 1808,[1] were the first thousand copies exhausted, and a second edition, better punctuated, the verse paragraphs numbered, and the notes relegated to the ends of the books, rendered possible. No further issue of the volume was called for until the publication of Southey's complete poems in 1837.[2]

The ill success of *Thalaba* was no indication of the attention which the poem attracted in literary circles. "Sa reputation est faite," wrote the poet in his sportive French, "mais sa fortune — helas! n'importe." A band of young wits in a Scotch lawyer's third-story flat in Buccleuch Place, Edinburgh, happened at this very time to be planning a new organ of Whig politics and criticism, and in October, 1802, the first number of their *Edinburgh Review* appeared. Of the new era in periodical publications marked by the *Edinburgh*, of the consequent eclipse of the *Monthly*, the *Critical*, and the lesser reviews, of the authority in criticism which it immediately assumed, it would be needless to speak here in detail. But in that first number, received with an acclaim that amazed even its editors, one of the most conspicuous and trenchant articles was a review

---

[1] *Warter*, II, 101, 107.

[2] In the *Works* the *Preface* to the first edition is reprinted under the caption, "Preface to the Fourth Edition." This is an error. There was no fourth edition.

of *Thalaba* by Francis Jeffrey himself in which that redoubtable law-giver to literature defined the tenets of the new
"sect" in poetry as deduced from their practices and as
illustrated by *Thalaba* and by the *Lyrical Ballads*. While
regretting that genius should be so misspent, Jeffrey condemned all three poets, and suddenly lifted the railings of
the *Anti-Jacobin* to the level of serious criticism. Thus
Southey became fixed in the public mind as a member, if
not the leader, of an actual conspiracy of poets later to
be known as "the lake school."

That Southey, Coleridge, Lamb, and Lloyd had been
associated together by the *Anti-Jacobin* as a group of
writers with peculiar and up-setting notions in politics as
well as poetry, we have already seen. The last number
of the original *Anti-Jacobin and Weekly Examiner* had appeared July 9, 1798, with the satire entitled *The New
Morality* as a parting broadside to all Jacobins, but especially to the Jacobin poets. In the same month, with the
same publisher and the same politics, though under far
different editorship, began *The Anti-Jacobin Review*. The
very first number proceeded to take advantage of the
popularity achieved by *The New Morality*, and published
an elaborate caricature by Gillray illustrating those lines
in the satire that describe the Jacobin newspapers, politicians, and poets, "tuning their harps to praise Lépaux."
The picture represents that gentleman as the leader of the
"theo-philanthropic sect of Marat, Mirabeau, and Voltaire."
Justice, Philanthropy, and Sensibility, all in suitable Jaco-
binical attitudes, watch over him. Before him stand tooting
figures to represent

> "*Couriers* and *Stars*, Sedition's Evening Host,
>   Thou *Morning Chronicle*, and *Morning Post*."

Then in the center of the picture, grouped about a "Cornucopia of Ignorance," labeled "*Analytical Review, Monthly*

Review, Critical Review," and belching pamphlets, are grouped the Jacobin authors. Most conspicuous of these is Southey with an ass's head standing in the immediate foreground at the mouth of the cornucopia. He is braying praises to Lépaux from a volume in his hand inscribed *Southey's Saphics* [sic],[1] and *Joan of Arc* is thrust into the pocket of his coat. In the background stands a similar figure holding before him *Coleridge's Dactylics*.[2] Finally, two frog-figures, representing Lloyd and Lamb, squat behind Southey in the picture, and croak from *Blank Verse by Toad and Frog*. Other men who were attacked in the poem are also represented: Priestley, Whitfield, Thelwall, Paine, Godwin, Holcroft, Erskine, Grey, Courtenay, Whitbread, and Leviathan Bedford hooked by Burke. Southey did not fail to see this production, and was half amused by it. "The fellow has not, however," he wrote (Aug. 29, 1798) to his brother, "libeled my likeness, because he did not know it, so he clapped an ass's head upon my shoulders." To Wynn he wrote (Aug. 15, 1798) more seriously that *The Anti-Jacobin* had stupidly lumped together men of opposite principles, who should have been shown welcoming the Director rather than Lépaux, and that the editors would have much to answer for in thus inflaming political animosities.

After this beginning one might have expected *The Anti-Jacobin Review* to become a consistent opponent of Southey and his brethren. This is not the case. They were, however, attacked in September, 1798, in another poem called *The Anarchists, — an Ode*, which, after representing Paine, Priestley, Thelwall, Godwin, and Holcroft praising anarchy, describes the Jacobin poets doing the same, and follows them with Fox, Norfolk, and Bedford.

[1] *Poems*, 1797, *The Widow*, 82.
[2] *Poems*, 1797, *The Soldier's Wife*, 81. The third stanza is accredited in a footnote to S. T. Coleridge.

"See! faithful to their mighty dam,
C[oleri]dge, S[ou]th[e]y, L[loy]d, and L[am]be,
In splay-foot madrigals of love,
Soft-moaning like the widow'd dove,
Pour, side by side, their sympathetic notes;
   Of equal rights, and civic feasts,
   And tyrant Kings, and knavish priests,
Swift through the land the tuneful mischief floats.
And now to softer strains they struck the lyre,
   They sung the beetle, or the mole,
   The dying kid, or ass's foal,
By cruel man permitted to expire." [1]

Of this attack Southey does not appear to have heard, and then but indirectly, until 1801. Writing in February from Lisbon, he said of *Thalaba*, "It is so utterly innocent of all good drift; it may pass through the world like Richard Cromwell, notwithstanding the sweet savour of its father's name. Do you know that they have caricatured me between Fox and Norfolk — worshiping Bonaparte? Poor me — at Lisbon — who have certainly molested nothing but Portuguese spiders." [2] Yet *The Anti-Jacobin* criticasters were henceforth sparing in their notice of the new poets. The second edition of *Joan of Arc* received but meager attention, [3] and that dealt with politics, not poetry. The *Poems* of 1799, however, were attacked on the score of style. In the prefatory note to the *English Eclogues* in that volume, Southey had written, "The following Eclogues, I believe, bear no resemblance to any poems in our language." The reviewer added, "No — nor to any poetry in any language," and then expressed disgust with the meanness of the subjects and the antiquated phraseology. This was

[1] *Anti-Jac. Rev.*, v. I, 365–367.

[2] I have found no such caricature of Southey and others worshiping Bonaparte in either of two copies of *The Anti-Jacobin Review* which I have examined.

[3] *Anti-Jac. Rev.*, June, 1799, v. 3, 120–128.

the last time that any of Southey's poetry was reviewed in the *Anti-Jacobin*, but in January, 1800,[1] thrown off his guard by anonymity and absence of politics, the reviewer of the *Lyrical Ballads* wrote a thoroughgoing puff, praising even *The Idiot Boy*.

When we turn to the reviews that compose the "cornucopia of ignorance," the *Monthly*, the *Critical*, and the *Analytical*, we find almost as little penetration as in the *Anti-Jacobin*. Nevertheless, the name of Southey occurs with some frequency upon their pages; those of Coleridge, Wordsworth, Lamb, and Lloyd more rarely, and then often in conjunction with Southey. The existence of some loose union or "school" among these young poets was now taken for granted, and they are singly or collectively charged with affected simplicity, antiquated phraseology, prosaic style, and vulgar subject matter. Thus the ground was prepared for Jeffrey, to whom it was left, by giving the new poets more serious and extended attention, to turn these carping jews-harps of criticism into the trumpet of a battle of books.

We have seen that the *Monthly*, the *Critical*, and the *Analytical* had all smacked their lips over *Joan of Arc*, and for sake of his politics had acclaimed the youthful author. This not only insured more attentive notice to his later works, but it also brought him the opportunity to become a reviewer himself, first in the *Critical* and later in the short-lived *Annual*, an organ conducted for Longman by Dr. Aiken, author of the review of *Joan* in the *Analytical*. The *Monthly* followed up its notice of *Joan* by another[2] in similar vein upon the *Poems* of 1797, in which it is said that true poetry, though with some negligence, is always to be expected from this youthful genius. The *Poems on the Slave Trade*, the inscription *For a Tablet on the Banks*

[1] *Anti-Jac. Rev.*, April, Jan., v. 5, 334.
[2] *Month. Rev.*, March, 1797, n.s.,v. 22, 297–302.

of a Stream, and *Botany Bay Eclogues* are all highly commended. A few months later the *Letters written during a
Short Residence in Spain and Portugal* were praised[1] for the
warmth of interest which the author took in "the general
welfare and true happiness of his fellow-creatures, in every
quarter of the habitable globe." Coleridge, meanwhile,
although receiving less notice than Southey, did not go
entirely without attention. His *Poems on Various Subjects*
(1796) was reviewed by the *Monthly* in June of the same
year.[2] The notice was brief, referring to him as an associate of Southey, and praising his sublimity and power.
In March, 1797, his *Ode on the Departing Year* (1796) was
mentioned[3] in perfunctory fashion, and a puff of his 1798
volume containing *Fears in Solitude, France,—an Ode,* and
Frost at Midnight appeared in May, 1799.[4] In this article
it is noteworthy that the reviewer takes occasion to commend literary as well as political heresy; here is an author,
he says in effect, who makes no use "of exploded though
elegant mythology, nor does he seek fame by singing of
what is called *Glory.*" With the review of the *Lyrical
Ballads* in June, 1799,[5] the *Monthly* struck a new note that
had rather more of what was to be the familiar sound of
criticism against the authors of that volume. "So much
genius and originality are discovered in this publication,
that we wish to see another from the same hand, written
on more elevated subjects and in a more cheerful disposition." On questions of politics, the poor, and the war,
this reviewer now took occasion to differ, and he insisted
that much of the volume was not to be regarded as poetry
because it had been imitated from such crude fourteenth-

[1] *Month. Rev.,* July, 1797, n.s.,v. 23, 302–306.
[2] *Ibid.,* June, 1796, n.s.,v. 20, 194–199.
[3] *Ibid.,* March, 1797, n.s.,v. 22, 342–343.
[4] *Ibid.,* May, 1799, n.s.,v. 29, 43–47.
[5] *Ibid.,* June, 1799, n.s.,v. 29, 202–210.

century models as Chaucer, and dealt too freely with low life. Of *The Ancient Mariner* he says that it is written "in imitation of the *style* as well as the spirit of the elder poets, [and] is the strangest story of a cock and a bull that we ever saw on paper; yet, though it seems a rhapsody of unintelligible wildness and incoherence . . . , there are in it poetical touches of an exquisite kind." As for *Tintern Abbey*, it is "poetical, beautiful, and philsosphical; but somewhat tinctured with gloomy, narrow, and unsociable ideas of seclusion from the commerce of the world." Southey's *Poems* of 1799 were reviewed at some length and in the same tone.[1] The poet was advised to labor longer, and he was condemned for prosiness, for his low vulgar style, his triviality, his use of "monkish" models, his imitation of "the rudest productions of the last two centuries," and for obsolete language. "Let Mr. Southey look up to the classic models, instead of the monkish trash which he has studied, and he will find reason enough for congratulating himself on his change of objects." In April of the same year the attack was pressed [2] with more vigor against *The Annual Anthology* for 1799. The ballads were again singled out for objection, and the author was advised, instead of imitating the "quaintness of the old writers," or seeking, as in *Bishop Bruno*, "a very indifferent resemblance of halfpenny ballads," to adopt Gay and Goldsmith as his models. Again Southey is said to be prosaic, obscure, bizarre, and to affect simplicity. The rimeless experiments and the *English Eclogues* came in for special condemnation. Of *The Last of the Family*, for instance, it is said that "Mr. S. has proved so very correct in his imitation of the gossiping Farmer James and Farmer Gregory that he has taken off much from the gravity as well as the interest of the piece." After this the *Monthly* neglected Southey for a

---

[1] *Month. Rev.*, March, 1800, n.s.,v. 31, 261–267.

[2] *Ibid.*, April, 1800, n.s.,v. 31, 352–363.

time, and it moderated its tone considerably in dealing with the second edition of the *Lyrical Ballads*.[1] Upon that occasion it even expressed a "hope that this will not prove the last time of our meeting this natural, easy, sentimental Bard, in his pensive rambles through the wilds and groves of his truly poetic, though somewhat peculiar, imagination."

Yet the unfriendliness of the *Monthly's* new attitude[2] toward the erstwhile Jacobin poets was plain and not without significance. Its criticism had now laid aside the tone of partisan puffery that had arisen about *Joan of Arc*, and confined itself more strictly to literary matters. Moreover, the traits in the *Lyrical Ballads* and in the 1799 volumes which the *Monthly* objected to were precisely those against which Jeffrey was at a later time to direct his shafts, — affected simplicity, prosaic style, and apish imitation of barbarous models.

The criticisms upon the new poets in *The Analytical Review*, — after, that is, its article upon *Joan*, — and of the orthodox *British Critic* were colorless and negligible, but not so with *The Critical Review*. Previous to *Joan of Arc* that organ had noticed,[3] though at first only in the spirit of perfunctory partisanship, the early volumes of Southey, Coleridge, and even of Wordsworth. Then, in February, 1796, *Joan of Arc* was received in its pages with what acclaim we have already seen, and after that the *Critical* accorded more vigorous attention to Southey and Coleridge. The latter's *Poems on Various Subjects* (1796) was noticed

[1] *Month. Rev.*, June, 1802, n.s.,v. 38, 209.

[2] Southey was anxious to discover the identity of his new critic in the *Monthly*, and mentioned the matter at least twice (July 5, 1800; Nov. 11, 1801) in his letters to Taylor, broadly hinting for information. Taylor suspected (Nov. 22, 1801) from internal evidence only that the reviewer may have been James Mackintosh or his wife. *Taylor*, I, 353, 378–379, 388–389.

[3] *Crit. Rev.*, July, 1793, 2d ser., v. 8, 347; Nov. 1794, 2d ser., v. 12, 260–262; April, 1795, 2d ser., v. 13, 420–421.

at length in June, 1796,[1] with general commendation, but
with certain exceptions to innovations in language and
versification. It was carefully noted by the reviewer that,
of Coleridge's *Effusions* in this volume, "the first half
of the fifteenth was written by Mr. Southey, the ingenious
author of *Joan of Arc*," and that, of the sonnets, three
were the work of Mr. Charles Lamb of the India House.
The *Critical's* account of Southey's *Poems* of 1797 adopts
the same tone that had been used toward *Joan*, for which
the poet is here said to be already well known. *The Triumph of Woman, Sonnets on the Slave Trade,* and *Botany
Bay Eclogues* are, for political reasons, singled out for
praise. "The same animated description, the same spirit
of benevolence, and the same love of virtue that pervaded
Mr. Southey's former poems will be found in this volume."[2]
When we come to the little book which Coleridge published
in 1798, containing *France,—an Ode,* we find that the *Critical*
mitigates its commendation, and asserts that the author
"too frequently mistakes bombast and obscurity for sublimity." It is further claimed now that "our lyric poets"
attempt too often "to support trifling ideas with a pom-
posity of thought," whatever that may mean. Nevertheless the second edition of *Joan of Arc* came in for very
flattering attention,[3] although the *Poems by S. T. Coleridge
To which are added Poems by Charles Lamb and Charles
Lloyd* were only briefly noticed,[4] and *Blank Verse* by
Charles Lloyd and Charles Lamb was but half-heartedly
praised.[5]

It is not impossible that Southey was himself responsible
for the two last-mentioned reviews, for he was by this time

[1] *Crit. Rev.*, June, 1796, 2d ser., v. 17, 209–212.

[2] *Ibid.*, March, 1797, 2d ser., v. 19, 304–307.

[3] *Ibid.*, June, 1798, 2d ser., v. 23, 196–200.

[4] *Ibid.*, July, 1798, 2d ser., v. 23, 266–268.

[5] *Ibid.*, Sept., 1798, 2d ser., v. 24, 232–233.

one of the *Critical's* regular contributors, and some volumes of poetry seem to have fallen to him for dissection. After six months at Bristol, in 1797, he had gone up to London near the end of the year for his first term of law, and on December 24 he said, "I write now for *The Critical Review.*" This connection undoubtedly continued during more than a year, for we know that he was the author of the review of the *Lyrical Ballads* in the October number, and in 1799 there are several references in his letters to show that he was regularly at work for Hamilton until interrupted by ill-health. In January, 1800, Southey had not reviewed a book for three months. This breach continued during the year of his second sojourn in Portugal, but in July, 1801, shortly after his return, he applied successfully for a renewal of the former arrangement, and wrote for the *Critical*, in spite of vicissitudes of the publisher costly to his contributors, until the close of 1803, when the editor ceased applying for Southey's criticism just at the time when the latter had found a better market for his wares with Longman and the *Annual*.[1] His hand in the *Critical* is probably not in every case to be distinguished from the dull fists of other hacks, but we can identify some of his work. Specific references in letters certainly indicate that he reviewed the *Lyrical Ballads*,[2] Landor's *Gebir*,[3] some part of Joanna Baillie's series of plays,[4] and a few obscurer publications. His statement in January, 1799, that he had some weeks before "killed off" a bundle of French books probably points to his responsibility for several articles appearing in December, 1798, in which political opinions characteristic of him were expressed in his characteristic, clear, rapid style.

---

[1] *Taylor*, I, 500.

[2] *Ibid.*, 223; *Crit. Rev.*, Oct. 1798, 2d ser., v. 24, 197–204.

[3] *Life*, II, 240; *Crit. Rev.*, Sept. 1799, 2d ser., v. 27, 29–38.

[4] *Ibid.* 240; *Crit. Rev.*, Sept. 1798, 2d ser., v. 24, 13–22, Feb. 1803, 2d ser., v. 37, 200–212.

Style and opinions also tend to show that Southey was the author of reviews of Kotzebue, Schiller, Ellis's *Specimens of Early English Poets*, and Anderson's *British Poets*. Finally, it may be noted that, during the months that Southey wrote for the *Critical*, there appeared in its pages accounts of various books of travel, such as those of La Pérouse and Mungo Park, which were later referred to in connection with *Thalaba*. To search much farther in the dusty files of the *Critical* for work of Southey's, however, would hardly prove profitable. His method of criticism was as a rule the usual one of summary and excerpt with a modicum of perfunctory comment but with less than usual acerbity. He quite frankly reserved "the lazy work of reviewing bad books" (Feb. 20, 1800) for the hours when he was too weary for other work, and he thought the *Critical* so miserably bad that he felt no impulse to write in any but an indolent way for it himself. He owned to great expectations that the *Edinburgh Review* would surpass its London rivals because English authors would be personally unknown to its reviewers, and confessed at the same time that he himself got the worthless poems of good-natured acquaintances, to whom he tried to give no pain but rather such milk-and-water praise of smooth versification and moral tendency as might take in some to buy. "I have rarely scratched without giving a plaister for it; except, indeed, where a fellow puts a string of titles to his name, or such an offender as — appears, and then my inquisitorship, instead of actually burning him, only ties a few crackers to his tail" (Dec. 22, 1802). The superficiality of Southey's criticism is exemplified even in his account of *Gebir*, great as his admiration of that poem was, for he gives merely a summary of the story interspersed with quotation and with praise which, though sincere, is certainly rather general. The faults of the work are said to be incoherence and obscurity. "Of its beauties, our readers must already be sensible. They are of the first order; every circumstance is displayed with a force and accuracy which painting cannot exceed. . . . We have read his poem with more than common attention, and with far more than common delight." This was enough to warm the heart of Landor and open the way for friendship, but it is not acute criticism. The most interesting of Southey's reviews in the *Critical* was that of the *Lyrical Ballads* in October, 1798.[1] This is famous for a little understood remark upon *The Ancient Mariner;* justice would also add that, except for this one ineptitude, Southey's opinion sums up about what later taste has felt concerning the book. He notes to begin with that the poems included in its pages were "to be considered as experiments," and in conclusion that "the experiment . . . has failed, not because the language of conversation is little adapted to 'the purposes of poetic pleasure,' but because it has been tried upon uninteresting subjects. Yet every piece discovers genius; and, ill as the author has frequently employed his talents, they certainly rank him with the best of living poets." Surely we should disagree with little in this opinion as far as it goes; yet it is even harsher than the article as a whole. One may not admit that *The Idiot Boy* and *The Thorn* fail because of their subjects, but fail they certainly do. Of the former Southey says, "It resembles a Flemish picture in the worthlessness of its design and the excellence of its execution," and *The Ancient Mariner*, in a notorious phrase, is also condemned for expending too much art upon matters of small moment. "Many of the stanzas are laboriously beautiful; but in connection they are absurd or unintelligible." Hence he can say, "We do not sufficiently understand the story to analyze it. It is a Dutch attempt at German sublimity. Genius has here been employed in producing a poem of little merit." Certain other pieces in

[1] *Crit. Rev.*, 2d ser., v. 24, 197–204.

the volume, on the other hand, were singled out for great praise; naturally they are the ones which most resemble those which Southey was himself writing at the time. Coleridge's *The Foster-mother's Tale* and Wordsworth's *The Female Vagrant* are attempts to do what Southey was trying to do in his *English Eclogues*. Coleridge's *The Dungeon* might have been a companion piece to his fellow-pantisocrat's inscriptions for martyrs of liberty. Wordsworth's *Lines left upon a Seat in a Yew-tree* are, of course, in the same manner and vein as those inscriptions of Southey's that deal with the worship of nature. Finally, *Tintern Abbey*, a poem of similar type, expresses supremely that mood of idealism, of self-sufficiency in the mystic contemplation of nature, to which Southey also had arrived. He quotes in great admiration the passage which begins with the sixty-sixth line of the poem as printed in 1798, which centers in the famous lines,

> "And I have felt
> A presence that disturbs me with the joy
> Of elevated thoughts;"

and which concludes with those in which the poet owns himself

> "Well pleased to recognize
> In nature and the language of the sense,
> The anchor of my purest thoughts, the nurse,
> The guide, the guardian of my heart, and soul
> Of all my moral being."

"In the whole range of English poetry," says Southey, "we scarcely recollect anything superior to a part of [this] passage."

At the time this review was written, its author, together with Lamb and Lloyd, was on the outs [1] with Coleridge, and knew his associate but slightly. Though Southey had as

---

[1] *Letters of the Wordsworth Family*, I, 122.

good a reason for writing reviews as that which Wordsworth gave for publishing his poems at this time, — namely
that he needed money, — nevertheless he would undoubtedly
have shown greater tact if he had written nothing about
the *Lyrical Ballads*. For what he wrote he has been bitterly and intemperately condemned [1] on the supposition that
his strictures were prompted by spite against Coleridge.
In view of all the facts this was probably not the case.
Though Southey often spoke without charity of his brother-
in-law's failings as a man, he frequently expressed just

[1] In the introduction to his edition of the *Lyrical Ballads*, Mr.
Thomas Hutchinson, whose conclusions are in the main accepted by
Professor Harper in his *William Wordsworth*, I, 381–382, and by Mr.
Thomas J. Wise in his *Bibliography of Wordsworth* 31, presents the
case against Southey most fully.   In addition to his objections to the
review itself, Mr. Hutchinson thinks that Southey tried to conceal
his authorship of the article, and especially that he warned Cottle to
sell out the copyright of the *Lyrical Ballads* because he intended to
attack the book in the *Critical*.   If concealment had been Southey's
purpose, he knew Cottle too well to have imparted the secret of his
authorship to him; as it was, Wordsworth learned the identity of
his critic from the bookseller upon his return from Germany in 1799,
though the precise date is uncertain.   (The date of Wordsworth's
letter upon the subject to Cottle from Sockburn is given in *Letters of
the Wordsworth Family*, I, 122 merely as 1799.)   That Cottle sold out
the *Lyrical Ballads* to Arch in London within a fortnight of publication
because Southey was going to attack the book is, from the evidence
available, but a conjecture.   An explanation at least equally plausible
and sufficient in itself to account for the sale is plainly suggested by
a letter of Coleridge to which Mr. Hutchinson refers.   (Coleridge to
Southey [Dec. 24], 1799, Coleridge *Letters*, I, 319.)   Joey had been
plunging as a publisher, and when Coleridge wrote, had evidently been
for some time fighting hard to keep his head above water.   Among the
books that he had put forth, only Southey's had been profitable.   In
1799 the publishing business was therefore wound up by the Bristol
Mæcenas, and all his copyrights sold to Longman.   It is possible, if
not highly probable, that the earlier sale of the *Lyrical Ballads* to Arch
was made to tide over a stringency preliminary to the final outcome of
Cottle's affairs, and may have had nothing to do with Southey's review.

admiration for his abilities.   We must remember that when
this review was written, the tone of periodical criticism was
even less urbane than that which its author adopted.   That
his opinions on *The Idiot Boy, Tintern Abbey,* and the experiments in diction did not have much reason in them, it
would be difficult to prove.   Coleridge, to be sure, had good
ground for thinking that *The Ancient Mariner* had been
unintelligently treated, but Lamb appears to have been the
only one at this time to treat it otherwise, and Wordsworth
spoke of it in his own way with as little appreciation as
Southey.[1]   That the greatest poet of the three should have
felt too much aggrieved at the objections to some of his pieces
to take with good grace the high commendation of others
and of his work as a whole, is no reason why we should agree
with him.   We may more than suspect that nothing but
unmitigated praise would have satisfied him at all.   Finally,
it must be noted that neither of the authors of the *Lyrical
Ballads* retained animosity toward their critic for what
might hastily have been thought treachery.

Southey's article on the *Lyrical Ballads* was the *Critical's*
first notable contribution to the recognition of the new sect
of poets.   Wordsworth thought that it injured the sale of
the book, but proof upon such a point is difficult to establish.   The unusual particularity of the criticism in this
review as well as the striking phrase on *The Ancient Mariner*
probably did their share toward pointing out the peculiarities in the poetry of Southey's associates, and, indeed, of
himself, for many knew him as Coleridge's collaborator and
friend in comparison with the number that knew him at
this time as a reviewer.   The succeeding productions of
the group as a whole were reviewed by the *Critical* with
increasing asperity and with emphasis upon their common
faults.   Southey's 1799 *Poems* were, to be sure, greeted[2]

[1] J. Mc L. Harper, *William Wordsworth,* I, 380, 383.
[2] *Crit. Rev.,* June, 1799, 2d ser., v. 26, 161–164.

with puffing references to the high rank of the author among youthful poets, but mild objections were set up against the too familiar thought and language of the *English Eclogues*. The review of the first *Annual Anthology* (1799),[1] which referred to Southey's sponsorship in the opening sentence, was more outspoken. In a left-handed compliment to the Eclogue, *The Last of the Family*, it is said that this is a "successful specimen of the author's talent in using a familiar vehicle of sympathy and instruction, without falling into that prosaic flatness which is frequently the consequence of such attempts." The critic then roundly damns the poems on a goose, a pig, and a filbert because they "have neither the humourous pomp of burlesque, nor the easy charm of nature." Some months later the foundation of a new school of poets was actually attributed by the *Critical* to Coleridge in a review[2] of his translation of *Wallenstein*. He was there exhorted to teach "his pupils" by precept and example that they should polish their effusions, that carelessness was not ease, and obscurity not sublimity. The same point was made against the second *Annual Anthology* (1800), a number of the poems in which, notably by Southey, Coleridge, Lloyd, and Joseph Cottle, were cited[3] as being "disgraced by that carelessness, or rather that affectation of carelessness, which we have often had occasion to notice and reprobate of late as absurd and pretended attempts at genuine simplicity and ease." More favorable mention, however, was accorded to *The Battle of Blenheim*, which was quoted in full, and of which it was said that it "archly conveys, in strains of poetic simplicity, a most affecting moral."

The drift of all this criticism is sufficiently obvious; the "lake school" was taking shape in the minds of its enemies.

---

[1] *Crit. Rev.*, Jan. 1800, 2d ser., v. 28, 82–89.

[2] *Ibid.*, Oct. 1800, 2d ser., v. 31, 175–185.

[3] *Ibid.*, Dec. 1800, 2d ser., v. 31, 426–431.

We have seen that the names of Southey and Coleridge had appeared together in their volumes of 1796 and 1797, and that for the sake of their principles the anti-ministerial organs had at first acclaimed, as the *Anti-Jacobin* had satirized, the two new poets that had suddenly blazed out together in the critical months of 1797. Now the opposition reviews, in 1798 and 1799, when the stress of political dissension had eased, and the two youths had mitigated some of their ardor, permitted partisan praise gradually to subside, and began to apply their characteristic attitude of mind to more strictly literary matters. They then found much that was incompatible with devotion to that constitution of the literary state which rested upon the prestige of Pope and Dryden. The practices of the new poets, of whom Southey was easily the most conspicuous, Coleridge his best-known associate, and Wordsworth practically unheard of, were discovered to be distinctly subversive, and both *Monthly* and *Critical*, with intermittent support from other quarters, began, as we have seen, to make charges that cover all the main points of rebellion which Jeffrey was soon to assemble, elaborate, and proclaim. These charges are easy to distinguish in the criticisms just surveyed. The school began and continued with innovation, sinister word. Its members used obsolete or vulgar language, they affected simplicity and achieved carelessness, they experimented with verse and became prosaic, they neglected the accepted models, and resorted to the imitation of ones that had been thought safely discarded. As for subject matter, so long as they used the merely sentimental and the semi- or the pseudo-heroic, they met with no disapproval, but the tendency grew to condemn, on the one hand, their use of themes from low or simple life, and on the other their attempts at sublimity, "enthusiasm," and lofty passion. The self-confidence of the new poets and their contempt of criticism account for much of the asperity of the later reviews, and Southey's air in London of personal aloofness from poetasters and criticasters helped to chill any warmth they may have felt in the beginning for the author of *Joan of Arc*.

Such was the situation when the *Edinburgh* appeared and at once appropriated to itself the leadership of criticism. Jeffrey made no break with the methods, style, or principles of his predecessors. Summary, excerpt, and verdict was his procedure as it had been theirs. Their tone of judicial, all-knowing finality, he now merely deepened and made more trenchant. Their assumption of a constitution and oligarchy in literature, he merely made more emphatic. In the first number[1] of the new *Edinburgh Review*, therefore, testifying in the act to the importance of the new poets, Jeffrey passed over the second edition of the *Lyrical Ballads*, preface and all, but made *Thalaba* the subject of his first literary review and the occasion for summing up the naggings of previous critics and for the delivery of a regular indictment against Southey's school for poetic treason.

He begins by laying down the constitution of that literary state before whose bar of criticism English poets were in succession to be summoned. The standards of poetry, he maintains, like those of religion, were fixed long ago, and are not lawfully to be questioned. Saints of the catholic church of the muses appeared early in its history; since then had come schism and heresy. The author before the court of criticism was said to belong to a recently established "sect of poets" and was looked upon as one of its chief champions and apostles. The sect was made up entirely of dissenters in poetry, and so serious was their heresy that it was proposed to make the review of *Thalaba* the occasion for considering the group as a whole. Their principles and the origin of their creed were then analyzed

[1] *Edin. Rev.*, Oct. 1802, v. 1, 63–83.

in detail. First the new poets were all said to betray the anti-social notions of Rousseau, his distempered sensibility, his discontent with the existing constitution of society, his paradoxical morality, and his perpetual hankering after some unattainable state of voluptuous virtue and perfection. At another point the principles of the new poets were said to be Calvinistic in origin. Their simplicity and energy were attributed to the influence of Kotzebue and Schiller, the homeliness and harshness of their verse and language to Cowper, their "innocence" to Ambrose Phillips, their quaintness to Quarles and Donne. Jeffrey had no doubt that from these models a complete art of poetry might be collected, by which "the very gentlest" of his readers might qualify themselves to compose a poem as correctly versified as *Thalaba* and to deal out sentiment and description "with all the sweetness of Lambe [sic], and all the magnificence of Coleridge." Then quoting from Wordsworth's preface the sentence about adapting to the uses of poetry "the ordinary language of conversation in the lower and middle classes of society," the critic declared the "most distinguishing symbol" of the whole group to be "an affectation of great simplicity and familiarity of language" leading, especially in subordinate parts of their work, to "low and inelegant expressions," to the "*bona fide* rejection of art altogether," and to a "bold use of . . . rude and negligent expressions." This style was to be condemned because "it is absurd to suppose that the author should make use of the language of the vulgar to express the sentiments of the refined." The different classes of society had different characters and sentiments as well as different idioms, and "the poor and vulgar may interest us, in poetry, by their situation; but never . . . by any sentiments that are peculiar to their condition, and still less by any language that is characteristic of it." By these strictures, Jeffrey confessed, he meant "no particular allusion to Mr. Southey."

Better examples of these faults were to be found "in the effusions of that poet who commemorates, with so much effect, the chattering of Harry Gill's teeth, [and] tells the tale of the one-eyed huntsman." Southey was, indeed, "less addicted" to this sort of thing "than most of his fraternity," but "at the same time, it is impossible to deny that the author of the *English Eclogues* is liable to a similar censure; and few persons will peruse the following verses without acknowledging that he still continues to deserve it." There followed two passages[1] from *Thalaba* in which the style does indeed drop to the flat tone of the lake poets at their worst. Such lines Jeffrey characterized as "feeble, low, and disjointed; without elegance, without dignity; the offspring of mere indolence and neglect," and he went on to condemn the disgusting homeliness of "odes to his college-bell" and "hymns to the Penates."

Another characteristic fault of the new sect of poets is one that was more frequently attributed to Southey by Jeffrey. "Next after great familiarity of language," he said, "there is nothing that appears to them so meritorious as perpetual exaggeration of thought. There must be nothing moderate, natural, or easy about their sentiments. . . . Instead of contemplating the wonders and pleasures which civilization has created for mankind, they are perpetually brooding over the disorders by which its progress has been attended." All their horror and compassion, accompanied by no indignation against individuals, was reserved for the vices of the vulgar, while for those whose sins were due to wealth they had no sympathy whatever. To such conceptions the new sect contrived to give the "appearance of uncommon force and animation" by wrapping them up in "a veil of mysterious and unintelligible

---

[1] *Thalaba*, Vol. I, Bk. III, 124–125; Vol. II, Bk. VII, 89–90. Jeffrey also singles out "Old Poulter's Mare," to which reference has been made above.

language, which flows past with so much solemnity, that it is difficult to believe that it conveys nothing of any value." To such a charge, even more than to the charge of apish simplicity, *Thalaba*, as well as Southey's early work, was plainly not invulnerable. There was, moreover, the versification, a perfect example of the heresies of the sect. It was declared to have no melody, to be merely prose. As for the story, it was an inconsistent, unconvincing, extravagant, confusing patchwork. The only praise to be accorded to the whole work was for the sentimental episodes dealing with Oneiza and Laila. Jeffrey concluded, therefore, with only grudging recognition for Southey's genius and insistence upon the faults that he shared with his brethren. His gifts were admittedly great, but his "faults are always aggravated, and often created, by his partiality for the peculiar manner of that new school of poetry, of which he is the faithful disciple, and to the glory of which he has sacrificed greater talents and acquisitions than can be boasted of by any of his associates."

To the charge that he was a party to any conspiracy for the formation of a new school of poets, Southey from the first offered denial, and of course there was no basis for supposing that the three men had jointly drawn up any articles of critical faith. But that the reviewers had created them into the "lake school" because they resided in the lake region was equally untrue. The accident of residence at a later time merely supplied a convenient name for the sect which had been defined before Southey and Coleridge had gone near Keswick, and before Wordsworth, the original "laker," was at all known to the world. Even at the time of Jeffrey's onslaught upon *Thalaba*, Southey's connection with what was not to be his home until 1803 was limited to one fleeting visit to Greta Hall in 1801. Yet in 1802 he himself recognized a kinship in spirit between himself and the author of *Tintern Abbey*, nay even the author of the preface to the second edition of the *Lyrical Ballads*, a kinship which, out of pure contentiousness, he was at pains to deny in 1837, and which the world has been prone to overlook. "*Vidi* the Review of Edinburgh," he wrote in December, 1802, to Wynn; "The first part is designed evidently as an answer to Wordsworth's Preface to the second edition of the Lyrical Ballads; and, *however relevant to me, quoad Robert Southey*, is certainly utterly irrelevant to *Thalaba*."[1] Here was an implicit acknowledgment that he shared the principles of that noted preface. Even before this and before his first visit to Keswick, in a letter to Coleridge in August, 1801, the same tacit agreement and a decided interest in Wordsworth are expressed. "I know not whether Wordsworth will forgive the stimulant tale of Thalaba,—'tis a turtle soup, highly seasoned, but with a flavor of its own predominant. His are sparagrass . . . and artichokes, good with plain butter and wholesome." Jeffrey's linking the three of them so publicly together, therefore, was not unflattering to Southey. "I am well pleased to be abused with Coleridge and Wordsworth: it is the best omen that I shall be remembered with them,"[2] and although he admits that he has no intimacy with Wordsworth, he does say, in words that sum up exactly the impression that we have already derived from his early poems, "In whatever we resemble each other, the resemblance has sprung, not, I believe, from chance, but because we have both studied poetry — and indeed it is no light or easy study — in the same school,— in the works of nature, and in the heart of man."

Southey at first took Jeffrey's broadside in what was for him fairly good part. He told[3] Taylor that, although the

---

[1] The italics are mine. See also Southey's letter to Bedford (Aug. 19, 1801) commending Wordsworth's *Michael* and *The Brothers*. Southey says he had never been so much or so well affected as by some passages in the latter poem.   [2] *Taylor*, I, 440.   [3] *Ibid.*

Edinburgh's principles were thoroughly false, they were ably pleaded, and the worst faults were those of negligence. Yet at another time he argued that the misrepresentation he had suffered from the new review was the result of an unfair attitude in the critic rather than inattention. Much water was to run through the mill between 1801 and 1837, when *Thalaba* was revised for the last time. In the preface to the final edition of the poem as it appeared in his poetical works (1837) Southey recalls that it was upon the original publication of this poem that his name was first associated with Wordsworth's, but he goes on to add that no two poets could be found more different, "the difference not being that between good and bad." "I happened to be residing at Keswick when Mr. Wordsworth and I began to be acquainted; Mr. Coleridge also resided there; and this was reason enough for classing us together as a school of poets. Accordingly, for more than twenty years from that time, every tyro in criticism who could smatter and sneer, tried his 'prentice hand' upon the lake poets; and every young sportsman, who carried a popgun in the field of satire, considered them as fair game."

Southey was forgetting much when he penned these misleading and ungracious words. Yet the success of the new Scotch review had emboldened others in their objections to the poetry of Southey and his friends, and the charges that Jeffrey trumpeted went echoing through the pages of periodical criticism. The first number of the Edinburgh appeared in June, 1802. In November *The Monthly Review*[1] noticed *Thalaba* rather lamely, prophesying that Southey would disgust many readers by his story and meter, and expressing a wish that he would advance toward a "more correct taste or a more manly style of composition." But the new *Annual Review*, published by Longman, with Arthur Aiken as editor and Southey himself as one of the

[1] *Month. Rev.*, Nov. 1802, n.s., v. 39, 240–251.

chief contributors, took up the hue and cry with more earnest. The first number, which was for the year 1802, but appeared about a year late, seized upon Lamb's luckless *John Woodvil*[1] as occasion to pillory the new school, the *Edinburgh*[2] having already, in its review of the same volume, though with no reference to the "sect," grouped Lamb with Coleridge. The writer[3] in the *Annual* was, according to Southey, Aiken's daughter, Mrs. Barbauld, and in no gentle fashion did the review summarize the play with sneering implication against the author's poetic gifts, theories, and friends. It concludes with a thorough scolding for poor Lamb and the school of poetry which he was accused of setting up. Implying that perhaps his disciples had been led astray by their disgust of the "Della Cruscans," the reviewer goes on to say that, not content with stripping poetry of superfluous embellishments, the new poets had stripped the muse of the common decencies of dress, and taught her to be a bold, affected, pouting, melancholy, discontented, fretful, deceitful little minx. Southey expressed great indignation at this translation of Jeffrey into the idiom of the respectable British female, and wrote[4] at once to Coleridge: "Why have you not made Lamb declare war upon Mrs. Bare-bald? He should singe her flaxen wig with squibs, and tie crackers to her petticoats till she leapt about like a parched pea for very torture. There is not a man in the world who could so well revenge himself." A few days later he wrote to Taylor[5] that, though Lamb's tragedy was a bad tragedy, albeit full of fine passages, Mrs. Barbauld's review was nothing but "Presbyterian sneer from one end to the other." To this

---

[1] *An. Rev.*, 1803, v. 1, 688–692.

[2] *Edin. Rev.*, April, 1803, v. 2, 90–96.

[3] Mr. E. V. Lucas states that later Lamb learned from Mrs. Barbauld herself that she had not written the review of his play. E. V. Lucas, *Life of Lamb*, I, 312.   [4] *Life*, II, 275.   [5] *Taylor*, I, 489.

Taylor replied, defending the lady, who was an old friend
of his, but scouting her notion that Lamb was to be lumped
with the new sect of poets. "It is . . . preposterous," he
says,[1] "to inveigh against the Southey school of writers in
analysing this play; for it is not of the school struck at.
It is quaint and affected, not simple and insipid; the diction
is artfully antique, not vulgarly natural."

The *Critical's*[2] account of *Thalaba*, written by Taylor himself during a brief service for Hamilton, did not appear until
December, 1803. Naturally it did not echo Jeffrey, but it
delivered a passing shot at him in the course of a laudation
of the witch's incantation in Book IX; "Greeks! Latins!
come with your pythonesses! Where is there a description
like this? Edinburgh Reviewers, tamers of genius, come
and vaunt couplets and habitual meters, and show us an
effort like this! Ghost of Boileau scowl! we will enjoy."

At the time of the publication of the *Metrical Tales*
(1805), which was noticed but insignificantly in the *Monthly*[3]
and not at all in the *Edinburgh*, Taylor's connection with
the *Critical* was off, and that organ opened the vials of
vituperation. This volume was a reprinting of those minor
pieces that Southey had been writing during the few years
past for the newspapers and *The Annual Anthology*. The
reviewer, although admitting that the poet possessed
"genius, fancy, no common powers of language and versification," nevertheless insisted[4] that "he has also many
faults which are highly reprehensible, the more so perhaps
because they are avoidable and voluntary. The greatest,
and indeed that which contains in itself the seeds of all
his other defects, is that he is an egregious poetical coxcomb. It seems to be his aim to strike out a new model

[1] *Taylor*, I, 491.
[2] *Crit. Rev.*, Dec. 1803, 2d ser., 1, 39, 369–379 and see above.
[3] *Month. Rev.*, Nov. 1805, n.s.,v. 48, 323.
[4] *Crit. Rev.* 3d ser., v. 4, 118.

for English poetry; to be as it were the founder of a new sect. But to this he has no pretensions; it is for Mr. Southey to follow received opinions." So the rest of the article prates of the faults "which are peculiar to Mr. Southey and his school" with particular objections to word-coining, the sonnet form, and above all to the rhyme-less, irregular meter. "In his 'Songs of the American Indians' . . . [he] treats us with that new-fangled and nondescript species of poetry, that prose-like verse or verse-like prose, which it is not possible sufficiently to reprobate." In spite of all this there is a sprinkling of praise for *The Old Man's Comforts* and the *English Eclogues*, but through-out the whole there is evident a particular animus against the poet-reviewer who had deserted to the *Annual*.

The limitations of the present book make it impossible at this time to enter in detail into the later criticism of the lake poets as well as to discuss the justice of that criticism and its effects upon the poets themselves and their reputations. Such a study would, nevertheless, be well worth making. We have seen that there had arisen about Southey, Coleridge, and their associates the notion that they were attempting to start a "new sect of poets." We have seen also that the peculiarities of these young writers and their friendly association together gave some basis for such a notion, but that there was no such formal con-spiracy as the legal mind of Jeffrey postulated. Several forces served to keep the "lake school" alive; Jeffrey's insistence, the chorus of minor critics, Southey's obstinacy, the conspicuous and increasing provincialism of the two most steadfast members of the group, perched upon their mountains and giving laws to England down below. As time went on Wordsworth won respect in spite of Jeffrey, and Southey took to writing epics, histories, reviews, biog-raphies, and treatises upon political philosophy, works superficially remote from the forgotten *English Eclogues* as

well as from the notorious *Excursion*. Wordsworth, therefore, eventually became, in the pages of periodical criticism,
the chief, practically the sole, representative of the lake
school, but this was not for several years to come. After
Thalaba, Jeffrey delivered his next edict (October, 1805)[1]
upon *Madoc*, repeating his former strictures more em-
phatically and elaborately, while in the same month the
Monthly[2] and a few months later *The Critical Review*[3]
echoed his thunders in less gentlemanly terms. Not until
October, 1807, was Wordsworth, whose *Poems in Two Volumes* appeared in that year, made the subject of an article
in the *Edinburgh*[4] which publicly defined his position as a
greater offender in the same class with Southey. Without
recounting the indictment in detail, we may note a few of
Jeffrey's remarks. The critic defied anyone to show a
worse poem than *Resolution and Independence* even in the
Specimens of the Later English Poets edited by Mr. Wordsworth's "friend Mr. Southey." Jeffrey further declared
that "All the world laughs at Elegiac Stanzas to a Sucking
Pig[5] — a Hymn on Washing-Day[6] — Sonnets to one's grandmother[7] — or Pindarics on Gooseberry-pie;[8] and yet, we are

[1] *Edin. Rev.*, Oct. 1805, v. 7, 1–27.

[2] *Month. Rev.*, Oct. 1805, n.s., v. 48, 113–122.

[3] *Crit. Rev.*, Jan. 1806, 3d ser., v. 7, 72–83.

[4] *Edin. Rev.*, Oct. 1807, v. 11, 214.

[5] Perhaps a reference to Southey's *The Pig* in *Metrical Tales*, 1805.

[6] Perhaps a reference to a poem called *Washing Day* by Mrs. Barbauld, written in blank verse after the model of Cowper's *Task*. *Washing Day* appeared in *Month. Mag.*, Dec. 1797, v. 4, 452 and in *The
Works of Anna Laetitia Barbauld*, 1825, 202–206.

[7] Sonnets on this subject by both Lamb and Lloyd appeared in
*Poems, by S. T. Coleridge, Second Edition. To which are now added
Poems by Charles Lamb and Charles Lloyd*. Jeffrey may also have had
in mind Lloyd's *Poem on the death of his Grandmother, Priscilla Farmer*,
1796, which also contained an introductory sonnet by Coleridge and
The Grandame by Lamb.

[8] *Gooseberry-Pie, A Pindaric Ode* in Southey's *Metrical Tales*, 1805.

afraid, it will not be quite easy to convince Mr. Wordsworth, that the same ridicule must infallibly attach to most
of the pathetic pieces in these volumes." And finally for
the first time public mention of the lakes was now made
in the *Edinburgh*; "this author [Wordsworth] is known to
belong to a certain brotherhood of poets, who have haunted
for some years about the lakes of Cumberland; and is
generally looked upon, we believe, as the purest model of
the excellences and peculiarities of the school which they
have been labouring to establish." After this Jeffrey
paused in his onslaughts, except for an occasional side-
thrust,[1] until the publication of *The Curse of Kehama* in
1810, when he could adopt only a tone of discouraged
resignation at his failure to win Southey from lakish
heresies.[2] Then, in 1814 and 1815, came *The Excursion*[3]
and *The White Doe of Rylstone*,[4] and the full force of critical
wrath fell upon Wordsworth. Curiously enough, of the
whole series of pronunciamentos on the lake school, the
two last named were the earliest to which Jeffrey gave
place in the selections from his writings in the *Edinburgh*
which he published in 1843, and these are the ones, therefore, by which his opinions upon the "sect" are best known
to later readers, although, aside from the fact that they
deal specifically with two of Wordsworth's most ambitious
efforts, they are in themselves less interesting and less
representative of Jeffrey's genuine though limited critical
acumen and sanity. Incidentally, the greater attention
which has been given to these later articles has helped to
obscure the close association that existed, in the character

[1] *Edin. Rev.*, Jan. 1808, v. 11, 411, Bowles's edition of Pope; April,
1808, v. 12, 133, *Poems* by George Crabbe, 1807; Jan. 1809, v. 13, 276,
Reliques of Robert Burns; April, 1809, v. 14, 1 Thomas Campbell's
Gertrude of Wyoming.

[2] *Ibid.*, Feb. 1811, v. 17, 429–465.

[3] *Ibid.*, Oct. 1815, v. 25, 355–363.

[4] *Ibid.*, Nov. 1814, v. 24, 1–30.

of their work and its reception by the public, between Southey and Wordsworth. This connection has been the more easily forgotten again, because it was the review of *Roderick* in June, 1815,[1] making no specific reference to the lake school whatever, which was the only one of his articles upon Southey that Jeffrey chose to preserve and reprint.

Before leaving this subject it will be well to add that other periodicals helped to keep alive the pother maintained by the *Edinburgh*. The *Critical*, in spite of Tory politics, became an offensive and violent auxiliary to Whig criticism, and the *Quarterly's* connection with Southey did not prevent it from challenging Jeffrey only lukewarmly in defense of the lake school. *Blackwoods* was bolder, denied the existence of any conspiracy, or of any resemblance between Southey and Wordsworth, but at the same time published articles on "The Lake School of Poets" consisting, to be sure, only of generous appreciation of Wordsworth. "Maga's" wits, furthermore, invented a whole series of "schools," such as "the leg of mutton school of poetry" or "the pluckless school of politics," to accommodate the peculiarities of various persons whom they wished, from time to time, to satirize. Of these the best known was, of course, "the Cockney school of poetry," created for the sake of Leigh Hunt and infamous for the sake of Keats. Finally, in this list of the figments of literary controversy, it is but just to mention that Southey himself, in the preface to his unhappy *Vision of Judgment* (1821), became the luckless inventor of "the Satanic school of poets," and thereby precipitated that quarrel with Byron from the effects of which his fame has never recovered.

Into the further history of that fame this is not the point at which to enter. The "lake school," in the sense of conspiracy which legalistic critics gave to the term, never existed. This fact, however, does not warrant several mis-

[1] *Edin. Rev.*, June, 1815, v. 25, 1–31.

apprehensions which have arisen. Jeffrey was far too clever a man not to perceive that popular judgment was correct in recognizing a definite point of wiew and certain definite literary peculiarities in the earlier writings of Southey which were only less conspicuously manifested in his compatriot Coleridge and carried to an extreme both of sublimity and absurdity in Wordsworth. The justice of Jeffreys strictures in matters of taste was recognized in practice, even though his authority was denied, by all three poets and not least by the greatest among them. Furthermore, it may be said again, if any of the group is to be excluded, it should not be Southey, and the criticism that would see a closer kinship between him and Scott betrays but a superficial understanding both of Southey himself and of that great man who, in true catholicity of mind, far excelled any of the lake school.

IV

The author of *Thalaba* returned from Lisbon to Bristol in June, 1801. He and his wife were restored in health, but still unsettled as to the future. Though penniless as a result of their year's excursion, they were not without resources. There was a head and a portfolio full of marketable material, and always there were friends. Southey's central problem was still to find means of independent support, and incidental to this was the question where to live and what to do with his family, particularly, now, what to do with his brother Henry.

The boy had passed something over a year under the tutelage of the Reverend Michael Maurice in Suffolk, where he had been placed by his brother upon the advice of William Taylor. The time had been spent profitably, and Taylor had a good report to make. But Henry was nearly eighteen, and it became necessary that his future should be more definitely provided for. He was a fine, spirited lad of very pleasing presence and sociable temper, a great favorite with Taylor. With the latter's counsel he now fixed his ambition upon the practice of medicine, and the question of providing the requisite funds was pressing. Southey at first thought of having the boy study in London, but on Taylor's advice Henry was finally apprenticed to a surgeon in Norwich named Philip Martineau. This involved a cost of a hundred pounds, and Southey cheerfully made ready to surrender the profits of *Thalaba* for the purpose, resigning thereby the hope of furnishing a house. Fortunately this sacrifice was unnecessary, for Mr. Hill came to the rescue, and after vainly attempting to persuade the protégé of William Taylor to accept the opportunity already declined by his elder brother to go to Oxford and enter the church, provided the money required for a medical education. Henry well repaid the interest of his friends and kindred. After further study at Edinburgh in 1804, he practiced his profession at Norwich and then with distinction in London. His relations with his brother, although naturally rather more filial in character than fraternal, were continuously warm and affectionate. Other members of the family were not in so hopeful a state in 1801. Margaret Hill, the cousin whom Southey loved dearly, and to whose support he had been for some time contributing, was evidently dying of consumption, and his mother was also failing more and more rapidly every day.

The question of deciding upon a home and a profession for himself had now to be approached anew by the poet, and the trying uncertainty was to continue for several years longer, though rendered less acute by the unmistakable fact that literature would always claim the major part of his attention, whatever might be the major source of his income. Before his return to England the futility of Southey's persisting in the law had become evident even to Wynn, and early in July the poet journeyed to Worcester to discuss the new plan that his old friend now suggested. This was that Wynn should use his influence to obtain for Southey the secretaryship to some legation in the south of Europe where climate would consort with health, and where leisure would permit literary pursuits. Pending some decision in this matter, the emancipated law student expected to spend the coming summer in Bristol, then to walk through North Wales in search of local color for *Madoc*, and afterwards to go to Keswick to see Coleridge. To the latter he had written from Lisbon, and confided his longing that they might at last live together. He feared a return of his old illness from the English climate, and wondered whether Coleridge's ailments did not have the same cause. Perhaps they might emigrate together after all, and find happiness in some southern place. An answer from his friend, urging him at once to come to Keswick, awaited his return to Bristol. Coleridge had three arguments in favor of Greta Hall. The first was the beauty of the surrounding scenery — the little River Derwent; the giant's camp of mountains; "massy Skiddaw, smooth, green, high;" Lodore; Derwentwater; Borrowdale. The next argument was the size and convenience of the house. The last was the near neighborhood of Wordsworth.

Such was Southey's invitation and first introduction to the lake country and his future home. He could not accept the invitation at once, partly because of the precarious state of his cousin's and of his mother's health, and partly because he was awaiting the early development of Wynn's new scheme. But the idea of again living with Coleridge took hold of him, and he pressed the suggestion that they emigrate together to a warmer climate. In the ensuing months the subject was thoroughly discussed in their letters. Constantinople, Palermo, Naples, even India, and the West Indies were thought of. Eventually Coleridge

tried his unhappy experiment of going to Malta in a position similar to that at first designed for Southey. Meanwhile the latter wrote day-dream pictures of the life they
would lead together at Constantinople, concluding, however, with something finer, if not more tangible. "Time
and absence make strange work with our affections; but
mine are ever returning to rest upon you. I have other
and dear friends, but none with whom the whole of my
being is intimate — with whom every thought and feeling
can amalgamate. Oh! I have yet such dreams! Is it quite
clear that you and I were not meant for some better star,
and dropped, by mistake, into this world of pounds, shill-
ings, and pence?" To all this Coleridge responded with
repeated exhortations to come to Keswick; "Do, do for
heaven's sake, come . . . the shortest way, however dreary
it may be; for there is enough to be seen when you get to
our house. If you did but know what a flutter the old
movable at my left breast has been in since I read your
letter." Rather than not see him, Coleridge, despite ill-
health, was ready to brave the journey to Bristol, and he
subscribed with a desperate heartiness to the scheme for
joint residence abroad. He would go anywhere, do anything, if Southey would but come and float with him on
Derwentwater. "Oh how I have dreamt about you!
Times that *have been*, and never can return, have been
with me on my bed of pain, and how I yearned towards
you in those moments, I myself can know, only by feeling
it over again."[1]

For any journey, however, as well as for the expense of
his cousin's illness, and for the payment of the debts in-
curred by the Portugal trip, Southey was in immediate
need of money. He offered *Madoc* to Longman for an
advance of fifty pounds, but upon being cheapened,—
Thalaba was not living up to expectations as a popular

[1] Coleridge, *Letters*, I, 356–358.

success,— summarily withdrew the offer. Reviewing again for the *Critical* was a more certain resource, but he even thought of once more "selling his soul" to Stuart of *The Morning Post*. The hope of publishing any of the history had to be deferred. A volume could have been prepared, but the historian must one day return to Lisbon, and what he might publish at this time would surely render him *persona non grata* in Portugal hereafter.

Not until the end of August, 1801, was Southey able to leave Bristol and go to Coleridge at Keswick, but he reached there at last, expecting to remain while the plans for going abroad settled themselves. What passed between the two men we do not know. The lake country disappointed Southey after the grander scenery of Cintra, and the climate seemed raw and cold, so that he conceived no desire to make his permanent residence at Greta Hall. His visit was, indeed, cut very short, for after a week or so, he left Edith with her sister, and joined Wynn at Wynnstay in Wales for a trip through the country of *Madoc*. With their old Westminster friend, Peter Elmsley, they tramped through a land of mountains, waterfalls and forests, ruined abbeys, castles, romantic bridges, and plunging streams. The poet in Southey rejoiced; the peaks were the highest he had seen, and walking gave him such sleep and hunger as he had not known. Upon his return to Wynnstay, however, a letter awaited him which ended his holiday, and demanded his translation to a new rôle. Wynn's efforts to obtain a place abroad for him had so far failed, and in the meantime Rickman had succeeded elsewhere. Through the latter's interposition Southey was now offered the place of private secretary to Michael Corry, chancellor of the Exchequer for Ireland, at a salary of about £350, half of which would be consumed by travel. Rickman himself held a government position in Dublin, where his company would make the annual six months'

stay of Corry's secretary at least tolerable. Southey accepted the offer immediately, and his services being required at once, went up to Keswick for a day or so, and
by October 10 was on his way to Dublin.

"A foolish office and a good salary," Southey said of his
secretaryship after he had resigned it, but he undertook it
with high hopes, fostered by Rickman, of the independence
he had so longed for. His duties, indeed, were nearly nil,—
a little copying, a little cooling his heels daily at Corry's
door, a little investigation on tithes and corn-laws, the rest
of his time free. In Dublin he was required to remain but
a short time, and he then set out for London with his
chief, stopping by the way at Keswick to get his wife. In
November London saw them again, and the secretary's
duties were as before. To be sure *The True Briton* and
other hostile organs printed sundry paragraphs on the
Jacobin turned office-holder, but these flea-bites were osten-
tatiously ignored. Thus the winter passed, not with entire
satisfaction, in an office of "all pay and no work." Then
it was intimated to the secretary that his services would
be appreciated as tutor to Corry's son, whereupon he
resigned, and about May first retired still another time to
Bristol. He would never again seriously attempt to earn
his bread save by literature.

On March 27, 1802, an event occurred which settled any
remaining doubts Southey may have had about his attitude
toward political affairs. Upon that day the "anti-Jacobin
war" came to a close with the Treaty of Amiens, and the
author of *Joan of Arc* felt in later years that English feeling[1]
had thereby at last been restored within him. England had
fought against the cause of liberty, and he had consistently
felt that her opposition had helped drive the revolutionists
into those excesses toward which their own corruption was
already tending. Now that his country had made peace,

[1] *Warter*, III, 319–321.

he expected that freer scope would be given to the better nature of France. When France should reject the opportunity thus afforded and Napoleon should attack England, Southey would have no doubt that the two countries had exchanged rôles, that tyranny infinitely monstrous was embodied in France and that England was fighting for liberty and natural goodness. The same passion for uncompromisingly and conspicuously committing himself that had made him write an anti-English epic at the age of nineteen would later make him the vehement *Quarterly* reviewer and Tory laureate.

Meanwhile the young man who turned his back once more upon London and returned to Bristol was seeking from Danvers and his mother simple human comfort. Southey had now lost his cousin, and on January 5, 1802, his own mother had died under his roof in London, whither she had gone to be with him. As he had now long schooled himself to do, Southey reined in his emotions hard. In a letter to Wynn, which, for the terseness of intense though restrained grief, is not to be surpassed, he says, "I calmed and curbed myself, and forced myself to employment; but, at night, there was no sound of feet in her bed-room, to which I had been used to listen, and in the morning it was not my first business to see her. . . . I have now lost all the friends of my infancy and childhood. The whole recollections of my first ten years are connected with the dead. There lives no one who can share them with me. It is losing so much of one's existence. I have not been yielding to, or rather indulging, grief; that would have been folly. I have read, written, talked; Bedford has been often with me, and kindly."

There were plenty of distractions in London. It had been a great pleasure to be with Rickman in Dublin; here there were more friends and acquaintances than were welcome. Longman invited him "to meet a few literary friends." He appears to have seen the Lambs frequently, Coleridge occasionally. The father of Maria Edgeworth invited him to Edgeworthtown, and he made a short visit to William Taylor at Norwich. Some acquaintances came to him with his new position, but comments upon them show the real attitude of the man toward general social converse of any kind. He was reserved, sensitive, ill-at-ease, and proud; his heart was in his literary work, and he was frankly in his present position only to help that work forward. After he had been a week in town, he wrote that the civilities that had been shown to him made him think despicably of the world, that one man congratulated him and another called upon him as though the author of *Joan of Arc* and of *Thalaba* had been made great by scribing for the Irish Chancellor of the Exchequer. Back to Bristol, therefore, Southey went with his wife and her sister, Mrs. Lovell, who had shortly before become a member of his household. By the first of June they had taken a furnished house in the same row on the Kingsdown Parade with their old friend Danvers. Here there was room for books, quiet for work, and conveniences for Edith, who expected confinement during the summer. This was to be the last of their temporary residences until September of the following year, when they finally made their way to Greta Hall for that visit that was to stretch out to the end of life. Meanwhile Southey took great pleasure in the near neighborhood of Danvers and his mother, a joy broken into by the death of the latter in the course of the winter. For a few summer weeks, Thomas Southey visited his brother's family, enforcing wholesome idleness and promoting good spirits. Then, in September, a daughter was born to the poet, named Margaret after Southey's mother, and the household was completely happy.

The years from 1801 to 1803, during which Southey, now settled in his own mind as to his ambitions and desires, was still unsettled in the world, were not years of literary harvest, nor yet of literary inactivity. The Hindoo romance which he had begun in Portugal immediately after finishing *Thalaba*, and which was to be followed by similar works on the Persian and on the "Runic" mythology, if he were granted but four years of life, was first delayed and then halted for several reasons. In the first place *Thalaba* had not sold. Published in the spring, but three hundred copies had been disposed of by November 20, 1801. Longman, as we have seen, did not rate highly the selling value of *Madoc*, and esteemed the prospects of *Kehama* no better. Then the attack of *The Edinburgh Review* upon *Thalaba* and the new sect of poets appeared in October, 1802. Such discouragement, coming partly when the secretaryship supplied daily wants, merely helped to foster in Southey the confidence that, if he missed popularity, he would the more surely win immortality. Consequently the new mythological romance could rest for a time while he turned his attention to correcting *Madoc*. When he arrived in Dublin in October, 1801, to assume his official position, the new secretary found Mr. Corry on the wing for London, and "what did I but open 'Madoc,' and commenced the great labour of rebuilding it." This poem had rested since the completion of the first draught in 1799; now it was put upon the anvil for thorough revision. Notes were to be compiled, and local color was to be supplied from the walk in North Wales with Wynn. Possibly the fortune of *Thalaba* and the criticisms of Taylor were not without influence. Certainly Southey proposed to revise the latter poem thoroughly for its next edition, and wrote to Taylor concerning *Madoc*, "I am correcting it with merciless vigilance, — shortening and shortening, distilling wine into alcohol." [1]

All poetic composition, however, was now put into a

[1] *Taylor*, I, 440.

parenthesis beside the work on the great history, to which the new salary permitted Southey to devote part of his time. In this task the man had at last really found himself and his happiness. To sit at home over old folios, digesting, taking notes, transcribing, compiling,— here was to be found that calm for the spirit which he had longed after. Of this fact he was himself fully aware. In November, 1802, he wrote[1] to Taylor from Bristol that he had for some time been abstaining from poetry. Old chronicles pleased him better because to delve in them never made "the face burn or the brain throb." Occasionally he would think of "a huge faery castle in the air," but when it came to write, "alas for the stately rhyme." So when some passing trouble with his eyes kept him from reading, Southey was annoyed because then he could write only poetry, and that was hard when prose pleased him better. The scope and the pleasure of the work upon Portugal had increased proportionately. Mr. Hill was buying books for it and moving them to England; Southey's own library was beginning to be embarrassingly large; and he was rummaging in all public collections to which he could gain access. Publication of any part of his labors had to be postponed for reasons already explained, and especially because he was now deep in the unsavoury history of the church and the monastic orders, an experience by which he confirmed in himself that hatred of popery which was to be one of the standing terrors of his life.

Unfortunately the income from the secretaryship lapsed in less than a year, and even while it lasted, it was insufficient for all needs, and had to be eked out by never-ending hack-work. "Drudge, drudge, drudge," Southey wrote to Taylor; "Do you know Quarles's emblem of the soul that tries to fly, but is chained by the leg to earth? For myself I could do easily, but not easily for others;

[1] *Taylor*, I, 429–430.

and there are more claims than one upon me."[1] For
several years to come, therefore, he had to "evacuate" for
The Morning Post "sundry indifferent verses, value one
guinea per hundred, according to the print-reckoning of six
score." Far more distasteful was the reviewing that had
to be done for *The Critical Review,* and for the new *Annual
Review* that Longman had set up under the editorship of
Dr. Aiken. Never was Southey to be free from such work,
and never was he to do it with a willing spirit. More to
his taste was another task that he undertook for Longman,
unwelcome only because it took time from the history.
This was a translation and abridgment of *Amadis of Gaul,*
begun in the spring of 1802, when the resignation of his
"foolish office" made him cast about for other sources of
money. It was done purely as a task, and he huzzaed like
a schoolboy as each chapter was knocked off. If it succeeded, the publisher was to proceed through the whole
catalogue of romances, but so meanly did Southey think of
this kind of literary service that he stipulated for an
anonymous publication. The wily Longman, well knowing
the worth of the translator's name on the title-page, acci-
dentally divulged his identity, much to Southey's disgust.
Still the returns were materially increased to £100 cash,
£50 when the edition should be sold, and half the profit on
future issues. This was substantially better than the pay-
ments from *Thalaba,* and the author pocketed his chagrin
after a futile attempt to disclaim his work. The translation itself, passing over Southey's antiquated speculation
concerning the original authorship, is one of his rare successes in genuine beauty. He skillfully condensed the text
into half its length by curtailing dialogue, avoiding repeti-
tion, and excising some of the moralizing, immorality, and
fighting, but thereby heightened the unity of the narrative
as a whole. His wide reading in such literature and his

[1] *Taylor,* I, 445.

sympathy with chivalric ideals enabled him to catch perfectly the spirit of romance and to clothe it in a style that carries the reader, if anything can, happily through the extravagances and involutions of the long-winded old story.

Now that literature was to be relied upon for sole support, some more regular resource than such casual tasks as *Amadis* had to be found, and Southey canvassed several schemes in the next year or two before settling down to reviewing for his bread and cheese. In November, 1802, William Taylor, just returned from Paris, where he had been joined by Henry Southey as his companion, proposed to Robert that he make his residence in Norwich, where rents were cheap, and offered the editorship of a Whiggish weekly newspaper, called *The Iris*, soon to be established in that place under his sponsorship. Southey declined to consider a removal to Norwich for a number of reasons. It was above all too inaccessible. He wished to be nearer London, the seaports that led to Portugal, and Hereford, where his uncle might settle or might have a house which his nephew could occupy. The editorship of a newspaper would be too confining, and finally, "Among the odd revolutions of the world you may reckon this, that my politics come nearer to Mr. Windham's than they do William Taylor's." Norwich, therefore, in spite of the attractions offered, was out of the question.

Nevertheless, a library and a nursery had to be housed in some fairly fixed habitation, and all Southey's new plans for work were accompanied by new plans for an establishment. The kind of place he would have liked is suggested by the words that he wrote to Bedford upon the latter's enforced removal from Brixton Causeway. The poet said that he loved best an old house with odd closets, cupboards, thick walls, heart-of-oak beams, chimney pieces, fire-places, and clipt yews. Probably he had no expectations of finding such an ideal realized by the place he looked for in Richmond in the spring of 1802, but he did hope that he would there find comfort for his work on the history and pleasure in the near neighborhood of John May. Far more alluring was the place that he considered in the fall of the same year for a residence in Wales. Eighty miles from Bristol was Neath, and eight miles up the vale of Neath was the house of Maes Gwyn, a journey of some thirty-six hours. "I shall have a house in the loveliest part of South Wales, in a vale between high mountains; and an onymous house . . . that is down in the map of Glamorganshire." (Nov. 28, 1802.) Arrangements for renting this establishment furnished were almost concluded when a dispute with the landlord about the kitchen resulted in the breaking off of the whole scheme. In after years Southey is said always to have spoken of Maes Gwyn with something like regret.

Another winter passed at Bristol, therefore, and in the next year still another literary scheme arose which promised to carry Southey's household back to London after all. This was a *Bibliotheca Brittanica,* and by July, 1803, we find Southey actively consulting Coleridge with regard to a design for a work of several eight-hundred-page quarto volumes forming a history of English literature or chronological account of all books in the British languages, with biography, criticism, and connecting chapters. Southey as editor and absolute director was to receive £150 per volume; contributors apparently were to receive four guineas per sheet. It was hoped to publish half of the first volume by Christmas 1804. Some of Southey's assistants were already enlisted; Sharon Turner, Duppa, William Taylor, Rickman, and Coleridge were among them. The plan at first promised well, and arrangements for publication were apparently settled with Longman, who was to advance £150 so that Southey could move to London, the more conveniently to carry on his editorial duties. John May was sent again to seek a house in Richmond, and even went so far as to secure the refusal of one place that promised sufficiently well. Such a scheme naturally appealed to the expansive genius of Coleridge, who took an influential hand in formulating it, but whose ambitions were too comprehensive for Southey's more practical mind. To the latter's first suggestions Coleridge responded with a proposal far more copious still which, if executed, would have included, not only an account of all English books, but of all books written upon subjects that had been written upon in English. In another connection Southey had written, "You spawn plans like a herring," and he replied to the new suggestion in similar vein. "Your proposal is too good, too gigantic, quite beyond my powers." With health and industry, Coleridge might, if he would, make such a work the most valuable of any age or country, but Southey alone did not feel himself capable of filling up such an outline; he must have a plan that he knew he could execute. As for relying upon Coleridge for whole quartos, the thought brought tears to his friend's eyes (Aug. 3, 1803).

Suddenly all hopes came to an end. The child Margaret, so gladly welcomed, a quick-limbed, bright-eyed baby, died when scarcely more than a year old. "Edith is suffering bitterly," he wrote; "I myself am recovering, perfectly resigned to the visitation, perfectly satisfied that it is for the best, perfectly assured that the loss will be but for a time. Never man enjoyed purer happiness than I have for the last twelve months. My plans are now all wrecked" (Aug. 29, 1803). For the *Bibliotheca*, somewhat to Southey's relief under the circumstances, was now frustrated. The general panic lest Bonaparte should invade England entered Longman's breast, and the grand new scheme had to be indefinitely postponed. This, of course, halted the plan for living at Richmond, and the Southeys were again all at sea. The one thing now was to escape from Bristol; "The place is haunted, and it is my wish never to see it again" (Sept. 8, 1803). After Edith had recovered, therefore, they started at once for the north, and after five days in Staffordshire with their Lisbon friend, Miss Barker, arrived at Greta Hall on the seventh of September. Southey hoped that the infant Sara Coleridge might afford some relief to Edith, might be 'grafted into the wound,' but it was a joyless coming and to no happy household. Poor Coleridge, caught in the grip of opium, was sick at heart and in body. The glory of his promise was slipping from his enervated fingers, and the bitterness of dissension had entered his home. He was in Scotland at this time, but hastened back (September 15, 1803),[1] wretchedly ill, to welcome his old friends. A few weeks later his companions, the Wordsworths, returned, and before long William came over from Grasmere, met his former critic, and wrote[2] that he liked him very much. So the visit of the Southeys at Greta Hall began. They had not intended to remain, but there were now no ties to draw them elsewhere, and it became evident in time that their departure would be long postponed. They had at last come home.

[1] Campbell, *Coleridge*, 140.
[2] *Letters of the Wordsworth Family*, I, 153, October 14, 1803.

CONCLUSION

SOUTHEY's youth had ended when he crossed the threshold of Greta Hall. His reputation as an author, his ideals and plan of life, his means of livelihood, in spite of temporary discouragement and embarrassment, were virtually fixed. In 1837 he wrote,

"Personal attachment first, and family circumstances afterwards, connected me long and closely with Mr. Coleridge; and three-and-thirty years have ratified a friendship with Mr. Wordsworth, which we believe will not terminate with this life, and which it is a pleasure for us to know will be continued and cherished as an heirloom by those who are dearest to us both. When I add, what has been the greatest of all advantages, that I have passed more than half my life in retirement, conversing with books rather than men, constantly and unweariably engaged in literary pursuits, communing with my own heart, and taking that course which, upon mature consideration, seemed best to myself, I have said everything necessary to account for the characteristics of my poetry, whatever they may be."

The ideals whose development in youth we have now traced and which such a way of life in manhood confirmed formed the staple of all the literary pursuits with which Southey's days were henceforth filled. Though living in retirement, he tried to apply these ideals to the questions and affairs of his own day in *The Annual* and then in *The Quarterly Review*, and in such works as his *Book of the Church*, his *Colloquies on the Progress and Prospects of Society*, and his *History of the Peninsular War*. His early interest in purely literary matters found expression in his *Life of Cowper* and in other writings in which he helped forward the study of English literature. The historical studies by which he sought to verify his preconceived ideals and to disseminate the learning that he loved he vainly tried to consummate in his vastly planned works upon the history of Portugal. Finally his passionate devotion to those ideals thus fortified by erudition he labored to express for all time in a great epic poem. Until the hand of death was upon him, he never was freed from poverty to serve his ambitions with all his powers but he kept his courage through long years of struggle and deferred hope by unflinching faith in the rectitude of his own purposes and in his own ability to achieve them. If he had succeeded, he would have become one of the standing examples of the sublime self-confidence of great genius. That his name became, instead, a by-word for renegade in life, and for a vanished reputation after death, is an irony acute enough to give any man pause in his pride. But it was a life worth living and worth remembering because, if for no other reason, of the spirit in which it was lived, a spirit that cannot in conclusion be better expressed than in the words of Thalaba on the way to the Dom-Daniel Caverns:

> "If from my childhood up, I have looked on
>   With exultation to my destiny,
>   If, in the hour of anguish, I have felt
>   The justice of the hand that chastened me,
>   If, of all selfish passions purified,
>   I go to work thy will, and from the world
>   Root up the ill-doing race,
>   Lord! let not thou the weakness of mine arm
>   Make vain the enterprise!"

APPENDIX A

WORKS OF ROBERT SOUTHEY

This list purports to be a contribution to a bibliography of Southey, and not a complete final list of all his works nor of all editions of his works. It includes the works of Southey as first published by or for him, and does not include contributions to periodicals. Unless otherwise stated, all information has been taken, either by the writer or by some other competent person, from the books themselves, but certain information concerning editions other than those in the first instance cited has been obtained from sources indicated as follows: *The Catalogue of the British Museum*,[1] *Book Prices Current*,[2] *American Book Prices Current*,[3] *Book Auction Records*.[4]

The Flagellant. London: printed for the authors; and sold by T. and J. Egerton, near Whitehall. MDCCXCII.

> Written by Southey and Grosvenor C. Bedford at Westminster School, and published in nine weekly numbers from March 1 to April 26. The first number was by Bedford. The fifth number, on the subject of flogging, was by Southey, and caused the author's expulsion from the school. There is a complete file of the nine numbers in the British Museum, and there is a file of numbers one through five in the library of Yale University.

The Fall of Robespierre. An Historic Drama. By S. T Coleridge, of Jesus College, Cambridge. Cambridge: Printed by Benjamin Flower, For W. H. Lums, and J. and J. Merrill; and sold by J. March, Norwich. 1794.

> The first act of this drama was written by Coleridge, the second and third by Southey. See T. J. Wise, *Bibliography of Coleridge* and E. H. Coleridge, *Complete Poetical Works of Samuel Taylor Coleridge*.

Poems: containing The Retrospect, Odes, Elegies, Sonnets, &c. by Robert Lovell, and Robert Southey, of Baliol College, Oxford. . . . "Minuentur atrae/ "Carmine curae." Hor. [Publisher's device] Bath, Printed by R. Cruttwell, and sold by C. Dilly, Poultry, London. MDCCXCV.

Joan of Arc, an Epic Poem, by Robert Southey. ΕΙΣ ΟΙΩΝΟΣ
ΑΡΙΣΤΟΣ ΑΜΥΝΕΣΘΑΙ ΠΕΡΙ ΠΑΤΡΗΣ. ΟΜΗΡΟΣ. Bristol:
printed by Bulgin and Rosser, for Joseph Cottle, Bristol, and
Cadell and Davies, and G. G. and J. Robinson, London.
MDCCXCVI.

> Second edition, Bristol 1798: Third, London 1806: Fourth, 1812:[4]
> Fifth, London 1817: Another, London 1853:[1] Another, Boston
> Mass. 1798.

Letters written during a short residence in Spain and Portugal, by
Robert Southey. With some account of Spanish and Portugueze Poetry. Bristol; printed by Bulgin and Rosser, for
Joseph Cottle, Bristol, and G. G. and J. Robinson, and Cadell
and Davies, London. 1797.

> Second edition, Bristol 1799: Third with title "Letters written
> during a journey in Spain, and a short residence in Portugal,"
> London 1808.

On the French Revolution, by Mr. Necker. Translated from the
French. In two volumes, Vol. I. [II.] London: Printed for
T. Cadell Jun. and W. Davies (Successors to Mr. Cadell) in the
Strand, 1797.

> Published without the translators' names. According to Southey
> (April 5, 1797, *Life* I, 307 note), the first volume was translated by
> Dr. John Aiken and son (probably Arthur Aiken), and the second
> by himself.

Poems by Robert Southey. Second Edition. Bristol: Printed by
N. Biggs, for Joseph Cottle, and sold in London by Messrs.
Robinsons. 1797. [Reverse of title-page]; Goddess of the
Lyre! with thee comes/ Majestic Truth; and where Truth
deigns to come,/ Her sister Liberty will not be far./ Akenside.

> This volume consisted partly of pieces reprinted from the *Poems*
> of 1795, and partly of new material.
> Third edition, London 1800: Fourth, London 1801: Fifth, London
> 1808: Another, Boston Mass. 1799.[1]

Poems, by Robert Southey. *The better, please; the worse, displease;
I ask no more.* Spenser. The second volume. Bristol: printed
by Biggs and Cottle, for T. N. Longman and O. Rees, Paternoster-Row, London. 1799.

This volume consisted partly of *The Vision of the Maid of Orleans*, being the original ninth book of *Joan of Arc* (1796) now reprinted as a separate poem, and partly of new material.
Second edition, London 1800: Third, 1801:[3] Fourth, London 1806.

The Annual Anthology. Volume I. 1799. [II. 1800.] Bristol: printed by Biggs and Co. for T. N. Longman and O. Rees, Paternoster-Row, London.

Edited anonymously and in part written by Southey. T. J. Wise, *Bibliography of Coleridge*, 192, notes that in all known copies of this book except Southey's own, now in the Dyce Library South Kensington Museum, Sig. B 8 (pp. 31-32) of Vol. I is missing. It contained *War Poem*, a poem sympathizing with the French in their victory at Toulon.

Thalaba the Destroyer, by Robert Southey. Ποιηματων ακρατης η ελευθερια, και νομος εις, το δοξαν τω ποιητη. *Lucian, Quomodo Hist. scribenda.* The first volume. [The second volume.] London: printed for T. N. Longman and O. Rees, Paternoster-Row, by Biggs and Cottle, Bristol. 1801.

Second edition, London 1809:[1] Third, London 1814: Fourth, London 1821: Others, London 1846, 1853,[1] 1860,[1] Boston Mass. 1812.

The Works of Thomas Chatterton. Vol. I. Containing his Life, by G. Gregory, D. D. and Miscellaneous Poems. London: printed by Biggs and Cottle, Crane-Court, Fleet-Street, for T. N. Longman and O. Rees, Paternoster-Row. 1803. Vol. II. Containing the Poems attributed to Rowley.
Vol. III. Containing Miscellaneous Pieces in Prose.

The preface is by Southey. The editorial work was done almost entirely by Joseph Cottle under Southey's direction.

Amadis of Gaul, from the Spanish version of Garciordonez de Montalvo, by Robert Southey, Vol. I. [II. III. IV.] [Half-title.]

Amadis of Gaul, by Vasco Lobeira. In four volumes. Vol. I. [II. III. IV.] London: printed by N. Biggs, Crane-court, Fleet-Street, for T. N. Longman and O. Rees, Paternoster Row. 1803. [Full-title.]

Second edition [?]: Third, London 1872.

Madoc, by Robert Southey. [device] London Printed for Longman, Hurst, Rees, and Orme. and A. Constable and Co. Edinburgh. M.D.CCC.V. [Half-title.]

Madoc, a Poem, in two parts. by Robert Southey. *Omne solum forti patria.* London: printed for Longman, Hurst, Rees, and Orme, Paternoster-Row, and A. Constable and Co. Edinburgh, by James Ballantyne, Edinburgh. 1805. [Full-title.]

> None of the three copies which I have examined contains both the title-pages. Second edition, London 1807: Third, 1812:[2] Fourth, London 1815: Fifth, London 1825:[1] Another, London 1853:[1] Another, Boston Mass., 1806.

Metrical Tales and Other Poems. by Robert Southey. Nos haec novimus esse nihil. London: printed for Longman, Hurst, Rees, and Orme, Paternoster-Row. 1805.

> This volume consisted of pieces by Southey reprinted from *The Annual Anthology.*
> Another edition, Boston Mass. 1811.

Letters from England: By Don Manuel Alvarez Espriella. Translated from the Spanish. In Three Volumes. Vol. I. [II. III.] London: Printed for Longman, Hurst, Rees and Orme, Paternoster Row. 1807.

> Published anonymously.
> Second edition, London 1808: Others, Boston Mass. 1807, New York 1808, 1836: translated into French, Paris 1817,[1] into German from the French, Leipzig 1818.[1]

The Remains of Henry Kirke White, of Nottingham, late of St. John's College, Cambridge. [Engraving. Drawn by Harraden Junr. Engraved by George Cooke]. /No marble marks thy couch of lowly sleep,/ But living statues, there are seen to weep;/ Affliction's semblance bends not o'er thy tomb,/ Affliction's self deplores thy youthful doom./ Ld. Byron. This drawing & Plate presented to the Work by a Lady an esteemed friend of the Author. Published by Vernor, Hood & Sharpe, Novr. 14, 1807. [Engraved title-page.]

The Remains of Henry Kirke White, of Nottingham, late of St. John's College, Cambridge; With an Account of his Life, by Robert Southey. In Two Volumes. Vol. I. [II.] London:

Printed for Vernor, Hood, and Sharpe; Longman, Hurst, Rees, and Orme; J. Deighton, T. Barrett, and J. Nicholson, Cambridge; and W. Dunn, and S. Tupman, Nottingham; At the Union Printing Office, St. John's Square, by W. Wilson. 1808. [Second title-page.] Vol. III. 1822.

This is the earliest edition in the British Museum and the earliest which I have seen, but the list of Southey's works given in *Life* VI, 397 gives the date of the first edition as 1807. (See also Allibone, *Critical Dictionary of English Literature.*) The earliest mention of the book in Southey's letters (*Life* III, 140) is of the date, April 22, 1808. It states that the first edition of 750 copies was sold in less than three months. Later editions in Great Britain and America have been frequent, the tenth appearing in London, 1823.

Palmerin of England, in four volumes. Corrected by Robert Southey, from the original Portugueze. [Half-title.]
Palmerin of England, by Francisco de Moraes. Vol. I. [II. III. IV.] London; printed for Longman, Hurst, Rees, and Orme, Paternoster Row. 1807. [Full-title.]

Translated by A. Munday from the French (1581) and extensively corrected by Southey from the original.

Specimens of the Later English Poets, with preliminary notices; by Robert Southey. In three volumes. London: printed for Longman, Hurst, Rees and Orme, Pater-noster Row. 1807.
Chronicle of the Cid, from the Spanish; by Robert Southey. London: printed for Longman, Hurst, Rees, and Orme, Paternoster-row. 1808.

Another edition, London 1846: another, London 1868:[1] another, London 1883: another, Lowell Mass. 1846.

The Curse of Kehama: by Robert Southey. ΚΑΤΑΡΑΙ, ΩΣ ΚΑΙ ΤΑ ΑΛΕΚΤΡΥΟΝΟΝΕΟΤΤΑ, ΟΙΚΟΝ ΑΕΙ, ΟΨΕ ΚΕΝ ΕΠΑΝΗΞΑΝ ΕΓΚΑΘΙΣΟΜΕΝΑΙ. ΑΠΟΦΘ. ΑΝΕΚ. ΤΟΥ ΓΥΛΙΕΑ ΤΟΥ ΜΗΤ. Curses are like young chicken, they always come home to roost. London: printed for Longman, Hurst, Rees, Orme, and Brown, Paternoster-row, by James Ballantyne and Co. Edinburgh. 1810.

Second edition, London 1812:[2] Third [?]: Fourth, London 1818: Others, London 1853:[1] London 1886:[1] New York 1811.

History of Brazil; by Robert Southey. Part the First. London; Printed for Longman, Hurst, Rees, and Orme, Paternoster-row. 1810.
Part the Second, 1817.
Part the Third, 1819.
Part the First, Second edition, 1822.

Omniana, or Horae Otiosiores. Vol. I. [II.] London: printed for Longman, Hurst, Rees, Orme, and Brown, Paternoster Row. 1812.

> Published anonymously. Forty-five contributions are by Coleridge, and are marked with an asterisk in the table of contents. The remaining number, two hundred and one, are by Southey. Some of the latter's contributions were previously published in *The Athenæum Magazine*.

The Life of Nelson. by Robert Southey./ . . . "Bursting thro' the gloom/ With radiant glory from thy trophied tomb,/ The sacred splendour of thy deathless name/ Shall grace and guard thy Country's martial fame./ Far-seen shall blaze the unextinguish'd ray,/ A mighty beacon, lighting Glory's way;/ With living lustre this proud Land adorn,/ And shine and save, thro' ages yet unborn."/ Ulm and Trafalgar. In Two Volumes. Vol. I. [II.] London: printed for John Murray, bookseller to the Admiralty and to the Board of Longitude, 50, Albemarle Street. 1813.

> Later editions have been very numerous. No less than twenty-two[1] appeared between 1843 and 1894, and there have been many others since in Great Britain and America.

Roderick, The Last of the Goths. by Robert Southey, Esq. Poet Laureate, and Member of the Royal Spanish Academy. London: printed for Longman, Hurst, Rees, Orme, and Brown. Paternoster-Row, by James Ballantyne and Co. Edinburgh, 1814.

> Second edition, London 1815: Third, London 1815:[1] Fourth, London 1816: Fifth, London 1818: Sixth, London 1826:[1] Another, Philadelphia 1815: Translated into French 1820, 1821; into Dutch 1823-1824.

Odes to His Royal Highness The Prince Regent, His Imperial Majesty The Emperor of Russia, and His Majesty The King of

Prussia By Robert Southey, Esq. Poet-Laureate. London:
Printed for Longman, Hurst, Rees, Orme, and Brown, Paternoster Row. 1814.

Second edition, London, 1821, with the title, "Carmen Triumphale,
for the Commencement of the year 1814. Carmen Aulica. Written
in 1814 on the Arrival of the Allied Sovereigns in England."

The Minor Poems of Robert Southey. *Nos haec novimus esse nihil.*
In three volumes Vol. I. [II. III.] London: printed for Longman, Hurst, Rees, Orme, and Brown, Paternoster-Row 1815.

Second edition, London 1823. In these volumes were reprinted the
Poems of 1797 and of 1799 and the *Metrical Tales* of 1805.

The Poet's Pilgrimage to Waterloo: by Robert Southey. Esq. Poet
Laureate, Member of the Royal Spanish Academy, and of the
Royal Spanish Academy of History. /Εὐανθεα δ'ἀναβάσομαι/
Στόλον ἀμφ' ἀρετᾷ /Κελαδέων./ Pindar. Pyth. 2. London:
printed for Longman, Hurst, Rees, Orme, and Brown, Pater-
noster Row. 1816.

Second edition, London 1816: Others, New York 1816, Boston
Mass. 1816.

The Lay of the Laureate. Carmen Nuptiale, by Robert Southey,
Esq. Poet Laureate, Member of the Royal Spanish Academy,
and of the Royal Spanish Academy of History. London:
Printed for Longman, Hurst, Rees, Orme, and Brown, Paternoster Row. 1816.

The Byrth, Lyf, and Actes of King Arthur; of his noble knyghtes
of the rounde table, theyr merveyllous enquestes and aduentures,
Thachyeuyng of the Sanc Greal; and in the end Le Morte
Darthur, with the dolorous deth and departyng out of thys
worlde of them al. With an introduction and notes, by Robert
Southey, Esq. Vol. I. [II.] [Engraving] London: printed from
Caxton's Edition, 1485, for Longman, Hurst, Orme, and Brown,
Paternoster-Row. by Thomas Davison, Whitefriars. 1817.

Wat Tyler. a Dramatic Poem. in three acts. "Thus ever did rebellion find rebuke." Shakespeare. London: printed for Sherwood, Neely, and Jones, Paternoster-Row. 1817.

This is apparently the first edition, for it was against "Sherwood
and others" that Southey tried to get an injunction restraining

them from publication of the poem (March 18, 19, 1817, Merivale *Reports* II 435).   In the trial it appeared that Sherwood printed the piece from a manuscript the history of which was obscure, but he denied having any property or copyright in the production, and Lord Eldon, in refusing the injunction, denied any rights to the author on the ground that the work was of a nature dangerous to the public welfare.   The consequence of this decision was the publication of numerous editions by numerous booksellers in London and elsewhere, some of which are here listed.

Wat Tyler; a dramatic poem.   A new edition.   With a Preface, suitable to recent circumstances.   /Come, listen to a Tale of Times of Old! / Come, for ye know me — I am he who sung/ The "Maid of Arc," and I am he who fram'd/ Of "Thalaba" the wild and wondrous song./   Southey!   /And I was once like this! . . . / . . . Twenty years/ Have wrought strange alteration./ Southey!!!   London: Printed for W. Hone, 67, Old Bailey, and 55, Fleet Street.   1817.

A slip of paper, sewed into the binding of the copy of this pamphlet which I have examined, contains the following:
Wat Tyler.   Price 3s 6d.   Printed for W. Hone, 67. Old Bailey and 55, Fleet Street.***   *This is the* Genuine Edition, *carefully and literally reprinted, verbatim,* (not a word being omitted), *carefully collated with the Original, and enlarged by the addition of a* NEW PREFACE, *suitable to present Circumstances.*   Orders should be given expressly *in these words* — "HONE'S EDITION of WAT TYLER, with a New Preface, 3s. 6d."
Other editions, London 1817, were published by John Fairburn,[1] W. T. Sherwin, T. Broom,[1] and by various other persons at dates uncertain.

A Letter to William Smith, Esq. M. P. from Robert Southey, Esq.   London: John Murray, Albemarle Street.   1817.

Third edition, London 1817: Fourth, London 1817.

The Life of Wesley; and the Rise and Progress of Methodism.   By Robert Southey, Esq. Poet Laureate, Member of the Royal Spanish Academy, of the Royal Spanish Academy of History, and of the Royal Institute of the Netherlands, &c.   Read not to contradict and confute; nor to believe and take for granted; nor to find talk and discourse: but to weigh and consider.   Lord Bacon.   In two Volumes.   London: Printed for Longman, Hurst, Rees, Orme, and Brown, Paternoster-Row.   1820.

Second edition, London 1820: Third, "with notes by . . . S. T. Coleridge . . . , and remarks on the life and character of J. Wesley, by . . . A. Knox. Edited by . . . C. C. Southey, London 1846:[1] Other editions, London 1858,[1] 1864,[1] 1889,[1] New York 1820.

A Vision of Judgement. by Robert Southey, Esq. LL.D. Poet Laureate; Member of the Royal Spanish Academy, of the Royal Spanish Academy of History, and of the Royal Institute of the Netherlands, &c. London: printed for Longman, Hurst, Rees, Orme, and Brown, Paternoster-Row 1821.

Another edition, London n. d.: Appeared also in "A Vision of Judgment; by Robert Southey, Esq. L.L.D. Author of Wat Tyler, also a Vision of Judgment; by Lord Byron. My bane and antidote are both before me. Third edition, London: printed and published by W. Dugdale, 23, Russel Court, Drury Lane, 1824." and in "The Two Visions or Byron v. Southey . . . New York 1823."

The Expedition of Orsua; and the Crimes of Aguirre. by Robert Southey, Esq. LL.D. Poet Laureate: Member of the Royal Spanish Academy, of the Royal Spanish Academy of History, of the Royal Institute of the Netherlands, of the Cymmrodorion, &c. London: printed for Longman, Hurst, Rees, Orme, and Brown, Paternoster-Row. 1821.

Reprinted from *The Edinburgh Annual Register*, v. 3, pt. 2.

History of The Peninsular War. by Robert Southey, Esq. LL.D. Poet Laureate, Honorary Member of the Royal Spanish Academy, of the Royal Spanish Academy of History, of the Royal Institute of the Netherlands, of the Cymmrodorion, of the Massachusetts Historical Society, &c. In Three Volumes. Vol. I. London: John Murray, Albemarle-Street. 1823. Vol. II. 1827. Vol. III. 1832.

A new edition in six volumes, London, Vols. I–IV 1828, Vols. V–VI 1837.

The Book of the Church. by Robert Southey, Esq. LL.D. Poet Laureate, Honorary Member of the Royal Spanish Academy, of the Royal Spanish Academy of History, of the Royal Institute of the Netherlands, of the Cymmrodorion, of the Massachusetts

Historical Society, of the American Antiquarian Society, of the Royal Irish Academy, of the Bristol Philosophical and Literary Society, &c.   In Two Volumes.   Vol. I. [II.] London: John Murray, Albemarle-Street.   MDCCCXXIV.

Second Edition, London 1824: Third, London 1825: Fourth, London 1837:[1] Fifth, London 1841:[1] Sixth, London 1848: Seventh, London 1859:[1] Others, London 1869,[1] 1885,[1] Boston 1825.

A Tale of Paraguay. by Robert Southey, Esq.LL.D.   Poet Laureate, Member of the Royal Spanish Academy, of the Royal Spanish Academy of History, of the Royal Institute of the Netherlands, of the Cymrodorion, of the American Antiquarian Society, of the Royal Irish Academy, of the Bristol Philosophical and Literary Society, &c. &c.   /Go forth, my little book!/ Go forth, and please the gentle and the good./   Wordsworth.   London: printed for Longman, Hurst, Rees, Orme, Brown, and Green, Paternoster-row, 1825.

Second edition, London 1828: another, Boston Mass. 1827.

Vindiciae Ecclesiae Anglicanae.   Letters to Charles Butler, Esq. comprising Essays on the Romish Religion and vindicating the Book of the Church. by Robert Southey, Esq. LL.D. Poet Laureate, Honorary Member of the Royal Spanish Academy, of the Royal Spanish Academy of History, of the Royal Institute of the Netherlands, of the Cymmrodorion, of the Massachusetts Historical Society, of the American Antiquarian Society, of the Royal Irish Academy, of the Bristol Philosophical and Literary Society, of the Metropolitan Institution, of the Philomathic Institution, &c. London: John Murray, Albemarle-Street. MDCCCXXVI.

All for Love; and the Pilgrim to Compostella. by Robert Southey, Esq. LL.D. Poet Laureate, &c. London: John Murray, Albemarle Street.   MDCCCXXIX.

Sir Thomas More: or, Colloquies on the Progress and Prospects of Society. by Robert Southey, Esq. LL.D. Poet Laureate.   Honorary Member of the Royal Spanish Academy, of the Royal Spanish Academy of History, of the Royal Institute of the Netherlands, of the Cymmrodorion, of the Massachusetts Historical Society, of the American Antiquarian Society, of the

Royal Irish Academy, of the Bristol Philosophical and Literary Society, of the Metropolitan Institution, of the Philomathic Institution, &c. Respice, Aspice, Prospice.— *St. Bernard.* With plates. in two volumes. London: John Murray, Albemarle-Street. MDCCCXXIX.

Second edition, 1831.

The Poetical Works of Robert Southey. Complete in one volume. [device] Paris Published by A.and W. Galignani N° 18, Rue Vivienne 1829.

Another edition, n. d.

The Pilgrim's Progress. with a Life of John Bunyan by Robert Southey, Esq. LL.D. Poet Laureate, &c. &c. &c. Illustrated with engravings. [device] London: John Murray, Albemarle-Street, and John Major, Fleet-Street. M.DCCC.XXX.

Second edition, London 1839: Others, London 1844, Boston Mass. 1832, New York 1837, 1846.

Select Works of the British Poets, from Chaucer to Jonson, with Bio-graphical Sketches by Robert Southey Esqr. L. L. D. [Device] London. Printed for Longman, Rees, Orme, Brown and Green. Paternoster Row, 1831.

Attempts in Verse, by John Jones, an old servant: with some account of the writer, written by himself and an introductory essay on the lives and works of our uneducated poets, by Robert Southey, Esq. Poet Laureate. London: John Murray, Albe-marle Street. MDCCCXXXI.

Another edition, London 1836.

Essays, Moral and Political, by Robert Southey, Esq. LL.D. Poet Laureate, &c. Now first collected: in two volumes. /Here shalt thou have the service of my pen, /The tongue of my best thoughts./ Daniel. London: John Murray, Albemarle Street. MDCCCXXXII.

Lives of the British Admirals, with an Introductory view of the Naval History of England, by Robert Southey, LL.D. Poet Laureate. Vol. I. [Engraving, H. Corbauld, del.— E. Finden, sc.] London: printed for Longman, Rees, Orme, Brown, Green

& Longman, Paternoster Row. and John Taylor, Upper Gower Street. 1833.

Vol. II. 1833.

Vol. III. 1834.

Vol. IV. 1837.

Continued by Robt. Bell, Esqr. Vol. V. 1840.

Letter to John Murray, Esq., "touching" Lord Nugent; in reply to a letter from his lordship, touching an article in the "Quarterly Review." by the author of that article. /"I have been libell'd, Murray, as thou know'st, /Through all degrees of calumny!"/ *Southey's Epistle to Allan Cunningham.* London: John Murray, Albemarle Street. MDCCCXXXIII.

Published anonymously.

The Doctor, &c. [device] Vol. I. London: Longman, Rees, Orme, Brown, Green, and Longman. 1834.

Vol. II [1834]

Vol. III. 1835.

Vol. IV. 1837.

Vol. V. 1838.

Vol. VI–VII. 1847, edited by John Wood Warter.

Third edition Vols. I–II, London 1839: Another, Vols. I–II, New York 1836: An edition in one volume edited by J. W. Warter, London 1848, 1853, 1856, 1862, 1864, 1865: Others, New York 1836, 1856, 1872.

Horae Lyricae. Poems, chiefly of the Lyric Kind, in three books. Sacred to devotion and piety,— to virtue, honour, and friendship.— to the memory of the dead. by Isaac Watts, D.D. to which is added a supplement, containing translations of all the Latin poems, with notes, by Thomas Gibbons, D.D. /—— Si non Uranie lyram/ Coelestem cohibet, nec Polyhymnia/ Humanum refugit tendere barbiton./ Hor. Od. I. Imitat. With a Memoir of the Author, by Robert Southey, Esq, LL. D. London: John Hatcherd and Son, Piccadilly; Whittaker and Co. Ave. Maria Lane; Simpkin and Marshall, Stationers' Court; Talboys, Oxford; Deighton, Cambridge; Oliver and Boyd, Edinburgh: and Cumming, Dublin. MDCCCXXXIV. *in* The Sacred Classics: or, Cabinet Library of Divinity. Edited by the Rev. R. Cattermole, B. D. and the Rev. H. Stebbing, M. A. Vol. IX.

Life and Works of William Cowper, by Robert Southey, Esq.
L. L. D. Vol. I. [Engraving, W. Harvey-E. Goodall] London:
Baldwin and Cradock, Paternoster Row. 1835. [Half-title].
The Works of William Cowper, Esq. comprising his Poems, Cor-
respondence, and Translations. With a Life of the Author, by
the editor, Robert Southey, Esq. LL.D. Poet Laureate, Etc.
London: Baldwin and Cradock, Paternoster Row. 1835.
[Full-title].
Vols. II–IX 1836.
Vols. X–XV 1837.

Second edition, London 1853–1855: Another, Boston 1839.

The Poetical Works of Robert Southey, collected by himself. In
ten volumes. Vol. I.[II.] London: printed for Longman, Orme,
Brown, Green, & Longmans, Paternoster-Row. 1837.
Vols. III–X 1838.

This edition, or various volumes of this edition, was reissued, with
and without date, in London by Longman at frequent intervals
during the ten or twelve years after the poet's death. Another
edition, New York 1839. An edition in one volume appeared in
London 1850,[1] 1863, 1873; Philadelphia 1846, New York 1848,
1853, 1856.

The Life of the Rev. Andrew Bell. D.D. LL.D. F. As. S. F. R. S. Ed.
Prebendary of Westminster, and Master of Sherburn Hospital,
Durham. Comprising the history of the rise and progress of
the system of mutual tuition. The first volume by Robert
Southey, Esq., P.L., LL.D. edited by Mrs. Southey. The two
last by his son, the Rev. Charles Cuthbert Southey, B.A., of
Queen's College, Oxford, perpetual curate of Setmurthy, and
assistant curate and evening lecturer of Cockermouth. In three
Volumes. Vol. I. [II. III.] John Murray, London; William
Blackwood & Sons, Edinburgh. M.DCCC.XLIV.

The Life of Oliver Cromwell.

In the list of Southey's works given in *Life*, VI, 397, this work is
mentioned as published in London, 1814. This is doubtless an
error. In *The Quarterly Review*, July 1821, v. 25, 279-347, there
appeared an article by Southey entitled *Life of Cromwell*, a review
of four works on Cromwell. This was reprinted in *Murray's Home
and Colonial Library*, London, 1844, along with Southey's *Life of
Bunyan*, q. v.

Oliver Newman: A New-England Tale (Unfinished): With Other
Poetical Remains. By the Late Robert Southey. [Edited by
H. Hill] London: Longman, Brown, Green, & Longmans,
Paternoster Row. 1845.

Robin Hood: a fragment. by the late Robert Southey, and Caroline
Southey. with other fragments and poems By R. S. & C. S.
William Blackwood and Sons, Edinburgh and London. M.DCCC.-
XLVII.

Southey's Common Place Book. [engraving E. W. Wyon] /Oderat
hic urbes: nitidâque remotus ab aulâ/ Secretos montes, et
inambitiosa colebat/ Rura: nec Iliacos coetus, nisi rarus, adibat./
Ovid Met XI 765. London. Longman, Brown, Green, &
Longmans, Paternoster Row 1849. [Half-title].

Southey's Common-place Book. First Series. Choice passages.
Collections for English manners and literature. Edited by his
son-in-law, John Wood Warter, B.D. Second Edition. London:
Longman, Brown, Green, and Longmans. 1850. [Full-title]
Second Series. Special Collections. 1849, 1850.
Third Series. Analytical Readings 1850.
Fourth Series. Original Memoranda, etc. 1850.

Journal of a Tour in the Netherlands in the autumn of 1815 by
Robert Southey with an introduction by W. Robertson Nicoll
[device] William Heinemann London M DCCCC III.

First edition, Houghton Mifflin Co., Boston, 1902.

APPENDIX B

A list of the works cited or probably referred to in the preface and notes to the first edition of *Joan of Arc*.

NOTE: Southey's usual practice was to refer to his source only by the last name of the author or in some other abbreviated way. In many cases, therefore, it has been impossible to trace his allusion with complete certainty. It has also been impossible in many cases to state exactly the edition used by Southey, but I have attempted to give the date of the first edition of each work cited and, in the case of foreign works, of the first English edition or translation, or of the first English edition or translation prior to the publication of the poem.

An asterisk signifies that the title occurs with the date indicated in the "Catalogue of the Valuable Library of the Late Robert Southey . . . which will be sold by auction . . . by . . . Sotheby & Co . . . [London] 1844."

Information has been taken, unless otherwise indicated, either from the books themselves or from the British Museum *Catalogue of Printed Books*.

BOOKS OF CURIOUS AND HISTORICAL INFORMATION

Andrews, James Pettit. The History of Great Britain connected with the Chronology of Europe; . . . London 1794*.

The notes which Southey cites from J. de Paris [sic] and from Mem. de Richemont [sic], and the note concerning the Prince of Orleans are taken verbatim from this work.

Clarendon, Hugh. A new and authentic History of England . . . to the close of the year 1767. London (1770?).

Clavigero, Francisco Saverio. Storia antica del Messico, . . . Cesena 1780*–81. Tr. into English by Cullen, London 1787.

Cranz, David. Historie von Grönland . . . Barby 1765. Tr. into English, London 1767.*

Fuller, Thomas. The holy and profane State*. Cambridge 1642;
London 1652. The Historie of the Holy Warre; . . . Cambridge
1639; 4 ed. 1651*.

> Southey Sale Catalogue gives the two preceding works together
> under the date Cambridge 1651.

Gillies, John. The History of Ancient Greece, . . . London 1786*.
Goodwin, Thomas. The history of the reign of Henry the Fifth,
. . . London 1704–03.
Grose, Francis. Military Antiquities . . . London 1786–88, 1812*.
Holinshed, Raphael. The Chronicles of England, Scotlande and
Irelande. London 1577.
Hume, David. The History of England . . . London 1754–1761
(*Dictionary of National Biography*); 1762; 1789*.
L'Averdy, Clément Charles François de. Notices et Extraits des
Manuscrits de la Bibliothèque du Roi, Paris 1790.

> Southey refers to this work in his preface but had not seen it at
> the time of the first edition of *Joan of Arc*.

Leemius, (Leem, Knute). de Lapponibus . . . Copenhagen 1767.
Mezéray, Fr. Eudes de. Histoire de France . . . Paris 1643–51.
Millin, Aubin-Louis. Antiquités Nationales . . . Paris 1790–(1799).
Monstrelet, Enguerrand de. . . . Des Croniques de France, . . .
(1380–1467). Paris (1500?).
Newton, Sir Isaac. Opticks . . . London 1704; many later editions.
Translated into French, Amsterdam 1720; Paris 1722.

> The Southey Sale Catalogue gives an edition Paris 1702, probably
> an error for 1722.

Paris, J. de. See Andrews, J. P.
Rapin-Thoyras, Paul de. Histoire d'Angleterre. La Haye 1724–
36. Tr. with notes by N. Tindal, London 1726–1731, 1732*.
. . . Acta Regia; or, An Account of the Treaties, Letters and In-
struments between the Monarchs of England and Foreign
Powers. Publish'd in Mr. Rymer's Foedera, . . . from the
French of M. Rapin, as publish'd by M. Le Clerc . . . London
1726–1727.
Richemont, Mem. de. See Andrews, J. P.

SOURCES OF LITERARY ILLUSTRATIONS

The following omissions have been made in this list: references in the preface to Homer, Virgil, Statius, Lucan, Tasso, Ariosto, Camoens, Spenser, Milton, Pope, Cowper, and Glover; references in the notes to Southey's portion of the poem to Quarles, Lucan, Goethe's *Werther, Revelations, Isaiah,* Coleridge's *Conciones ad Populum* and *Poems* (1796), and an essay in *The Flagellant* by P [eter the] H[ermit], pseudonym of G. C. Bedford; a reference in the notes to Coleridge's portion of the poem to his Greek *Ode on the Slave-trade* with a translation by Southey.

Boileau-Despréaux, Nicolas.   Satires du sieur D****.   Paris 1666–68.

. . . Œuvres . . . (gravés de Picart.)   Amsterdam 1718, La Haye 1722*.

Chapelain, Jean. La Pucelle ou la France Delivrée . . . Paris 1656*.

Southey refers to this work in his preface but had not seen it at the time of the first edition of *Joan of Arc.*

Churton, Ralph.   Eight Sermons . . . preached . . . Oxford . . .1785 at the lecture founded by John Bampton.   Oxford 1785.

Cottle, Amos S. Icelandic Poetry, or the Edda of Saemund translated into English verse, . . . Bristol 1797*.

D'Aubignac, Hedelin, abbé.   La Pucelle d'Orléans, tragédie en prose . . . Paris 1642.[1]   (*Bibliothèque National; Catalogue Gènéral.*)

Mesnardière, Jules de la; or, Mainardière, Pilet de la; attrib. to. La Pucelle d'Orléans, Tragédie.   Paris 1642.[1]

Mistère du siége d'Orléans, . . . manuscrit conservé à la Biblioth. du Vatican . . . (pub. 1862).[1]

Modern Amazon, The.[1]   Southey probably refers to the following: Le jeune, le P., canon of Orléans.   L'Amazone française . . . par le P. Neon dit le Philopole [Pseud. for above].   Orléans 1721;   Rouen 1729.   (Pierre Lanéry D'Arc, *Le Livre d'Or de Jeanne d' Arc.*)

Orleans, The Prince of.   See Andrews, J. P.

Voltaire, F. Arouet de.   La Pucelle.   1755;   many later eds. (Lanéry as above).

Southey refers to this title in his preface, but had not read the work itself.

[1] Southey mentions these titles in his preface, but it does not appear that he had seen the works themselves.

APPENDIX C

A list of the works cited or probably referred to in the notes to the first edition of *Thalaba*.

NOTE: See note to Appendix B.

BOOKS OF ANTIQUARIAN AND CURIOUS INFORMATION

Abyssinian historian.

> The note in which allusion is made to an Abyssinian historian is taken practically verbatim from James Bruce, q. v.

Admirable Curiosities etc. See Burton.

Aelianus. See Mexia.

Argens, Jean-Baptiste de Boyer, Marquis d'. Lettres juives, . . . La Haye 1736; Eng. trans. London 1739, Dublin 1753, London 1766–65.

Buffon, G. L., Leclerc, Comte de. Histoire Naturelle des Minéraux . . . Paris 1783–88. Many later editions and translations.

Burnet, Thomas. Telluris Theoria Sacra. London 1681–89; trans. into English by the author with additions, London 1684–89 (*Dictionary of National Biography*). Many later editions.

Burton, R. (pseud. of Nathaniel Crouch.) Admirable Curiosities, Rarities, and Wonders in Great Britain and Ireland . . . 10th. ed. London 1737.

Carlos Magno, Historia do Imperador, etc. See Turpin.

Davies, J. History of Magic. See Naudé.

Eleazar, Rabbi.

> Reference unlocated.

English Martyrologe, The. (John Watson?) . . . 1608.

Fuller, Thomas. See Appendix B.

Garcia Lasso de la Vega . . . Los Commentarios Reales, que tratan del origen de los Yncas, Reyes que fueron del Peru, . . . Lisboa 1609; trans. into Eng. London 1688.

Godwin, [or Godwyn], Thomas. Moses and Aaron. Civil and Ecclesiastical Rites, used by the ancient Hebrews; . . . 1625 (*Dic. Nat. Biog.*); second ed. London 1626.

Grimstone, Edward. A Generall Historie of the Netherlands . . . London 1608*.

Grose, Francis. A Provincial Glossary; with a collection of . . . popular Superstitions, London 1787; enlarged 1790.

Heeren, [Heering], Professor, of Göttingen. On Transplanting the Camel to the Cape of Good Hope; . . . *Month. Mag.* v. 8, Jan. 1, 1800.

Jortin, John. Sermons, 7 vols., London 1787.

Leonardus, Camillus. Speculum Lapidum, Venetiis 1502; The Mirror of Stones; . . . Now first translated into English. London 1750.

Lettres Juives. See Argens.

Margarita Philosophica. See Reisch.

Matthew of Westminster. See Paris.

Mexia, Pedro. The treasurie of auncient and moderne times, . . . (from) . . . Pedro Mexia and Francesco Sansovino, (etc) . . . London 1613–19*.

Naudé, Gabriel. Apologie pour tous les Grands Personnages qui ont esté faussemment soupçonnez de Magie. Paris 1625; trans. into Eng. by John Davies of Kidwelly (*Catalogue of the Library of Peabody Institute, Baltimore*) as The History of Magick, by way of apology for all the wise men who have unjustly been reputed magicians, . . . London 1657.

Nuremburg Chronicle. See Schedel.

Paris, Matthew. Historia Major (or Chronica Majora). First printed London 1571; many later editions. Continuous with Flores Historiarum, first printed London 1567; with additions London 1570. Ascribed to Matthew of Westminster.

Reisch, Gregorius. Margarita Philosophica, . . . Strasbourg 1504 (1505 n. s.); Basileae 1535*.

Saxonis Grammatici Historiae Danicae libri XVI. Stephanus Iohannis Stephanius summo studio recognovit, . . . Sorae 1644–45; another ed. Lipsiae 1771.

Schedel, Hartmann.   Nuremburg Chronicle, Nuremburg 1493.

Setphanius [sic].   See Saxonis.

Smellie, William.   The Philosophy of Natural History, Edinburgh 1790–99*.

Treasury, . . . See Mexia.

Tristan L'Hermite, Fr.   Plaidoyers historiques; . . . Paris 1643; Lyon 1650 (*Manuel du Libraire* . . . J. C. Brunet).

Turpin, archevêque de Reims (Attributed to).   Cronique et Histoire . . . du . . . Roy Charles le grãt . . . Paris 1527.   Many later editions and translations.

> Southey quotes the title in Portuguese and may have used the translation into that language by J. Moreira de Carvalho, Lisbon 1800–1799.

Universal History, An, from the earliest account of time to the present: compiled from original authors . . . 23 vols. London 1736–65; another ed. 1747–; an ed. in 26 vols. 1740–65*.

ORIENTAL AND PSEUDO-ORIENTAL SOURCES

Arabian Nights Entertainments, trans. from A. Galland, Les Mille et Une Nuits, Contes Arabes, traduits en François . . . 1704–; another ed. in Le Cabinet des Fées 1785–86; trans. into English 1713 (fourth ed.); many later eds. and translations.

Arabian Tales.   La suite des Mille et Une Nuits, Contes Arabes, tr. par Dom Chavis et M. Cazotte, in Le Cabinet des Fées, . . . Paris 1788–89; trans. into English by R. Heron 1792; another ed. 1794.

Asiatic Researches, . . . Calcutta 1788–1839 (*Catalogue of the Library of Congress*); 12 vols. 1801–11*.

Bahar-Danush; or, Garden of Knowledge, . . . Inatulla, Trans. from the Persic . . . by Jonathan Scott, Shrewsbury 1799*.

Beckford, William.   Vathek, . . . trans. from the French with notes by S. Henley, London 1786*; pub. in French 1787.

Caherman Nameh or History of Caherman.   Quoted from D'Herbelot, q. v.

Carlyle, J. D. Specimens of Arabian Poetry . . . Cambridge 1796.

D'Herbelot, Barthélémi, concluded by Antoine Galland.   Bibliothèque Orientale, . . . La Haye 1777–79.   First ed. Paris 1697; Maestricht 1776*.

Ferdusi. See Jones, Traité sur la Poésie Orientale.

Hafez. Quoted from Jones, Poeseos, q. v.

Hau Kiou Choan; or, the pleasing History. A translation from the
  Chinese . . . [by James Wilkinson] London 1761 (Ed. by Thomas
  Percy).

> *Dic. Nat. Biog.* states that this work was translated by Percy from
> a Portuguese manuscript.

Jones, Sir William.
  Traité sur la Poésie Orientale, 1770 (*Dic. Nat. Biog.*).

> Includes an abstract of Channamé [Ferdusi] with illustrative
> extracts in French.

  Poems, consisting chiefly of translations from Asiatic Languages,
    . . . [with] . . . two Essays on the Poetry of the Eastern
    Nations, and on the Arts called Imitative, 1772; 1777.
  Poeseos Asiaticae Commentariorum libri sex . . . London 1774;
    Lipsiae 1777.
  Works. ed. by Lord Teignmouth and Lady Jones, 6 vols. 1799;
    two supplementary vols. 1801; Memoirs 1804; Works (in-
    cluding all the above) 13 vols. 1807; an ed. with date not
    given, 13 vols*.

Koran. See Sale.

Lamai. Quoted from D'Herbelot, q. v.

Moallakat. See Jones.

Marraci, Ludovicus. Alcorani textus universus . . . in Latinum
  translatus, . . . Patavii 1698; Leipzig 1721.

Poeseos Asiaticae Commentarii. See Jones.

Sale, George. The Koran, commonly called the Alcoran of Mohammed, trans. into English immediately from the original
  Arabic, with Explanatory Notes, taken from the most approved
  commentators, to which is prefixed a Preliminary Discourse,
  London 1734; new ed. Bath 1795*.

Scott, Jonathan. See Bahar-Danush.

Scott, Major.

> Identity not established. Southey may refer to Jonathan Scott
> (see Bahar-Danush) or to his brother Major John Scott-Waring,
> author of several works on affairs in British India.

HISTORIES AND DESCRIPTIONS OF STRANGE LANDS, AND BOOKS OF TRAVEL

Ambassadors' Travels. See Olearius.

Astley, T. A New General Collection of Voyages and Travels . . . London 1745–47. Includes, The Journey of Anthony Gaubil, Jesuit, from Kanton to Pe-king in 1722.

Bartolomeo, Fra Paolino da San (Philipp Weredin). Viaggio alle Indie Orientali. Romae 1796; trans. into German 1798 (Kayser, *Bücher-Lexicon*); trans. into English from the German by W. Johnston, London 1800* (*Lib. Cong.*).

Bruce, James, of Kinnaird. Travels to discover the source of the Nile, . . . (in the years) . . . 1768–1773. Dublin 1790*.

Chandler, Richard. Travels in Asia Minor, . . . Oxford 1775 (*Lib. Cong.*); London 1776; 1817*.

Chardin, John. Voyages . . . en Perse, et autres lieux de l'Orient, Amsterdam 1711; enrichis de Figures . . . nouvelle ed. Amsterdam 1735 (*Lib. Cong.*); an ed. of the first portion of the work, London 1686; the first vol. trans. into Eng. 1686. Also in Harris, q. v.

Chénier, Louis Sauveur de. Recherches historiques sur les Maures, et histoire de l'Empire de Maroc, Paris 1787; trans. into Eng. London 1788.

Churchill, Awnsham and John. A Collection of Voyages and Travels, . . . London 1704–32; 1732; 1744*, 1752.

Dampier, William. A New Voyage round the World . . . 1697*– 1709. Also in Harris, q. v.

Quoted by Southey as History of the Buccaneers.

De La Roque, Jean. Voyage de Syrie et du mont Liban: . . . Paris 1772; Amsterdam 1723*.

D'Ohsson, I. de M. Tableau général de l'Empire Othoman . . . Paris 1787–1820; trans. into English, Philadelphia 1788; London 1789 (Lowndes, *Bibliog. Manual*).

Du Halde, Jean Baptiste. Description . . . de L'Empire de la Chine . . . Paris 1735; trans. into English by R. Brooks, London 1736.

Fryer, John. New account of East India and Persia . . . 1672–81, London 1698*.

Gaubil. See Astley.

Gemelli-Careri, Giovanni Francesco. Giro del mondo . . . Napoli 1699–1700; trans. into English in Churchill, q. v.

Greaves, John. Pyramidographia: or, a description of the pyramids in Aegypt, London 1646. Also in Churchill, q. v.

Guys, Pierre Augustin. Voyage littéraire de la Grèce, ou Lettres sur les Grecs, . . . Paris 1771; nouvelle éd. . . . augmentée . . . 1776; third ed. 1783* (Lib. Cong.).

Hakluyt, Richard. The Principal Navigations, Voyages, Traffiques, and Discoveries of the English Nation . . . etc. 1598–1600*. Includes:

The voyage of M. John Eldred to Tripolis in Syria by sea, and from thence by land and river to Babylon, and Balsara. Anno 1583.

The voyage of Master Cesar Frederick into the east India . . . 1563.

The voyages of M. Anthony Jenkinson.

The voyage of . . . Ralph Fitch . . . to Goa in the East India, . . . etc. . . . 1583–1591.

Voyage of . . . Odoricus to Asia Minor, Armenia . . . &c.

Certain letters in verse, written out of Moscovia by George Tuberuile . . . 1568.

Hanway, Jonas. An Historical account of the British Trade over the Caspian Sea; with Journal of Travels . . . London 1753*.

Irwin, Eyles. A series of adventures in the course of a voyage up the Red-Sea, . . . in . . . 1777 . . ., London 1780.

Jackson, John. Journey from India towards England in the year 1797 . . . London 1799.

Jenkinson. See Hakluyt.

Knolles, Richard. The Generall Historie of the Turkes . . . London 1603; 1610*.

Mandeville, Sir John. The Voiage and trauayle of, . . . London 1568. (The first English edition appeared about 1500.) Many later editions, among them one in London 1725.

Mandelslo. See Olearius.

Marigny, L'abbé Augier de.

Histoire des Arabes sous le gouvernement des Califes, Paris 1750*; trans. into English, London 1758.

Histoire des Révolutions de l'Empire des Arabes, Paris 1750–52*.

Morgan, John.   A complete history of Algiers, London [1728*]–1731.

Nieuhof, Jan.   Het Gezantschap der Neêrlandtsche Oost-Indihesc Companie aan den grooten Tartarischen Cham . . ., Amsterdam 1665; 1693*; trans. into French, Leyden 1665*; into Latin, Amsterdam 1668*; into English, London 1669; 1673.   Also in Astley and in Churchill, q. v.

Niebuhr, Carsten.

> Beschreibung von Arabien . . . , Copenhagen 1772; trans. into French, Copenhagen 1773; Amsterdam 1774*.

> Reisebeschreibung nach Arabien . . . Copenhagen 1774; trans. into French, 1776–80*; into English, Edinburgh 1792.

> Recueil de questions . . . par Michaelis . . . , Amsterdam 1774* (*Brunet*).

> In the Southey Sale Catalogue the three works marked * are included together under the date, Copenhagen 1774.

Norden, Frederic Louis.   Voyage d'Egypt et de Nubie . . . Copenhague 1755; trans. into English . . . by P. Templeman, London 1757.

Odoricus.   See Hakluyt.

Olearius, Adam.   The Voyages and Travels of the Ambassadors sent by Frederick Duke of Holstein, to the Great Duke of Muscovy, and the King of Persia . . . 1633–1639 . . . whereto are added the Travels of John Albert de Mandelslo . . . from Persia into the East Indies . . . Faithfully rendered into English by John Davies of Kidwelly, London 1662*.   Also in Harris, q. v.

Park, Mungo.   Travels in the Interior districts of Africa . . . 1795 . . . 1797 . . . appendix . . . by Major Rennell, London 1799.

Pausanius.   Description of Greece . . . (Translated by Thos. Taylor.)   London 1794;   1824*.

Pérouse, J. F. Galaup de la.   Voyage . . . auteur du Monde . . . rédigé par M. L. A. Milet-Mureau, Paris (1797); 1798; trans. into English by J. Johnson, London 1798, 1799; another translation, London 1798.

Pococke, Richard.   A Description of the East . . . London 1743–45.

Pontoppidan, Erik.   The Natural History of Norway . . . (Trans. from the Danish of 1552, 1753), London 1755.

Purchas, Samuel.

    Purchas his Pilgrimage; . . . London 1613; 1614; 1617; 1626; n.d*.

    Purchas his Pilgrimes, (Haklytus Posthumus), London 1625.

Rauwolf.

    The note alluding to Rauwolf is quoted verbatim from the notes to the Universal History, q. v.

Russell, Alexander. The Natural History of Aleppo . . . London 1756; second ed. . . . enlarged . . . notes by Pat. Russel, London 1794*.

Shaw, Thomas. Travels . . . (in) . . . Barbary and Levant, Oxford 1738; second ed. with improvements, London 1757*.

Sonnerat, Pierre. Voyage aux Indes Orientales et à la Chine . . . 1774–81, Paris 1782; trans. by F. Magnus into Eng. Calcutta 1788–89*.

Sonnini de Manoncourt, C. N. S. Voyage dans la Haute et Basse Égypte, . . . Paris (1799); trans. into English by Hunter, London 1799*.

Tavernier, Jean Baptiste. Les Six Voyages . . . Paris 1676; 1692* (Brunet); "Made into English by J. P." (J. Philips and E. Everard), 1684. Also in Harris, q. v.

Tournefort, Joseph Pitton de. Relation d'un Voyage du Levant, . . . Paris 1717; Amsterdam 1718*; trans. into English, London 1718.

Turbervile. See Hakluyt.

Valle, Pietro della. Viaggi . . . in tre parti, . . . la Turchia, la Persia, e l'India, Roma 1650; Venice 1667*; trans. into English London 1665*.

    Southey's reference to this author is found in full in the notes to the Universal History, q. v.

Vasconcellos, Simão de. Vida do . . . padre Joseph de Anchieta . . . , do Brasil, Lisboa 1672*.

Volney, C. F. Chassebœuf, comte de. Voyage en Syrie et en Egypte . . . 1783–1785, 1787; seconde éd. revue et corrigée, Paris 1787; trans. into English, London 1787; 1805*.

SOURCES OF LITERARY ILLUSTRATIONS

NOTE: Southey makes references to the following authors or works which have been omitted from this list: *The Old Testament* and the *Apocrypha*, Euripides, Ariosto, *Don Quixote*, Gower, Shakespeare, Spenser, Jeremy Taylor, Gibbon, Erasmus Darwin, Bürger, and Dr. Frank Sayers.

Boccage, Marie-Anne du. La Colombiade . . . Paris 1756; Londres 1758; Paris 1758*.

Brébeuf. See Lucanus.

Gongora, Luis de. Obras . . . Madrid 1627 (Heredia, *Catalogue de la Bibliothèque*); Bruselas 1659*.

Leonardo de Argensola, Lupercio i Barolome. Rimas . . . Zaragoza 1634.

Lesuire, Robert-Martin. Le Nouveau Monde, . . . Paris 1781; 1800.

Lucanus, Marcus Annæus. Pharsalia, cum supplemento T. Maii. . . . [Edited by J. Goulin] Paris 1767*; trans. into French by G. de Brébeuf Paris and Rouen 1655-54; trans. into English [with continuation] by Thomas May, London 1627; 1659-57*.

Old Poulter's Mare.

A poem quoted by Southey as a ballad of which he prints "only an imperfect copy from memory." The source of the poem has not been found. It is evidently not a genuine ballad.

Roberts, William Hayward. Judah Restored: a poem, London 1774*.

Sylvester, Joshua. [Guillaume de Salluste, seigneur] Du Bartas. His devine Weekes and Workes translated . . . London 1605-06.

Uziel, Jacopo. David: poema Heroica. Venetia 1624*.

INDEX